WORKING MEMORY

Working memory is the cognitive system in charge of the temporary maintenance of information in view of its ongoing processing. Lying at the centre of cognition, it has become a key concept in psychological science. The book presents a critical review and synthesis of the working memory literature, and also presents an innovative new theory – the Time-Based Resource-Sharing (TBRS) model.

Tracing back the evolution of the concept of working memory, from its introduction by Baddeley and Hitch in 1974 and the development of their modal model, Barrouillet and Camos explain how an alternative conception could have been developed from the very beginning, and why it is needed today. This alternative model takes into account the temporal dynamics of mental functioning. The book describes a new architecture for working memory, and provides a description of its functioning, its development, the sources of individual differences, and hints about neural substrates. The authors address central and debated questions about working memory, and also more general issues about cognitive architecture and functioning.

Working Memory: Loss and reconstruction will be essential reading for advanced students and researchers of the psychology of memory.

Pierre Barrouillet is Professor of developmental psychology at the University of Geneva, Switzerland, and Director of the Archives Jean Piaget. He is also associate editor of the *Journal of Experimental Psychology: Learning, Memory, and Cognition*. His research investigates the development of numerical cognition, conditional reasoning, as well as the functioning and development of working memory.

Valérie Camos is Professor of developmental psychology at the Université of Fribourg, Switzerland. She created and currently heads the Fribourg Center for Cognition, a multidisciplinary research centre. She was associate editor of the *Journal of Cognitive Psychology* and is currently associate editor of the *Quarterly Journal of Experimental Psychology*. Aside from her research on working memory, she is also interested in numerical cognition.

Essays in cognitive psychology

North American Editors:

Henry L. Roediger III, *Washington University in St. Louis*
James R. Pomerantz, *Rice University*

European Editors:

Alan D. Baddeley, *University of York*
Vicki Bruce, *University of Edinburgh*
Jonathan Grainger, *Université de Provence*

Essays in Cognitive Psychology is designed to meet the need for rapid publication of brief volumes in cognitive psychology. Primary topics will include perception, movement and action, attention, memory, mental representation, language and problem solving. Furthermore, the series seeks to define cognitive psychology in its broadest sense, encompassing all topics either informed by, or informing, the study of mental processes. As such, it covers a wide range of subjects including computational approaches to cognition, cognitive neuroscience, social cognition, and cognitive development, as well as areas more traditionally defined as cognitive psychology. Each volume in the series will make a conceptual contribution to the topic by reviewing and synthesising the existing research literature, by advancing theory in the area, or by some combination of these missions. The principal aim is that authors will provide an overview of their own highly successful research programme in an area. It is also expected that volumes will, to some extent, include an assessment of current knowledge and identification of possible future trends in research. Each book will be a self-contained unit supplying the advanced reader with a well-structured review of the work described and evaluated.

Published

Working Memory
Barrouillet and Camos

Extraordinary Memories of Exceptional Events
Schmidt

Psychology of Eyewitness Identification
Lampinen, Neuschatz and Cling

The Tip of the Tongue State
Brown

Mnemonology
Mnemonics for the 21st Century
Worthen and Hunt

Principles of Memory
Surprenant and Neath

Emotional Memory across the Lifespan
Kensinger

Space and Sense
Millar

Hypothetical Thinking
Evans

Associative Illusions of Memory
Gallo

Working Memory Capacity
Cowan

Semantic Priming
McNamara

The Déjà Vu Experience
Brown

Saying, Seeing and Acting
Coventry and Garrod

Space, Objects, Minds and Brains
Robertson

Visuo-spatial Working Memory and Individual Differences
Cornoldi and Vecchi

The Creativity Conundrum
Sternberg et al

Hypothesis-testing Behaviour
Poletiek

Mental Models and the Interpretations of Anaphora
Garnham

Forthcoming

The Mnemonic Benefits of Retrieval Practice
Butler and Kang

Flashbulb Memory
Weaver

For updated information about published and forthcoming titles in the *Essays in Cognitive Psychology* series, please visit: **www.psypress.com/essays**

WORKING MEMORY

Loss and reconstruction

Pierre Barrouillet and Valérie Camos

LONDON AND NEW YORK

First published 2015
by Psychology Press
27 Church Road, Hove, East Sussex BN3 2FA

and by Psychology Press
711 Third Avenue, New York, NY 10017

Psychology Press is an imprint of the Taylor & Francis Group, an informa business

© 2015 Psychology Press

The right of Pierre Barrouillet and Valérie Camos to be identified as the authors of this Work has been asserted by them in accordance with sections 77 and 78 of the Copyright, Designs and Patents Act 1988.

All rights reserved. No part of this book may be reprinted or reproduced or utilised in any form or by any electronic, mechanical, or other means, now known or hereafter invented, including photocopying and recording, or in any information storage or retrieval system, without permission in writing from the publishers.

Trademark notice: Product or corporate names may be trademarks or registered trademarks, and are used only for identification and explanation without intent to infringe.

British Library Cataloguing in Publication Data
A catalogue record for this book is available from the British Library

Library of Congress Cataloging-in-Publication Data
Barrouillet, Pierre.
Working memory : loss and reconstruction / Pierre Barrouillet and Valerie Camos.
pages cm
Includes bibliographical references.
ISBN 978-1-84872-265-1 (hb) – ISBN 978-1-84872-266-8 (softcover) – ISBN 978-1-315-75585-4 (ebk) 1. Short-term memory. I. Camos, Valérie. II. Title.
BF378.S54B37 2015
153.1'2–dc23
2014014270

ISBN: 978-1-84872-265-1 (hbk)
ISBN: 978-1-84872-266-8 (pbk)
ISBN: 978-1-315-75585-4 (ebk)

Typeset in Bembo
by Cenveo Publisher Services

Printed and bound in Great Britain by
TJ International Ltd, Padstow, Cornwall

CONTENTS

The structure of the book   *viii*
Preface   *ix*
About the cover   *xiii*

1. What is working memory?   1
2. Time and working memory   19
3. Time-based resource sharing   41
4. Working memory loss   71
5. Working memory reconstruction   94
6. A working memory architecture   117
7. Working memory in development and individual differences   146
8. Controversies and prospects in working memory   170

Epilogue: Searching for working memory   189

References   *193*
Index   *217*

THE STRUCTURE OF THE BOOK

Chapters

- Preface
- 1. What is WM?
- 2. Time and WM
- 3. Time-based resource sharing
- 4. WM loss
- 5. WM reconstruction
- 6. A WM architecture
- 7. WM in development and individual differences
- 8. Controversies and prospects in WM
- Epilogue

Topics

- The core of the book presenting the antagonistic processes of WM
- Our model: Its original and its new elaboration
- The key developmental questions at the root of our work and our own investigations and responses
- The past and future of WM
- Introducing and concluding words

PREFACE

In one of the most famous pages of his *Pensées*, the French philosopher and mathematician Blaise Pascal was asking how it is that a man distressed at the death of his wife can totally forget his sadness and seem so free from all painful thoughts. We need not wonder, said Pascal, our man has been served a ball, and he is occupied in returning it to his partner. Also, Pascal amusingly asked how this man could think of his own affairs when he has such an important matter in mind. The answer is simple and well known: distraction. Pascal, obviously, was not writing a monograph on cognitive psychology nor was he interested in describing cognitive processes; he was addressing a moral and religious question. Although thinking is the privilege of man, his dignity, and what he is obviously made for, he spends his entire life thinking of dancing, singing, hunting, following a ball, solving algebra problems, or making money, without ever thinking on what being a man means. The reason, according to Pascal, is that man knows that he will be miserable if he meditates on self and that, for the purpose of happiness, it is better not to know himself. But what makes diversion so efficient in forgetting what we are? Pascal suggests that it is a limitation of our mind, which he describes as lucky for us according to the world and our happiness, but not according to our salvation. This limitation means that a single thought is sufficient to occupy us because we cannot think of two things at the same time. This theme of diversion is persistent in the classical literature and can be traced back at least to Montaigne in his *Essays*, with a less moral and more humanistic flavour.

Though these readings might seem remote from the literature usually studied by cognitive psychologists, Pascal's and Montaigne's thoughts on distraction and diversion were at the source of the ideas that led to the model of working memory presented in this book.

Distraction might be the consequence of a key process by which thoughts rapidly succeed each other in mind, delineating a functioning of the cognitive system in which time is the main constraint. In the same way as following a ball is sufficient to attenuate and dissolve sorrowful thoughts, we surmised that a simple but continuous activity should have dramatic consequences on concurrent threads of thoughts and should jeopardise any possibility to simultaneously keep in mind even the most relevant information. The idea that diversion plays a crucial role in cognition is not new. In the homepage of his website, our eminent colleague Dylan Jones writes 'Distraction is the price we pay for being able to focus on an event of interest while also gleaning some information from other sources of information'. The same idea seems also to lie at the heart of the rationale of the paradigms used to study working memory (complex span and Brown-Peterson tasks) in which people are asked to maintain a series of items for further recall while performing an intervening activity. However, our intuition was that the crucial point in diverting attention was the continuity of this diversion. Let attention go back to its initial object, even surreptitiously, and most of the effects of distraction would vanish. But we reasoned that if a mere diversion was sufficient, complex activities like sentence comprehension or solving equations should not be needed. As Pascal noted, chasing a ball is sufficient to forget one's sorrows. Thus, we started to create tasks in which people had to remember some letters while performing very simple, elementary activities, but under temporal constraints to induce some continuity in the occupation of attention.

In a first attempt, one of us designed such a task, which he called the *continuous operation span* task. Letters to be remembered, the number of which varied from one to five, were successively displayed on screen, each letter being followed by four very simple operations consisting of adding or subtracting one to an ongoing count that never exceeded ten. In a moment of unrealistic optimism in his own capacities, he set the pace of this distracting task to one operation per second. After all, decades of research on mental arithmetic had shown that everybody is able to add or subtract one to a small number in less than one second. The result was quite hurtful for the designer of the task. He was at best able to recall two letters. Fortunately, younger individuals (including one of us) proved more efficient, but the difficulty of the task remained surprising. We soon discovered that it became far easier and recall performance was better when the time constraint was relaxed and the arithmetic task presented at a slower pace. This was the beginning of a programme of research that is still in progress, which has provided us with some insights about the structure and functioning of working memory for verbal as well as for visuospatial information, how it develops through age, how it differs between individuals, and what are its neural bases. The present book is an attempt to synthesise and integrate the results that we have obtained during this last decade within a hopefully comprehensive and coherent theoretical framework that we have named the Time-Based Resource-Sharing (TBRS) model.

The first chapter goes back to the introduction of the concept of working memory in cognitive psychology and to the seminal study by Baddeley and Hitch (1974). We will argue that Alan Baddeley and Graham Hitch's interpretation of their results, which provided the impetus for an impressive research programme and set the stage for the following 40 years of working memory studies and theorising, could have taken another route. Baddeley and Hitch concluded that the two functions of working memory, processing and storage, were underpinned by different systems, but a neglected alternative solution, also supported by the results, could have been that a unique mechanism is in charge of both functions in alternation, making temporal factors one of the main determinants of working memory functioning. The second chapter focuses on the relatively neglected role of time in working memory theories until the formulation by John Towse and Graham Hitch of their switching model. Towse and Hitch (1995) put forward a provocative hypothesis: the detrimental effect that processing has on concurrent maintenance would not result from some resource sharing between the two functions but simply from the effect of time, with memory traces suffering time-related decay during processing. Our own investigations in the domain started with the test of this hypothesis. It turned out that the switching model proved inadequate, but the results revealed a surprising capacity, even in children, to coordinate activities and apparently to do two things at the same time that required an explanation. This led us to design the TBRS model and a new paradigm of temporally constrained working memory span tasks that are presented in Chapter 3. Our results revealed that storage capacity systematically varies as a linear function of the cognitive load of concurrent processing, a relation that we describe as the law relating processing to storage. This law reflects the balance between the antagonistic processes of loss and reconstruction of working memory representations. Accordingly, Chapter 4 focuses on the loss side of this process and the problem of the sources of forgetting in working memory, whereas the following chapter addresses the key question of the mechanisms by which forgetting is counteracted and information maintained within working memory. Overall, the studies of the reciprocal effects of processing on storage, and of storage on processing, point towards a new working memory architecture described in Chapter 6.

The TBRS model was initially conceived in the context of developmental studies, and we never stopped exploring the construction and evolution of short-term and working memory functioning. Does the time-based resource sharing that characterises adults' functioning account also for working memory in school-aged children? And in preschoolers? Do these young children use some mechanisms for counteracting forgetting and how these mechanisms develop? These questions are addressed in Chapter 7 where we present our own conceptions concerning the intricate problem of the factors of working memory development and the recurring question of the relationships between developmental and individual differences. Working memory is a field of research attracting a great interest nowadays, with hotly debated questions. A final chapter focuses on some of these issues. Beginning by the controversies elicited by the loss-reconstruction hypothesis of the TBRS model, the chapter moves to the key question of the limitations of working memory, ending with the core problem of the genuine existence of a working memory as a separate memory system.

This book and the studies it reports would not have been possible without the dedication and enthusiasm of young researchers who worked with us through the years. We express our gratitude for their help to all of them, and more especially to

Sophie Bernardin, Raphaëlle Bertrand, Lucie Corbin, Isabelle Dagry, Sebastien De Schrijver, Annick De Paepe, Nele Dewaele, Kevin Diependaele, Nicolas Dirix, Vinciane Gaillard, Nathalie Gavens, Alessandro Guida, Egbert Hartstra, Prune Lagner, Naomi Langerock, Raphaëlle Lépine, Vanessa Loaiza, Annalisa Lucidi, Gérome Mora, Anne-Laure Oftinger, Gaën Plancher, Benoît Perriard, Sophie Portrat and, last but not least, Evie Vergauwe. Finally, we would also like to thank all the colleagues who helped us to refine our ideas and proposals through insightful discussions, friendly advice and, for some of them, constant and stimulating criticisms. Among those our memory has been able to retrieve, we are grateful to Alan Baddeley, Charles Brainerd, Marcel Brass, Nelson Cowan, Randall Engle, Graham Hitch, Christopher Jarrold, Stephen Lewandowsky, Baptist Liefooghe, Robert Logie, Akira Miyake (who suggested to us the name of the model in June 2002), Klaus Oberauer, Pierre Perruchet, Scott Saults, John Towse, and André Vandierendonck, as well as our past and present colleagues from the LEAD-CNRS at the Université de Bourgogne where we previously worked, and the Departments of Psychology of University of Geneva and University of Fribourg. The work presented in this book also benefitted from the support of grants mainly from the Agence Nationale de la Recherche, the Institut Universitaire de France, and the Fonds National Suisse de la Recherche Scientifique. Finally, Jacqueline Thurillet-Camos deserves special thanks for having hosted, fed (!) and taking care of us during the many peaceful weeks we spent writing up this book in Burgundy.

Pierre Barrouillet and Valérie Camos
Jallanges
July-August 2013/January-February 2014

ABOUT THE COVER

These four sandcastles are a metaphor of working memory functioning as described by the Time-Based Resource Sharing model in which four representations are stored in working memory. They are ephemeral in nature, can be degraded and may be lost. They can also be reconstructed by active processes, but only one castle can be (re)built at a time. Thanks to Calvin Seibert for this marvellous piece of art.

Further information about the TBRS model can be found at www.tbrsmodel.com

1
WHAT IS WORKING MEMORY?

According to Baddeley (2003), the first mention of the term 'working memory' can be traced back to Miller, Galanter and Pribam (1960). Does this mean that this date has to be taken as a corner stone of psychological science, marking the discovery of a central mechanism for cognition that was lying in the hidden recesses of our mind, running unnoticed until then? In introducing their remarkable and still indispensable book *Models of Working Memory*, Miyake and Shah (1999) recalled that working memory was proclaimed by Goldman-Rakic (1992, p. 111) as 'perhaps the most significant achievement of human mental evolution' and labelled by Haberlandt (1997, p. 212) as the 'hub of cognition'. How could the most significant achievement of human mental evolution have been left in such neglect for almost one century by scientific psychological research? The answer lies of course in the advent and success of the cognitive revolution and the ensuing deep transformation of our conception of mind functioning. Instead of an impenetrable learning device storing stimulus-response associations, the emergence of cognitive science in the 1950s disseminated the view of the mind as a system for processing information. The advent of computers proved that it was at least theoretically possible to envision human cognition as a system operating on symbolic representations in compliance with a predetermined programme, and successful computational simulations of a range of cognitive activities gave credence to this view. However, as the first theoretical elaborations made clear, the need for a system able to maintain representations of the information to be processed, to execute the successive instructions of the programme and control for their correct completion while rapidly accessing relevant knowledge from long-term memory was inherent to the information processing approach. If the idea of a mind simply connecting stimuli and responses by one-to-one switches was to be abandoned, Tolman (1948) emphasised the need for a central control room working over and elaborating incoming stimuli into cognitive maps of the environment. Surprisingly, the task of identifying this 'hub of cognition' was fraught with difficulties. Within the conceptual apparatus of psychology at the advent of the cognitive revolution, short-term memory was the unique conceivable solution. The impact of Baddeley and Hitch's (1974) chapter in Volume 8 of *The Psychology of Learning and Motivation* edited by G. H. Bower is probably due to the fact that they provided evidence that short-term memory was not the controlling executive system described by Atkinson and Shiffrin (1971) and delineated a new and original structure for working memory.

On the need for a working memory in the information-processing approach to cognition

At the turn of the 1950s, it became evident that behaviour could not entirely be described and explained in terms of stimulus-response links. As Tolman (1948) demonstrated, even rats in mazes behaved as problem solvers, using cognitive maps instead of memorised sequences of actions. This strongly suggested that a level of mental representation might be hypothesised in accounting for a large variety of cognitive phenomena ranging from perception to formal reasoning. As Gardner (1985) claimed, demonstrating the validity of this approach was the major accomplishment of cognitive science. It is usually assumed that a first and decisive step in this revolution was the introduction by Shannon and Turing, both in 1950, of the idea that machines could authentically think. Shannon (1950) anticipated that it should be possible to conceive of electronic machines playing a very difficult game like chess, and thus thinking, while Turing (1950) imagined that such a machine might produce responses that could not be distinguished by any interrogator from those produced by a human being. Turing (1950) described these machines as consisting of three parts, a store of information corresponding to human memory in which information is broken up into small packets or chunks, an executive unit carrying out individual operations contained in some 'book of rules', and a control verifying that the instructions maintained in the store have been correctly obeyed. The strength of Turing's idea was that the digital computer he envisioned should be conceived as a universal machine able to mimic any discrete state machine if suitably programmed. Accordingly, Newell and Simon (1956; Newell *et al.* 1958) showed that it was possible to simulate the cognitive processes involved in chess playing with heuristic programmes using a flexible information-processing language.

The fact that these simulations were successful strongly suggested an isomorphism between the basic organisation of human problem solving and the list structures for representing instructions that Newell and his collaborators used in programming their computer. Miller *et al.* (1960) called the cognitive structures corresponding in mind to the programmes in a computer 'Plans'. They assumed that when the decision is made to execute a Plan, it is taken out of dead storage and brought into the focus of attention for controlling what they called a segment of information-processing capacity. Miller and colleagues (p. 65) emphasised that 'something important' happens to the selected Plan during this process and that its special cognitive status required some machinery for its maintenance and execution. This machinery was described as a 'working memory' in a paragraph that we shall exhaustively quote here for its visionary character.

> The parts of a Plan that is being executed have special access to consciousness and special ways of being remembered that are necessary for coordinating parts of different Plans and for coordinating with the Plans of other people. When we have decided to execute some particular Plan, it is probably put into some special state of place where it can be remembered while it is being executed. Particularly if it is a transient, temporary kind of Plan that will be used today and never again, we need some special place to store it. The special place may be on a sheet of paper. Or (who knows?) it may be somewhere in the frontal lobes of the brain. Without committing ourselves to any specific machinery, therefore, we should like to speak of the memory we use for the execution of our Plans as a kind of quick-access, "working memory". There may be several Plans, or several parts of a single Plan, all stored in working memory at the same time. In particular, when one Plan is interrupted by the requirement of some other Plan, we must be able to remember the interrupted Plan in order to resume its execution when the opportunity arises. When a Plan has been transferred into working memory we recognize the special status of its incompleted parts by calling them "intentions".
>
> *(Miller et al. 1960, p. 65)*

Apart from the relationships between working memory and attention (but as we saw above, Plans being executed are brought into the focus of attention), several key aspects of the modern conception of working memory are already present in this first description, such as the links between working memory and consciousness, its dual function of processing and storage through the need of remembering Plans while being executed, the fast access to the stored information, and even hypotheses about a cerebral localisation in the frontal cortex. The limited capacity of working memory is among the rare characteristics omitted by Miller and colleagues in their description. However, from its very inception, the information-processing approach emphasised the limitations of the cognitive system that any theoretical or computational model should reflect (Turing 1948). Needless to say, Miller was more than anybody else aware of the strong limitations of the information-processing system, suggesting in his famous article 'The magical number seven, plus or minus two' that the mean capacity of the channel for a range of stimulus variables was 2.6 bits with a standard deviation of only 0.6 bit, corresponding to a mean of 6.5 distinguishable alternatives and a total range from 3 to 5 categories, which he considered as a remarkably narrow range (Miller 1956). Interestingly, but according to Miller quite coincidentally[1], the span of immediate memory was approximately equivalent and limited to about seven chunks.

Thus, conceiving the mind as a system that processes information following some internal programme instead of a learning device storing stimulus-response associations led to the necessity to conceive of a machinery with the capacity to represent the information to be processed, to remember it while executing the operations listed in the programme, and to control the outputs of these processes. Miller et al. (1960) coined the expression 'working memory' to describe such a system and identified its main characteristics, but they did not go further in describing its structure. The information-processing approach required a working memory, but what was the best candidate for this role within the conceptual toolbox of psychology in the middle of the twentieth century? Quite naturally, the response was 'short-term memory'. As Atkinson and Shiffrin (1971) noted, the distinction between short-term memory and long-term memory that was introduced at the end of the nineteenth century by Ebbinghaus (1885) or James (1890) was largely discarded by behaviourism, but was reintroduced during the 1950s, receiving considerable theoretical developments. A variety of models of short-term memory were proposed (for example, Broadbent 1958; Waugh and Norman 1965; Atkinson and Shiffrin 1965) that presented a sufficient degree of similarity to be summarised by Murdock (1967) into a synthesis he named the 'modal model', in which were distinguished three main levels: a sensory store, a primary and a secondary memory. The model designed by Atkinson and Shiffrin (1968) was probably the most influential version of this 'modal model'. They suggested that the entire memory system could be described in terms of a flow of information into and out of a short-term storage and the control that the subject can exert on that flow. In their model, information was first processed by sensory systems (visual, auditory or haptic for example) and entered into the short-term store where a variety of control processes could code the incoming information in different ways, maintain a limited number of items through rehearsal, copy these items into a long-term store, retrieve knowledge from this long-term store or make decisions for action. Atkinson and Shiffrin (1971) stressed that their account did not require the assumption that short-term and long-term stores involve different physiological structures or different neural substrates. Short-term memory could simply be the activated part of long-term memory, an idea that has been endorsed by several modern theories of working memory. More important in their view was what distinguishes the two stores, with two key and unique properties of short-term memory that would contain the thoughts and information of which we are currently aware, and that would be where control processes take place, these properties turning short-term memory into working memory. This was perfectly in line with Miller et al.'s (1960) suggestion to designate by the terms 'working memory' the memory used for remembering that part of the Plan currently executed that have special access to consciousness.

A seminal study: Baddeley and Hitch (1974)

Atkinson and Shiffrin were not isolated in assigning a crucial role to short-term memory in complex cognition such as learning (Peterson 1966), language comprehension (Rumelhart et al. 1972) or problem solving (Hunt 1971). However, it remained unclear at the time that the different roles of memory in information processing could be fulfilled by a single unitary system of short-term memory.

For example, Posner (1967) agreed that because any information processing requires is to keep track of incoming information and bring this information into contact with stored knowledge, some short-term memory system was needed to fulfil these functions. However, he noted some ambiguity in the short-term memory literature of this time, which used a single mechanism for the ephemeral representation of a stimulus, the retention of new information over brief periods of time and the activation of information from long-term memory needed by complex cognition (what Hunter 1964 described as an operational memory), while there was no evidence that these three functions had identical limitations. In line with Posner, Baddeley and Hitch (1974) observed that, despite the fact that short-term memory had been frequently assigned the role of operational or working memory, empirical evidence for this hypothesis was remarkably sparse, opening their chapter by assuming that 'we still know virtually nothing about its [short-term memory] role in normal human information processing' (Baddeley and Hitch 1974, p. 47). Empirical evidence was not only sparse but often contradicted the idea that short-term memory played any role in complex cognition and processes like concept formation (Coltheart 1972) or retrieval (Patterson 1971). According to Baddeley and Hitch, the strongest evidence against the hypothesis equating short-term memory with working memory was the neuropsychological observations of Shallice and Warrington (Shallice and Warrington 1970; Warrington and Shallice 1969) who extensively studied patient K. F. who had a greatly reduced short-term memory capacity but preserved performance in learning, memory or comprehension. Thus, Atkinson and Shiffrin's hypothesis of a short-term storage acting as a working memory lacked empirical support. Consequently, Baddeley and Hitch presented a series of experiments that attempted to answer two main questions. The first concerned the existence of a common working memory system shared by reasoning, comprehension and learning. The second, if such a system existed, concerned its relations with short-term memory. This study played, and is still playing, such a role in how cognitive psychology conceives working memory that we will present it in some detail here. We will see that the way Baddeley and Hitch interpreted their results had a strong and enduring impact on cognitive psychology, whereas other interpretations, at least as plausible as those they endorsed, would have led to a totally different view of working memory structure and functioning.

Baddeley and Hitch (1974) ran a first series of experiments that addressed the role of short-term memory in reasoning, language and comprehension. They reasoned that if these processes share some common working memory system corresponding to the short-term memory described by Atkinson and Shiffrin (1971), and taking for granted that short-term memory has a limited capacity, then absorbing some of this capacity by a memory load should have a detrimental effect on concurrent cognitive processes. For this purpose, they asked participants to perform a reasoning task while holding items in memory using a preload technique. The reasoning task consisted in presenting a sentence that described the order of occurrence of two letters that immediately followed the sentence (for example, 'A is not preceded by B – AB'). The difficulty of this task was varied by using passive sentences and introducing negations. Participants were asked to decide as quickly as possible whether the sentence correctly described the order in which the letters were presented by pressing appropriate keys for 'true' and 'false' responses. In a first experiment, participants were asked to perform this reasoning task while holding zero, one or two letters. This first experiment revealed no effect of memory load on solution times. This would suggest either that the memory system involved in maintaining the letters is not relevant for the reasoning task or that the memory preload was not sufficient. Thus, this preload was increased in a second experiment in which participants were asked to perform the reasoning task while maintaining either zero or six letters. Contrary to what occurred with two letters, holding six letters had a significant effect on solution times that increased from 2.73s to 4.73s. The fact that a preload of two letters left the reasoning task unaffected, whereas a preload that approached the memory span for many subjects resulted in a trade-off between reasoning and recall, suggested that the reasoning task involved short-term memory, but did not seem to require all the available short-term storage space.

Another aspect of these results that drew the authors' attention was that the effect of memory load only occurred when a particular stress was put on the memory part of the task, participants being told that only if their recall was completely correct could their reasoning performance be scored. This memory stress could have led participants to consolidate memory traces by quickly rehearsing the letter list before entering the reasoning task. This conjecture was supported by the fact that the slowing down in reasoning produced by the memory preload did not vary with the complexity of the sentence (either active or passive, affirmative or negative), something contradicting the hypothesis of a unique resource shared by memory and reasoning. Baddeley and Hitch surmised that participants adopted a strategy of time-sharing between rehearsal of the memory list and reasoning. In this case, the effect of memory load on reasoning would not necessarily be indicative of a competition between the two processes for a limited storage capacity. Indeed, the tasks might have competed for the use of the articulatory system without having overlapping storage demands.

In order to prevent the complete shift of attention from the memory to the reasoning task, Baddeley and Hitch decided in a third experiment to use a concurrent load procedure requiring participants to repeat cyclically a six-digit sequence during the reasoning task, with the sequence changed from trial to trial. This condition was compared with three other conditions in which, while solving the reasoning problems, participants either remained silent, repeated the word 'the' (an articulatory suppression method introduced by Murray in 1967), or cyclically repeated the familiar counting sequence 'one-two-three-four-five-six'. The three articulation conditions varied in storage demand from the mere repetition of a same word, which probably imposes low storage demand, to the six-digit sequence repetition, which presumably makes greater short-term storage demand. The results revealed that both the repetition of the same word or the familiar counting sequence produced a slight slowing down of the reasoning task (3.13s and 3.22s respectively, compared with 2.79s for the silent condition), while the effect was more pronounced with the digit sequence repetition task (4.27s). This suggested that the interference created by the memory task was not entirely to be explained in terms of competition with the articulatory system, short-term memory load being a much more important factor. Accordingly, the effect of memory load was greater for the difficult problems (i.e., negative passive sentences), suggesting the competition for a common resource. Baddeley and Hitch concluded that the rate at which the reasoning process is carried out is determined by the spare short-term storage capacity, the interference between storage and processing occurring within a limited capacity 'work space'. However, the small effect of articulatory suppression on the reasoning processes, along with related results from Hammerton (1969), suggested some resemblance between the reasoning and the memory span tasks in the use of an articulatory component. This hypothesis was tested by studying, on the reasoning task, the effect of phonemic similarity that had already been observed in the memory span task (Baddeley 1966; Conrad and Hull 1964). A fourth experiment manipulated the phonemic similarity of the letters involved in the problems (for example, FS or TD vs. MC or VS), as well as their visual similarity (for example, OQ or XY vs. MC or VS). Whereas visual similarity had no effect at all, phonemically similar letters induced lower reasoning performance, revealing the utilisation of phonemically coded information in the verbal reasoning task as it is the case in the memory span task. Baddeley and Hitch concluded from their investigation of the role of working memory in reasoning that their verbal reasoning task, which showed effects of concurrent memory load, articulatory suppression and phonemic similarity, depended on the use of a short-term store having the same characteristics typically observed in the memory span task. However, the magnitude of the effects along with the insensibility of reasoning processes to memory loads limited to three items led them to temper their conclusion: the system responsible for the memory span seemed to be only a part of working memory[2].

Baddeley and Hitch (1974) concluded from their studies that, in line with the working memory hypothesis, verbal reasoning and language comprehension relied on the operation of a common system that has something in common with the mechanism responsible for the memory span, all the tasks being susceptible to disruption by a concurrent memory load. However, they noted at the same time that this disruption, even with near-span concurrent memory load, 'was far from massive' (Baddeley and Hitch 1974, p. 75). In this restriction lie most of the developments of the future multiple-component model of working memory. The small and non-significant effect of three-item memory load strongly suggested that, although short-term memory and working memory overlap, a considerable component of working memory was not taken up by the short-term memory span tasks. Baddeley and Hitch suggested that this component, which they considered as the core component of working memory, consisted of a limited capacity 'work space' that could be divided between storage and control processing demands, with a trade-off between the two functions. Along with this flexible work space, working memory would also contain a component dedicated to storage, a relatively passive phonemic buffer that makes few demands on the central processing space. Thus, the span of immediate memory would be set by two factors: the capacity of the phonemic buffer (named in some places of their chapter 'phonemic loop', though the mechanism of the phonological loop was not yet described), and the ability of the central executive component to supplement it. In this initial version of the model, when the capacity of the phonemic buffer was exceeded, it was assumed that the executive component might 'devote more of its time to the problem of storage', by recoding information to facilitate its rehearsal or devoting more attention to retrieval through the use of contextual cues facilitating the interpretation of deteriorated phonemic traces. However, this did not mean that the central component of working memory might be conceived as a flexible work space with storage and processing capacities. When discussing the allocation of this work space, Baddeley and Hitch cautiously stated that it would be unwise to regard working memory as an entirely flexible system of which any part could be allocated either to storage or processing. Two reasons were advocated. Firstly, it might be theoretically difficult to distinguish between the two functions. Secondly, the low level of interference created by infra-span memory loads indicated that some part of working memory that is used for storage is not available for processing. Though they exclusively focused on verbal memory, Baddeley and Hitch (1974) reviewed a series of studies on visual memory (Baddeley et al. 1973; Brooks 1968; Kroll et al. 1970) from which they concluded that it was clear that auditory and visual short-term storage use different subsystems. Accordingly, they suggested that the central processor plays the same role in visual as in verbal memory, but with a separate peripheral memory component based on the visual system.

Thus was, in a single book chapter, delineated one of the most influential models of cognitive psychology. The modal model was clearly inadequate in the role of working memory. The magnitude of the interference effects created by near-span memory loads proved far smaller than expected if a single unique system was in charge of maintaining memory items while performing concurrent cognitive tasks. Instead, a variety of systems was needed, with at least a controlling central system in charge of implementing and supervising processing activities, while storage would be carried out by separate slave systems. This fragmentation of working memory into a series of specialised systems was fraught with consequences. Of course, it was assumed that the system responsible for verbal span in some way overlaps with working memory, but it is worthy to note that the solution adopted to conceptualise this overlap actually preserved the separation between the systems. The central executive was assumed to supplement the storage system by facilitating its rehearsal activities through information recoding and providing retrieval cues for interpreting degraded memory traces, a process akin to the modern concept of redintegration (Hulme et al. 1997). In other words, from its very first inception, the model that would become the standard model of working memory contained the seeds of a separation between the functions of processing and storage.

Processing, storage and their relationships

Processing and storage relationships within the multi-component model: towards the separation

The successive versions of the multi-component model that followed Baddeley and Hitch's initial proposal further accentuated the separation between processing and storage. A first step towards a complete separation was taken in the book *Working Memory* authored by Alan Baddeley in 1986. While reviewing the studies presented in the 1974 book chapter, Baddeley (1986) illustrated the inadequacy of the modal model of Atkinson and Shiffrin and the need for a multi-component model in a further unpublished study by Baddeley and Lewis who used the same reasoning task as previously described with memory preloads varying from 0 to 8 digits. This study was run in a small sample of seven female participants over five days. As in the studies reported in Baddeley and Hitch (1974), there was an effect of concurrent load on verification times, with increasing memory load resulting in a smooth increase of reasoning times (Figure 1.1). However, this study offered a series of new and highly interesting findings. First, though five days of practice led to a substantial improvement in verification times, this improvement did not remove or interact with the influence of memory load. Baddeley reasoned that if processing and storage were sharing a common space or resource, it could have been expected that a concurrent memory load would have impacted less and less on an increasingly automated reasoning process. Second, the difficulty of the reasoning task (i.e., positive/negative and active/passive sentences) did not interact with memory load on verification times, a lack of interaction that Baddeley found difficult to interpret. Third, when analysing memory performance, it appeared that a noticeable error rate in recall (19 per cent) only appeared in the eight-digit load condition. Thus, the reasoning task elicited virtually no decrement in memory. In the other way round, the memory task had no effect at all on reasoning accuracy, as Figure 1.1 makes clear. Finally, when simultaneously considering performance on the two tasks, the hypothesis of a common pool of resource shared by processing and storage would have predicted a trade-off between the two. However, the opposite was observed, with lower memory performance associated with longer, and not shorter, reasoning times.

Overall, Baddeley (1986) concluded that these findings created a major problem for a conception of working memory based on the modal model in which a unique short-term memory would be devoted to storage and processing activities. As he noted, such a model would have presumably predicted that a difficult reasoning task and the maintenance of digit sequences equivalent to subjects' span should have had disastrous reciprocal effects when performed concurrently. Nothing of this sort occurred. Of course, the impact of memory load on reasoning times certainly suggested that some limited capacity memory system influences reasoning, a finding consistent with the concept of general working memory. However, Baddeley noted that when he began this line of research with his colleagues, they expected clear and strong effects of concurrent memory load on cognitive processes such as reasoning,

10 What is working memory?

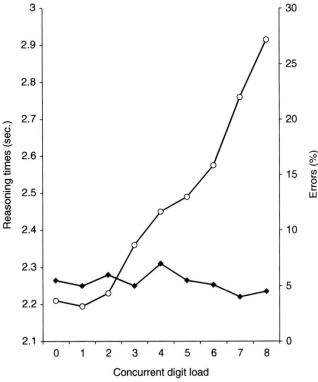

FIGURE 1.1 Response times (empty circles) and errors rates (filled diamonds) as a function of a concurrent memory preload in a reasoning task in Baddeley and Lewis's study reported in Baddeley (1986). From *Working Memory* (1986, p. 67) by A.D. Baddeley, Oxford, England: Oxford University Press. Copyright 1986 Oxford University Press. Adapted with permission

sentence comprehension or retrieval. On the contrary, they 'found the cognitive system to be much more robust than anticipated' (Baddeley 1986, p. 69); hence the abandonment of the modal model for a multi-component view with each working memory function supported by specialised and distinct systems. Thus, in the 1986 book *Working Memory*, the specific function of the central executive was suggested to be the control of attention, and possibly the function of consciousness, but its putative role in supplementing the slave systems in their storage function when overloaded was no longer mentioned. Conceived of as the Supervisory Attentional System (SAS) theorised by Norman and Shallice (1986), the central executive was assumed to act as an overall controller used to consciously bias the activation of some action schemata when automatic conflict resolution between competing potential actions no longer works. For example, the schemata usually used for driving must be overridden when driving on a snowy road, something that requires all our attention. Thus, equating the central executive with the control of action led to unambiguously associate it with the processing function of working memory.

Later on, the storage capacity of the central executive was explicitly abandoned by Baddeley and Logie (1999) who put forward three reasons for doing so, two of them empirical in nature. The first reason was that, from a theoretical point of view, Baddeley and Logie were reluctant to give the central executive the capacity to supplement and, hence, mimic the capacities of the slave systems, rendering the system too powerful and too flexible to be productively investigated. Interestingly, this point was already present in Baddeley and Hitch (1974) who noted that regarding working memory as an entirely flexible system would make difficult the theoretical distinction between the processing and storage functions. Second, from an empirical viewpoint, there was growing evidence that working memory can store information in systems other than the peripheral slave systems, such as long-term memory. For example, Wilson and Baddeley (1988) observed densely amnesic patients who had preserved immediate recall of a prose passage. Finally, and probably most importantly, empirical work seemed to offer little support for the original view of processing and maintenance activities sharing a common resource or work space. Baddeley and Logie (1999) reported a study by Logie and Duff (1996) who had participants performing a demanding processing task and a memory task either alone or concurrently. As a processing task, participants were requested to verify as many arithmetic sums (for example, 9 + 6 = 15 or 5 + 8 = 12) as they were able in a 10-s period. Beginning with two-equation trials with 5s per equation, the number of equations to verify was progressively increased until the subject was no longer able to verify all the equations presented. The memory task consisted of a word span task. In the dual task condition, participants were required to perform the arithmetic task with each equation accompanied by an unrelated to-be-remembered word. The results revealed that the memory task had virtually no effect on the number of arithmetic equations participants were able to verify in the 10-s period, while the arithmetic task had in turn little effect on recall performance of the series of words. Being at odds with the idea of a trade-off between processing and storage, these results were, according to Baddeley and Logie (1999), more readily accounted for by assuming that words were retained in a distinct subsystem devoted to storing verbal information (i.e., the phonological loop), while on-line processing activities involved in arithmetic problem solving were supported by the central executive. Baddeley and Logie claimed to have observed a similar pattern of results in three other experiments, 'offering little support for the view that processing and storage demands compete for a single resource' (Baddeley and Logie 1999, p. 39).

Thus, the successive refinements of the multi-component model led to a separation of the functions of processing and storage. Initiated by a study of the potential effects of storage on concurrent demanding activities like reasoning, learning and comprehension, the search for a cognitive system able to act as a working memory, as defined by Miller et al. (1960), ultimately led Baddeley and his colleagues to split working memory into a collection of systems subserving specific functions. However, this option was not retained by a series of alternative models that privileged the hypothesis of a unitary working memory system.

The trade-off hypothesis

Whereas the multi-component view tended towards an increasing separation between the different functions of working memory, several other theories assumed that processing and storage share a common resource or supply resulting in a perfect trade-off. One of the most prominent of these theories was proposed by Case (1978, 1985 and 1992). Case suggested that one should consider the total processing resources of an individual, i.e., her working memory capacity, as a 'total processing space' that could be indifferently used for storage or processing purpose. Thus, this total space might be divided into a 'short-term storage space', a hypothetical amount of space for storing information, and an 'operating space', referring to the hypothetical amount of space available for carrying out mental operations. As we will see in the next chapter, one of the most counterintuitive hypotheses put forward by Case was that the total processing space would remain constant across development, from birth to adulthood. Within this account, the well-documented developmental increase in short-term memory spans would result from an increase in processing efficiency. More efficient operations would require a smaller and smaller part of the total processing space with age, with a correlative increase of the space available for storage, resulting in a perfect trade-off between the two functions and an increase in short-term memory spans. This hypothesis was supported by the fact that, in a counting span task in which children had to count arrays of dots presented in immediate succession while maintaining the successive totals for further recall, the maximum number of totals that children were able to recall was a direct function of the efficiency of their counting procedures (Case *et al.* 1982). We will discuss these findings in greater detail in the next chapter when analysing Towse and Hitch's (1995) criticisms of this conception, but now we will concentrate on the explanation proposed by Case and colleagues of these phenomena. When discussing the psychological basis for this trade-off, they envisioned two possibilities. The first was to assume a mechanism of 'attentional interference' by which the attention allocated to operations is no longer available for attending to the stored information. Thus, inefficient operations requiring a higher amount of attention would prevent children from attending to the to-be-remembered totals, leading to their forgetting. However, an alternative explanation would be to consider a mechanism of 'temporal interference' rather than attentional interference. According to this account, it could be assumed that the time spent to execute difficult operations reduces the number of items that can be rehearsed in the phonological loop through a mechanism that the authors did not detail. However, advocating the results of unpublished pilot studies, Case *et al.* (1982) rejected this latter possibility and favoured the attentional over the temporal account.

Interestingly, Daneman and Carpenter (1980) envisioned the same hypotheses when discussing the relationships between processing and storage in reading comprehension, an activity that mainly involves relating the information that is currently processed with previously read information, such as in computing pronominal reference. There is little doubt that this kind of computation is easier if the required previous information is still active in working memory. Daneman and Carpenter's hypothesis was that good and poor readers make the same computations, but that they differ in the speed or efficiency with which they perform them, this speed or efficiency having a direct impact on the amount of information that can be concurrently maintained in an active state. Like Case, Daneman and Carpenter reasoned that less efficient computations consume more of the attention otherwise available for storage, leading to a trade-off. The other possibility they envisioned was that faster reading-related tasks would result in shorter periods during which information in working memory is subjected to temporal decay. Contrary to Case, Daneman and Carpenter did not choose between the two possibilities, focusing on the finding that individuals with high reading spans, and thus higher working memory capacities, were also better at reading comprehension. The same resource sharing as described by Daneman and Carpenter (1980) occurs in Just and Carpenter (1992) who developed a related conception in their theory of comprehension.

The most elaborated account of the 'attentional interference' hypothesis put forward by Case was probably proposed by Anderson *et al.* (1996) within the ACT-R model (Anderson 1993). This model assumes that the fundamental limitation of working memory is on the amount of attention that can be distributed among objects to produce activation. The consequence of a limited total amount of source activation is that two competing tasks that require source activation will interfere with each other. Anderson *et al.* (1996) tested this hypothesis in an experimental design close to that used by Baddeley and Hitch (1974) in which subjects were asked to hold lists of either two, four or six digits (and even 8 digits in a second experiment) while solving arithmetic equations of various degrees of difficulty. For example, in a first experiment, simple equations involved one transformation (for example, $3x = 6$ or $3 + x = 9$) whereas complex equations involved two transformations (for example, $3x - 2 = 7$). Interestingly, in a condition named 'substitution', the two first digits of the memory load might be introduced as constant values in the equation (for example, $ax - 2 = b$, where a and b stood for the two first to-be-remembered digits). Not surprisingly, as the memory and the arithmetic tasks get more difficult (more digits to be remembered or more complex equations), performance decreased in each task in terms of accuracy and latency but, more interestingly, increasing difficulty in one task affected the other task. Moreover, the need for substitution resulted in less accurate and slower equation solving. These results were consistent with the hypothesis that as more source activation was needed to maintain memory items in an active state, lower source activation was available to retrieve arithmetic facts from declarative long-term memory. In the same way, as equation solving needed more transformations and retrievals, a smaller amount of source activation remained available for keeping memory items active. Computational simulations based on the ACT-R architecture proved successful in simulating the data, whereas a separate capacity model assuming one capacity for digit span and a different capacity for equation solving failed in simulating the effect of equation difficulty on digit span.

In summary, though the model elaborated by Baddeley and his colleagues, that rapidly became a kind of modal model of working memory, tended towards a strict separation between functions subserved by distinct cognitive systems, a range of alternative approaches of working memory assumed that processing and storage competed for a unique resource shared within a unitary system. Not surprisingly, it is within this second tradition that were elaborated tasks to assess working memory capacity. Based on the trade-off hypothesis, these complex span tasks require the performance of some concurrent activity such as counting arrays of dots (Case et al. 1982), reading sentences (Daneman and Carpenter 1980) or solving arithmetic equations (Turner and Engle 1989) while maintaining series of items for further recall. The capacity of these tasks to predict high-level cognition and fluid intelligence is now well established (for example, Engle et al. 1999; Kane et al. 2004; Kane et al. 2007; Kyllonen and Christal 1990). Even if it was subsequently demonstrated that the addition of some processing component to simple span tasks is not necessary to achieve a good predictive power (Colom et al. 2006; Engle et al. 1992; La Pointe and Engle 1990; Unsworth and Engle 2007a), it is worth noting that the introduction of a processing component in the complex span tasks was initially motivated by the idea that properly measuring working memory capacity required taxing its processing component to 'obtain a more marked trade-off between processing and storage' (Daneman and Carpenter 1980, p. 451).

Trade-off or not trade-off?

It could come as a surprise that a seemingly simple, though central, question such as the existence of interference between processing and storage did not yet receive a clear and definitive answer. One of the reasons is probably that this answer is a matter of appreciation. Remember that Baddeley and Hitch (1974) did observe an effect of memory load on reasoning, if not on accuracy, at least on latencies (Figure 1.1). In the same way, Baddeley et al. (1984) found an effect of memory load on the sentence-verification task. However, these effects were deemed 'far from massive' (Baddeley and Hitch 1974, p. 75). Similar results of mild dual-task disruption, either mutual or only in one direction, were obtained later on by Baddeley and his research group (for example, Cocchini et al. 2002; Duff and Logie 1999, 2001; Logie and Duff 2007). When it reached significance, the observed impairment was interpreted as 'minimal' (Duff and Logie 1999), 'negligible' (Duff and Logie 1999) or 'modest' (Cocchini et al. 2002; Duff and Logie 2001; Logie and Duff 2007). This neglect of small but often robust effects is well illustrated by the study conducted by Duff and Logie (2001) who saw their results as a refutation of the trade-off hypothesis. They used approximately the same dual-task paradigm as in the study by Logie and Duff (1996) that we described above in which participants were presented with an arithmetic task, a word span task, and their combination. Instead of verifying a maximum of equations in the 10-s period, participants read and verified short sentences. The dual-task condition resembled Daneman and Carpenter's reading span: during the 10-s period participants verified a maximum of sentences while maintaining their last word. Whereas the verification span and the word span were about 4.75 when performed in isolation, the verification span dropped to 3.6 and the word span to 3 in the dual-task condition. This means that the word span task increased the mean time needed to verify a sentence from 2.11s to 2.78s, while the verification task resulted in a decrease of the word span of about 37 per cent. It is clear that the conclusions that were drawn from these findings by Duff and Logie on the independence of processing and storage depend on the expectations that underpinned their investigation. Indeed, as surprising as it may seem, empirical findings usually considered as supporting the trade-off hypothesis, such as those by Anderson *et al.* (1996), do not reveal stronger interference effects. Increasing memory load from two to six digits in Anderson *et al.* (1996, Experiment 1) involved a decrease in complex equation solving of about 5 per cent (from approximately 93 per cent to 88 per cent of correct responses). In Experiment 2, where digit load varied from two to eight, the decrease in percent correct solution was negligible whatever the difficulty of the equations, while the increase in solution times was of 0.33s and 0.69s per memory item for simple and complex equations (without substitution) respectively. These increases were actually modest when compared with the solution times observed at the smallest digit load (for example, more than 20s for complex problems). As Baddeley claimed, it could be concluded from these results that the cognitive system proves 'much more robust than anticipated', but what was anticipated?

Manifestly, Baddeley and Hitch (1974) as well as Duff and Logie (2001) based their anticipations on a conception of working memory as a limited space or supply that could be exhausted in the same way as a physical space can be fully occupied or a finite quantity of energy totally consumed. If working memory was such a static device providing a certain space for storing mental objects, or such a finite container of energy, there is no doubt that a near-span memory load would almost exhaust the available capacity and have a dramatic effect on concurrent activities. However, such a dramatic effect was never observed, even when results were interpreted as supporting the trade-off hypothesis (for example, Anderson *et al.* 1996). This means either that processing and storage are fuelled by specific and separate resources, as Baddeley and Logie (1999) concluded, or that the physical metaphor of the container is misleading. In the remainder of this book, we will argue and provide evidence that the second of these alternative propositions must be preferred.

A neglected alternative solution

How are people still able to solve reasoning problems or arithmetic equations while remembering about eight digits; why is their memory performance not dramatically affected by a concurrent task? One response could be that working memory is not a static container in which the space or energy allocated to one activity is no longer available for doing something else, but a dynamic system in which successive states can alternate as rapidly as thoughts follow each other in our mind. If psychological notions have to be taken seriously, and if working memory is literally a memory, this means that it should be able to maintain some items, without any cost, at least for a short period. After all, this is what a memory usually does. It is fortunate that we do not have to permanently reactivate the entire content of our long-term memory to find the kitchen in our house or remember the name of our partner. Of course, you could argue that these are permanent, long-term memories that do not need any allocation of resources, and you are right. Let us suggest another example – please try to add 45 to 78. A good way to solve this problem is to add 8 and 5 first, then 70 and 40, and finally to add the two resulting sums. Now, when adding 70 and 40, there is absolutely no reason to suppose that something in your mind is trying to continuously maintain 13 in an active state. Because 13 is stored in working memory, and because working memory is a memory, maintaining 13 for a short moment does not require the continuous allocation of resources. Of course if, for some reason, the calculation of 70 + 40 takes too long, it is possible that 13 will be lost, but you can verify that usually it is still there at the end of the computation, ready for use, something that is less certain if you try to calculate 3845 + 8078. In other words, items stored in working memory, as in any other type of 'memory', do not require a continuous allocation of resources for their maintenance. This idea was nicely illustrated by La Pointe and Engle (1990, p. 1130) who wrote that our working memories provide 'the texture and context to our cognitive life at any given moment' without being necessarily in the window of consciousness. We are aware that these considerations could sound like trivialities, but it seems that Baddeley and Hitch (1974) and most of their followers had in mind something like an hypothesis of continuous allocation of space or resource when they anticipated the dramatic effect of concurrent memory load on reasoning or comprehension: 'The modal model would surely suggest that a subject who is loaded to the limit of his span digits should have so little processing capacity left that his reasoning performance should disintegrate' (Baddeley 1986, p. 69).

If reasoning performance does not 'disintegrate', it is probably because reasoning and storage do not continuously share a limited space or energy, as Baddeley and Hitch (1974) reasoned. As we noted above, even the results usually considered as supporting the trade-off hypothesis are poorly convincing. There were conditions in the Anderson *et al.*'s (1996) study in which increasing memory load from two to eight digits did not have any effect on equation solving accuracy (for example, simple and complex equations without substitution in Experiment 2). If storage and processing shared some limited source activation, the consumption of the energy needed to produce activation of eight memory items should have strongly depleted the resources needed for solving equations. However, at the same time, increased memory load had a systematic effect on reasoning or solving times in Baddeley and Hitch's (1974) studies, in Baddeley and Lewis (reported in Baddeley 1986, see Figure 1.1), as well as in Anderson *et al.* (1996). As Baddeley and Hitch (1974, p. 76) cogently noted, 'our data suggest that a trade-off exists between the amount of storage required and the rate at which other processes can be carried out'. What the data suggest is that it is not some space or energy that processing and storage are sharing, but the temporal accessibility to these resources in a system in which storage and processing activities alternate. Suppose a sequential functioning of working memory and consider once more Figure 1.1. Any activity related to the storage and maintenance of memory traces would postpone concurrent processing for a duration commensurate with the amount of information to be maintained in an active state. This is exactly what Figure 1.1 reflects. More memory items take longer to be stored and consolidated, resulting in a smooth increase in reasoning times with the number of digits. Because the reasoning task takes only about 2s, it is probably not necessary to postpone it when few memory items have to be maintained, hence the absence of effect of memory loads of one and two digits. This hypothesis also explains why memory load only affects reasoning times, but not accuracy. A sequential functioning means that all the working memory resources, whatever the meaning given to the term 'resources', are available at any point in time whatever the type of ongoing activity. Thus, when working memory is switched into processing mode and resources are allocated to processing, the number of digits previously presented cannot affect reasoning accuracy. In the same way, this explains why there was no interaction between memory load and difficulty of the reasoning task in Baddeley and Lewis's study: more difficult problems take longer to be solved, but this extra time cannot be affected by memory load. This would also explain why five days of training did not abolish the effect of memory load on reasoning. Increasing reasoning efficiency should not have any impact on the efficiency of the activities related to the storage of memory traces. It is not so surprising that these activities took longer for eight digits than they did for one digit, even after five days of practice, leading to the postponing of reasoning activities and resulting in still longer reasoning times. Finally, Baddeley emphasised the fact that, contrary to any prediction based on the trade-off hypothesis, longer reasoning times were associated with lower, and not higher, recall performance. This would not come as a surprise if memory traces suffer from some damage when working memory is switched to processing mode, with longer processing phases resulting in more degraded memory traces. Interestingly, it is exactly this later hypothesis and the role of time in working memory functioning that motivated the switching model proposed by Towse and Hitch (1995). Because this model and the studies conducted by John Towse and Graham Hitch constituted our main source of inspiration and motivated our first inquiries concerning working memory functioning, we shall present their views and main discoveries in some detail in Chapter 2.

Conclusion

The abandonment of behaviourism at the turn of the 1950s and the advent of the information-processing approach to cognition generated a theoretical need for a machinery able to maintain and execute plans for action while holding the relevant information available for processing, a machinery that Miller *et al.* (1960) suggested calling 'working memory'. Within the conceptual toolbox of psychology at this time, the short-term store hypothesised by the modal model was the most promising candidate for this role. However, Baddeley and colleagues' investigations of the effects of memory load on concurrent processing led to the conclusion that the short-term memory of Atkinson and Shiffrin's (1968) modal model was not a working memory, processing and storage being probably subserved by different systems fuelled by their own resources. However, similar findings were taken by other researchers as evidence for a trade-off between the two functions, pointing towards unitary conceptions of working memory. Whatever the conclusion one favours, the effects of memory load on processing are far from being as dramatic as the conception of processing and storage sharing a common mental space or pool of energy would have predicted. The cognitive system proves much more robust than anticipated. Although the problem of the relationships between processing and storage tends to be sometimes forgotten nowadays, with the study of working memory through the extensive use of paradigms requiring the mere recognition of stimuli few hundreds of milliseconds after their presentation with no processing involved (for example, Luck and Vogel 1997), it remains the key question for a cognitivist view of the mind in which the only purpose of the temporary maintenance of information is its processing. As Conway *et al.* (2005, p. 771) cogently noted, 'a working memory system would be unlikely to evolve for the sole purpose of allowing an organism to store or rehearse information while it was doing nothing else. A more adaptive system would allow the organism to keep task-relevant information active and accessible in memory during the execution of complex cognitive tasks'.

Our thesis is that processing and storage do not compete for a limited mental space or mental energy but for the temporal availability of a central system in charge of both functions. The aim of this book is to describe the machinery that makes possible the alternation of the two functions, producing the smooth and continuous flow of thoughts that one experiences. Conceiving working memory as an alternation between the maintenance of information and its transformation puts emphasis on the temporal constraints that bear upon this mechanism and reintroduces time as the main factor of working memory functioning. This is the focus of the next chapter.

Notes

1 Miller considered the equivalence as coincidental because the two kinds of limitations are different, absolute judgements being limited by the amount of information whereas immediate memory is limited by the number of items.
2 A second series of experiments explored the role of short-term memory on comprehension of prose passages. As observed with the reasoning task, introducing phonemic similarity in the prose passages or adding a concurrent memory load of six items impaired performance, but a load of three or less had no effect. Baddeley and Hitch (1974) also studied the role of working memory on free recall, coming to the conclusion that it is involved in the process of transferring information into long-term memory but might have nothing to do with the recency effect.

2
TIME AND WORKING MEMORY

As we have seen, when investigating the effects of memory load on concurrent activities, Baddeley and his colleagues concluded on the existence of separate specialised systems for processing and storage fuelled by their own resources. Surprisingly, effects of a comparable amplitude were taken by others as evidence for a trade-off between functions sharing a limited pool of attention or activation (Anderson et al., 1996). What is worth noting is that, in both cases, psychologists reasoned that any working memory activity required, from its onset to its completion, the continuous allocation of a constant amount of resources that would consequently be no longer available for other activities. It seems that the temporal dynamics of the interplay between working memory functions was forgotten, and that the possibility of an alternation between functions within the same system was neglected, as if time was not an essential dimension of cognitive functioning. This is not to say that temporal factors were totally neglected in working memory studies. This chapter focuses on these studies. The role of time was mainly taken into account through its damaging effects on storage, as it is the case in the phonological loop model developed by Baddeley (1986), but was also studied in relation to the processing function, and used as an index of processing efficiency, as in Case's (1985) theory. Temporal aspects were even at the centre of the task-switching model proposed by Towse and Hitch (1995), which inspired our own theory.

Temporal constraints in the articulatory loop functioning

Baddeley (1986) escaped the dilemma created by the preserved capacity to solve reasoning problems while holding six or seven digits in short-term memory by assuming that the system storing digits was different from the system involved in reasoning. He proposed that verbal information is maintained in a phonological store whereas reasoning is carried out by some central executive. Though this conception departed from the modal model, the working memory model inherited from its predecessor the hypothesis that maintenance within the phonological store was not a passive but an active process. The phonological loop model is based on the idea that memory traces are subject to temporal decay, but this decay might be counteracted by a speech-based mechanism of articulatory rehearsal by which information is read out in the phonological store, refreshed through subvocal speech, and then fed back into the store. It is worth noting that verbal rehearsal involves an inner speech programme and thus does not necessarily require overt articulation (Baddeley and Wilson 1985). Two main findings support the articulatory loop model. The first is that memory performance degrades when reactivation through subvocal rehearsal is prevented by a concurrent articulation. Murray (1967) observed that the recall of digit or consonant sequences visually presented was strongly affected by the repeated utterance of an unrelated word like 'the' during presentation. This effect, that occurs also when memory items are auditorily presented (for example, Baddeley *et al.* 1984), varies with the articulatory demand. It increases with the articulatory complexity of the material to be uttered (Macken and Jones 1995) but disappears when the concurrent production does not necessitate articulation, the production of a continuous vowel sound (for example 'aaaaah') having no effect, whereas its repetition does ('ah', 'ah', 'ah', Saito 1997). Articulatory suppression is still frequently used to prevent maintenance of information through verbal rehearsal (for example, Cowan *et al.* 2012) and we have used it in many of our experiments in order to investigate the implication of the articulatory loop in memory performance (see Chapter 5). The second finding concerns an effect known as the word length effect (Baddeley *et al.* 1975). Recall performance is far better when subjects are asked to recall sequences made of short words such as 'sum', 'day', 'wit', 'harm' and 'peg', than of long words such as 'university', 'aluminium', 'representative', 'opportunity' and 'organisation'. The explanation is straightforward within the articulatory loop model. Because memory traces suffer from temporal decay within the phonological store, recall performance is a direct function of the time taken to rehearse memory items and avoid their complete loss. Indeed, perfect recall depends on the possibility to rehearse the entire list before the traces of the first items have suffered from an irreparable decay. Hence, memory for long words is poorer because they take longer to articulate. In line with this account, it was established that the effect depends more on articulation duration than on the length of the words in terms of syllables (Baddeley *et al.* 1975; Ellis and Henneley 1980) and that it is abolished by articulatory suppression provided that suppression occurs during both presentation and recall of the memory items (Baddeley *et al.* 1984).

The findings related to the word length effect introduced time as one of the main determinants of working memory, spans depending on the rate at which memory items can be rehearsed. Accordingly, Baddeley *et al.* (1975) were able to predict spans on the basis of the rate at which words could be read, individuals being able to remember as many words as they are able to read out in about 1.8s. As could be expected, the relationship between reading rates and spans held across participants, with a significant correlation of .685; those individuals who are slower in reading words have also lower spans. Interestingly, this relationship between articulatory rate and spans was also explored with success in the developmental domain. Studying the relationship between processing efficiency and memory span, Nicolson (1981) replicated the phenomena reported by Baddeley *et al.* (1975), but in samples of children aged 8, 10 and 12. For all age groups, word span for words varying in length from one to four syllables was roughly equal to the number of words that children were able to read in approximately 2s. It is worth noting that the processing efficiency (namely reading speed) assessed by Nicolson did not exactly correspond to the rate of articulation that plays a critical role in the phonological loop model according to Baddeley (1986). Indeed, especially in children, other factors than articulation rate can affect reading rates, such as, for example, reading abilities. More convincing evidence of the role of articulation in children's memory span was provided by Hulme *et al.* (1984) who asked 4-, 7- and 10-year-old children as well as adults to repeat 10 times pairs of words of short (one-syllable words), medium (two-syllable words), and long (three- and four-syllable words) spoken duration. Participants were also asked to recall lists of words the length of which was adapted to their age (adults were presented with lists of six words, whereas children aged 10 and 7 studied lists of five words and 4-year-old children lists of four words). The mean number of words recalled was plotted as a function of articulation rate for each age group and each type of word, each group contributing three points (i.e., short, medium and long duration words). It appeared that recall performance was a quasi-perfect linear function of speech rate, children and adults being able to recall as many words as they can articulate in 1.5s (Figure 2.1). The same relationship between articulation rate and recall was observed by Hitch *et al.* (1989). A second experiment involving 8- and 10-year-old children analysed the source of the observed developmental differences in articulation rate. It revealed that older children are faster in repeating words, not because they pack more closely the individual words they have to repeat, but simply because they articulate individual words more rapidly. The conclusions drawn by Hulme *et al.* from these findings were straightforward. There is no need to postulate an increase in short-term capacity to explain memory span development. It is the increase in speech rate, considered as reflecting rehearsal rate, which leads to the developmental increase in short-term memory spans.

Of course, the interpretations of the findings related to word length and articulatory rates in terms of a temporal decay of memory traces counteracted by a mechanism of verbal rehearsal did not remain unquestioned. Though the hypothesis of a temporal decay of memory traces is part of several computational models of immediate serial recall (Anderson *et al.* 1998; Burgess and Hitch 1999; Henson 1998; Page and Norris 1998), it is far from being universally endorsed and has been the object of strong criticisms by several scholars (Brown and Lewandowsky 2010; Lewandowsky *et al.* 2009; Nairne 2002). We shall go back to this central issue in Chapter 4. In the same way, it has been argued that the word length effect does not provide evidence for decay in short-term memory (Lewandowsky and Oberauer 2008).

22 Time and working memory

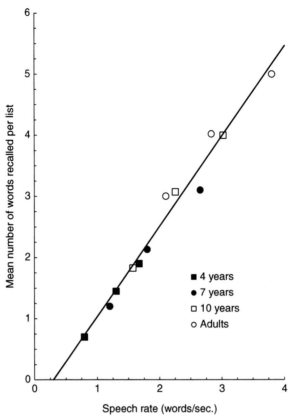

FIGURE 2.1 Relationship between number of words recalled and articulation rate in different age groups with linear regression line. Adapted with permission from C. Hulme, N. Thompson, C. Muir, and A. Lawrence (1984), *Journal of Experimental Child Psychology*, 38, p. 244, with permission from Elsevier

Nonetheless, studies in adults as well as in children clearly indicate a close relationship between memory span and articulatory rate for which the hypothesis of a verbal rehearsal mechanism counteracting the temporal decay of memory traces provides a simple and plausible account. Though this relationship was interpreted by Baddeley and his colleagues as a strong confirmation of the temporal constraints in phonological loop functioning, it received an entirely different explanation by defenders of the hypothesis of a trade-off between processing and storage in working memory.

Time as an index of processing efficiency in the search for a trade-off

There was, in the 1970s, a controversy with regard to the causal factors of memory span development during childhood. Some researchers such as Pascual-Leone (1970; see also Halford and Wilson 1980) suggested that cognitive development was underpinned by an increase in cognitive capacities conceived as an 'M space', some mental attention, energy or power available for maintaining information and simultaneously implementing task-relevant mental schemes on this information. This 'M space' or 'M power' clearly corresponds to what we are nowadays used to calling working memory capacity. Importantly, an additional hypothesis put forward by Pascual-Leone was that the growth in 'M Power' was not controlled by experiential but by epigenetic factors. Hence, an alternative account was to assume that there was no change in mental capacity, the developmental increase in memory spans being due to the development of mnemonic strategies and chunking (Chi 1978; Dempster 1978). We have seen that Nicolson (1981) and Hulme et al. (1984) rejected the hypothesis of an increase in capacities, concluding from their results that the increase in articulation rate (to be accurate, Nicolson evoked a reading rate that he considered as a measure of processing speed) was sufficient to account for memory span development. Case (1978) adopted an intermediary and original position in this debate. He assumed that there was no developmental increase in cognitive capacities, what he called total processing space, while he rejected the idea that memory span development could be explained by strategic factors or some increase in verbal rehearsal efficiency. As we have seen in Chapter 1, and contrary to Pascual-Leone's hypothesis of an increase in M space, Case assumed that the total processing space remained constant across age. Within this account, the developmental increase in memory spans would result from a trade-off between processing and storage. Short-term memory capacities would depend on a short-term storage space corresponding to that residual part of the total processing space left unoccupied by operating space, the amount of cognitive resources needed by mental operations. Processing becoming more and more efficient with age through practice and maturation, operations would require less and less attentional resources, leaving an increasing part of the total processing space available for storage purposes.

What makes things intricate is that Case assessed processing efficiency through processing speed in the same way as Hulme et al. (1984) tested the phonological loop hypothesis by assessing articulatory rates. In order to test their trade-off hypothesis, Case et al. (1982) attempted to measure storage space and operational efficiency independently. Storage space was assessed by measuring memory spans whereas processing efficiency was assessed by measuring the speed at which certain operations could be executed. It is worth noting that the processing/storage trade-off approach applies not only to working memory span tasks, requiring the performance of some secondary intervening task while maintaining memory items, but also to simple span tasks like the word span task that apparently involves only storage requirements. In this latter task, processing would consist in basic input-output operations such as identification of memory items. For example, Chi (1977) demonstrated that developmental differences between kindergarteners and adults in their memory of pictures are strongly reduced when presentation times are shortened for adults, indicating that part of their superiority relies on their higher speed in identifying and processing the pictures. Thus, Case and colleagues presented children ranging in age from 3 to 6 years with a word span task in which they had to recall lists of two to seven concrete and frequent nouns. Operational efficiency was assessed by measuring the time children took to repeat each of the nouns used in the memory task when presented in isolation, with reaction times measured from the end of the presentation of the noun and the onset of a subject's response. Note that, in their study, Hulme et al. (1984) used the same task of repeating words in isolation along with the repetition of three words to assess articulation rates. Case et al. observed a monotonic and linear relation between spans and repetition speed that remained significant even when age was partialled out (Figure 2.2, panel A). This first result supported the hypothesis of a relationship between short-term storage space and processing efficiency. The second experiment was critical in that it tested the hypothesis that, when equated in processing efficiency, two different age groups should exhibit identical spans. Indeed, if spans increase with age because operational efficiency increases, equating operational efficiency across ages should abolish any developmental difference in span. For this purpose, university-educated adults were presented with the same tasks previously used in children, but with less familiar material made of nonsense words (for example, 'loats', 'dast', 'thaid', or 'flim'). The mean reaction time of adults in the repetition task proved very close to that of the 6-year-old children in the previous experiment. Interestingly, and in line with Case et al.'s predictions, their memory span for this unfamiliar material was also very close to the span observed in children (4.36 and 4.49 respectively). Thus, the results of this second experiment clearly indicated the existence of a causal relation between the speed at which words were processed, interpreted by the authors as an index of processing efficiency, and memory spans. Exactly as the trade-off hypothesis predicts, whatever the age, short-term memory spans are a direct function of the speed at which the basic operations required by the memory span task can be executed. These findings corroborated the conclusion of a review of the literature by Dempster (1981) who analysed 10 possible sources of individual and developmental differences in memory span and concluded that only one of these sources, namely item identification, played a major role.

Case et al. (1982) went further in extending their investigation to complex span tasks (what they called in their article 'tests of M space' to refer to tasks in which memory items must be transformed by some operation prior to storage or retrieval). They used the counting span test, a task in which the operation consists of counting arrays of dots printed on cards presented one at a time. The products of the successive counts constitute the items to be stored and recalled. The task begins with only one card, but the number of cards in the series is progressively increased, memory load becoming greater and greater. The maximum set size at which a child is able to recall in correct order the successive totals constitutes his or her counting span, which Case et al. considered as reflecting the subject's M space, or total processing space. In order to prevent rehearsal, children were asked to avoid any pause when a new card was presented and to begin immediately to count. The operational efficiency was independently assessed before the counting span test by measuring children's maximum speed of counting. In order to prevent counting by subitising small groups of dots and thus alleviating the cognitive load of the task, the dots to

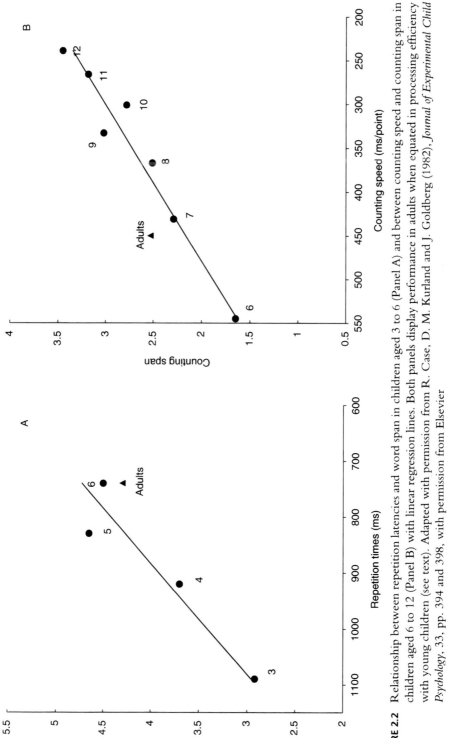

FIGURE 2.2 Relationship between repetition latencies and word span in children aged 3 to 6 (Panel A) and between counting speed and counting span in children aged 6 to 12 (Panel B) with linear regression lines. Both panels display performance in adults when equated in processing efficiency with young children (see text). Adapted with permission from R. Case, D. M. Kurland and J. Goldberg (1982). *Journal of Experimental Child Psychology*, 33, pp. 394 and 398, with permission from Elsevier

be counted, which were green, were randomly displayed along with yellow dots that broke up the visual patterns of the green dots. Moreover, in both tasks (i.e., the counting span test and the measure of counting speed), children were instructed to point to each dot with his or her finger while counting out loud.

As it could be expected, counting speed strongly increased with age. Whereas the time needed to count a dot was 545ms in kindergartners, it dropped to 239ms in sixth graders, revealing a strong age-related increase in processing efficiency. More interestingly, counting spans were a direct function of this processing efficiency (Figure 2.2 panel B). In line with the trade-off hypothesis, recall performance increased from kindergarten to grade six as counting times decreased, with a correlation of −.69 that was still significant when age was partialled out. Following the same logic as in the first part of their study, Case et al. predicted that equating processing efficiency across age should abolish the developmental difference in memory span. Thus, as in their second experiment, they taught a group of graduate and undergraduate students to count using an unfamiliar sequence of nonsense numbers: 'rab', 'slif', 'dak', 'leet', 'roak', 'taid', 'fap', 'flim', 'moof', 'zeer'. When asked to count arrays using this new sequence, adults were of course slower than usual and were as slow as first graders when counting with the canonical number sequence, taking about 450ms per dot. More importantly, as Case's theory predicted, rendering counting more demanding for adults in the counting span test abolished developmental differences in spans, adults and first graders exhibiting counting spans that did not significantly differ (2.53 and 2.29 respectively). Case and collaborators drew two main conclusions from these results. First, the fact that developmental differences in span were abolished when processing efficiency was equated across age suggested that there is no substantial increase in total processing space with development. Second, provided that processing speed is a reliable index of operational efficiency and adequately reflects the operating space needed, developmental differences in short-term storage space are no longer significant when operating spaces are equated across age. This was taken as evidence of a trade-off between storage space and operating space within a fixed and limited total processing space.

At this point, it is worth emphasising the differences between the interpretations that Case et al. (1982) on the one hand and Hulme et al. (1984) on the other made of the same phenomena. Both research groups observed a strong correlation between short-term memory spans and processing rates. Within the phonological loop model favoured by Hulme et al. (1984), time has a causal role on memory performance. It is because memory traces decay with time that their faster restoration through verbal rehearsal increases recall performance. Higher rates of articulation would allow for the restoration of more memory items per unit of time, resulting in longer sequences of items that can be restored and put back in the phonological store before their complete loss. Thus, older children would have higher spans because they are faster at rehearsing verbal memories. The explanation of the same relationship by Case et al. (1982) is totally different. Time within their approach does not play any causal role, but is only used as an index of processing efficiency. Based on proposals by Logan (1976) and Shiffrin and Schneider (1977), Case and colleagues assumed that any increase in efficiency results in a decreased attentional load, which results in turn in an increase in processing speed. The idea here is that slowness reveals inefficient operations that require a substantial amount of attention that is no longer available to attend to memory traces resulting from previous operations. The hypothesised mechanism is not one of time-constrained rehearsal that counteracts temporal decay, but one of attentional interference resulting in a trade-off between processing and storage. Faster articulation in older children is not related with higher memory spans because it allows for more rehearsal, but because it is associated with lower attentional demand of the operations involved in the span task.

Case was not isolated in thinking that processing efficiency and identification processes were the source of the developmental differences in short-term memory. In a review of the literature that we already evoked above, Dempster (1981) challenged the received view that the word length effect, as well as the correlation between articulation rate and serial recall, unambiguously testified for the existence of a capacity-limited phonological loop, and argued that the word length effect may reflect item identification processes. Identifying long words would require more time and capacity than identifying short words, resulting in a lower number of memorised words. Hitch *et al.* (1989) tested this latter hypothesis in 8- and 11-year-old children who were asked to recall lists of visually presented words of one, two or three syllables with and without articulatory suppression. Articulation rates, reading rates and word identification times were also measured. A strong word length effect affected recall performance in both age groups, but this effect disappeared under articulatory suppression. This suggested that the word length effect is related to the maintenance of words through articulatory rehearsal, as the phonological loop hypothesis assumes. However, developmental differences could not be entirely explained by differences in rehearsal efficiency because they were not entirely abolished when articulatory rehearsal was prevented. More importantly, and in line with the phonological loop model, articulation rates proved to be a far better predictor of spans than identification times. When plotted on articulation rates, mean spans for the three word length conditions fell into the same line for both age groups. Similar results were obtained by Hitch *et al.* (1993) in children aged 5, 8 and 11 with words presented auditorily, and not visually as in Hitch *et al.* (1989). Once again, articulation rate was a better predictor of word span than identification time, with a quasi-perfect linear relation between articulation rate and word span whatever the age of the participants.

There is no doubt that these results were at odds with the trade-off account of the developmental increase in working memory spans as measured by the immediate serial recall procedure. This is not to say that all was perfectly in line with the phonological loop model. As Hitch *et al.* (1989) observed, articulatory suppression did not abolish developmental differences, suggesting the existence of a second component of short-term memory span along with the phonological loop. When considering that 8- and 11-year-old children were still able to recall more than three words under articulatory suppression in Hitch *et al.* (1993), this second component was not to be neglected. Hitch *et al.* (1989, 1993) suggested that it might reflect some general workspace as in Case's theory. Another envisioned possibility was the intervention of a long-term memory component. Hulme *et al.* (1991) found a length effect for both words and pronounceable non-words, their recall being a function of the rate at which these materials could be articulated. However, there was also a clear advantage for words over non-words that was independent of length and that testified for the intervention of a long-term component independent of the phonological loop.

Thus, although the studies by Hitch *et al.* (1989, 1993) supported the phonological loop model, they left unresolved several issues. Besides the fact that the phonological loop model revealed itself insufficient to account for all the phenomena related with short-term memory spans, Case *et al.* (1982) extended their investigations and conclusions far beyond immediate recall. They showed that the same relationship between span and processing efficiency holds even when the measured efficiency does not correspond to processes involved in identifying and encoding the memoranda, but to concurrent activities that compete and interfere with storage, as is the case in their counting span test. The phonological loop model had very little to say about these findings, the multi-component model having left underspecified the relationships between processing and storage and the precise mechanisms by which they could interfere with each other. Clearly, a new model was needed, which was proposed by John Towse and Graham Hitch some years later.

The task-switching model

The phonological loop model accounts for the word length effect and the correlation between articulation rates and spans by assuming that articulatory rehearsal counteracts the temporal decay of memory traces. Expressed the other way round, this model assumes that verbal memory traces decay as long as they are not being articulated by the loop. Because articulatory rehearsal is a serial process (one can only utter one word at a time), a given memory trace decays as long as the articulatory loop is occupied by articulating other memory items or any other material. Consequently, short-term memory spans in the immediate serial recall paradigm correspond to the number of items that can be articulated and restored within a period of time equivalent to the complete decay and loss of a memory trace. The solution adopted by Towse and Hitch (1995) to account for Case *et al.*'s (1982) findings without resorting to any trade-off or resource-sharing hypothesis was to extend this logic to complex span tasks such as the counting span test, and to assume that to-be-remembered items (i.e., the successive totals) suffer from temporal decay while the subject is performing the processing component of the task (i.e., counting the arrays).

What Case *et al.* (1982) clearly established is that there is a correlation between mean counting spans and counting speed. As we have seen, they interpreted this relationship as evidence for a trade-off between processing and storage: faster counting in older children means that this operation is less attention-demanding, leaving more attentional resources available for storage purpose. However, Towse and

Hitch (1995) wisely noted that faster counting in older children also means shorter counting durations, and shorter counting durations involve a shorter period of storage in the counting span test paradigm. Indeed, recall that subjects are asked to count successive arrays while retaining their totals. Thus, the delay between encoding and recall of a given memory item is determined by the time taken to count the subsequently presented arrays, with faster counting corresponding to shorter delays. In other words, Towse and Hitch noted that, in the counting span test used by Case et al. (1982), the cognitive cost of the counting activity and the temporal period of storage are confounded. As they suggested, it might be supposed that the strength of the memory traces weakens as their delay of retention increases. Thus, higher spans in older children would not result from higher processing efficiency, but from the fact that they benefit from shorter delays of retention due to their faster counting. Towse and Hitch pointed out that their alternative memory decay hypothesis strongly differs from Case's account. There would be no need to resort to notions such as resource sharing between operating and storage space within a limited total processing space, or to notions such as cognitive load to account for the difficulty of the counting span task. A mere hypothesis of temporal decay while performing a concurrent task would be sufficient.

To decide between the competing hypotheses, Towse and Hitch (1995) conceived an astute experimental design that disentangled cognitive cost and duration of the counting activity. We have seen that, in Case et al.'s counting span test, the green dots to be counted were displayed along with yellow dots to be ignored. Differing in colour, targets are easy to distinguish from distracters. Towse and Hitch decided to vary the difficulty of the counting task by manipulating the discriminability of the targets. They contrasted an easy condition, named 'feature', in which blue square targets were mixed up with orange triangles, and a more difficult condition, named 'conjunction', in which blue square targets were presented alongside blue triangles; targets and distracters only differing by their shape while sharing the same colour. They verified in a preliminary experiment that the conjunction condition elicited longer counting times and higher error rates, from which they concluded that it involved a higher cognitive cost. The critical experiment involved children aged 6, 7, 8 and 11 who performed a counting span task under three conditions: the feature and conjunction conditions described above with a number of targets per card varying between 3 and 7, and a 'feature slow' condition identical to the feature condition except that the number of targets was increased and varied between 6 and 10. This last condition was designed to create a situation in which the difficulty of counting was the same as in the feature condition (same target/distracter discriminability) whereas its duration was the same as in the conjunction condition due to the greater number of targets to be counted.

What do the two models predict? According to the trade-off hypothesis, recall performance depends on the attentional demand of the processing component of the task. Thus, the conjunction condition in which counting is more difficult would yield lower spans than the two other conditions that should not differ from each other. By contrast, according to the memory decay hypothesis defended by Towse and Hitch, recall performance depends on the duration, and not the difficulty, of the intervening counting task. Consequently, the conjunction and the feature slow conditions should not differ from each other and should elicit lower spans than the feature condition. In other words, both hypotheses, though for different reasons, predict better recall performance in the feature than in the conjunction condition, but they differ concerning the feature slow condition. Whereas the memory decay hypothesis predicts lower spans for the feature slow than the feature condition, the trade-off hypothesis predicts similar spans in both conditions. The results unambiguously favoured the memory decay hypothesis. First of all, it was verified during the span task that the conjunction and the feature slow conditions involved equivalent but longer counting times than the feature condition. Concerning recall performance, counting spans were significantly higher for the feature than for both the conjunction and feature slow conditions that did not differ significantly from each other. This pattern was observed at all ages. According to Towse and Hitch, a simple explanation of this phenomenon was to suppose that instead of trading storage space for processing, children might alternate between the counting activity during display presentation and storage activities at display offset. In this view, the successive totals would be passively stored with no attempt to actively maintain them during the counting of each array (Hitch and Towse 1995). Suffering from temporal decay, the record of totals would decline during counting, with longer counting periods resulting in more decay and poorer recall performance. Based on results by Guttentag (1984, 1989), Hitch and Towse suggested that this serial resource-allocation strategy is adopted by children to cope with the demands inherent to time sharing in performing the dual task. Instead of the resource sharing, counting span performance would involve a resource switching.

This task switching hypothesis and the importance of temporal factors was further explored in a variety of complex span tasks by Towse et al. (1998). For this purpose, they adapted a paradigm initially developed by Cowan et al. (1992) to assess the contribution of output decay in the word length effect. Cowan et al. (1992) reasoned that saying long words at recall takes longer and hence delays output of the following memory items. They tested this hypothesis by having participants recall lists containing short and long words placed either at the beginning or the end of the lists. As the hypothesis of trace decay at output would have predicted, long words in the early part of the lists resulted in poorer recall. Following the same idea, Towse et al. (1998) designed a counting span task in which they manipulated the numerosity of the first and last cards in the sequences. Sequences beginning with a card with a large numerosity (and ending with a small card) were contrasted with sequences beginning with a small card and ending with a large card, the numerosity of the intervening cards remaining unchanged. Towse et al. (1998) noted that in terms of cognitive difficulty of counting, the two types of sequences were equivalent as the same cards were presented. By contrast, they differed in terms of delay of retention. As Figure 2.3 makes clear, the retention duration is longer for sequences ending with a large rather than a small card. Because only count products have to be retained, the time taken to count the first card has no impact on retention duration,

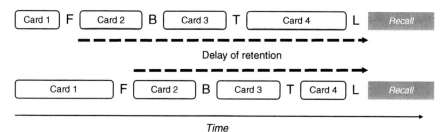

FIGURE 2.3 Illustration of the difference in delays of retention created by manipulating the order of presentation of cards varying in numerosity in a counting span task. Adapted with permission from J. N. Towse, G. J. Hitch and U. Hutton (1988), *Journal of Memory and Language*, 39, p. 198, with permission from Elsevier

but a large last card increases the likelihood of forgetting. Children aged 6, 7, 9 and 10 performed a counting span task with sequences ending either with a small card with a mean of four target squares or a large card containing a mean of seven targets. The results revealed that the large last cards took longer to count and, as the task switching model predicted, elicited lower spans, an effect that did not interact with age.

Subsequent experiments applied the same logic and design to the operation span task initially designed by Turner and Engle (1989) and the reading span task (Daneman and Carpenter 1980). For example, in the operation span test, children were presented with either short (for example, 7 + 1 =?), intermediate (for example, 5 + 0 + 1 =?) or long (for example, 8 + 0 + 1 − 1 =?) arithmetic problems and asked to remember the answers for further recall. Series with a first short and a last long problem were contrasted with series beginning with a long and ending with a short problem, with the intermediate problems in the intermediary positions. In the reading span task, children read a series of sentences in which the last word was missing but was strongly invited by the meaning (for example, 'the dog wagged his __'). They were asked to produce the missing words and recall them at the end of the series. The critical manipulation contrasted series beginning either with a short or a long sentence and ending with a long or a short sentence, respectively. As the task switching model predicted, in both tasks, series ending with a long problem or a long sentence resulted in lower spans, whatever the age of the children.

A longitudinal follow-up of this study was subsequently published by Hitch *et al.* (2001) in which children who participated in Experiment 3 in Towse *et al.* (1998) were tested one year later with the same operation and reading span tasks. Not surprisingly, working memory spans had increased during the year elapsed but, once again, for both tasks, spans were lower when the last processing episode took longer. Hitch *et al.* (2001) also observed a linear relationship between span and on-line measures of processing speed in both tasks but, interestingly, the two relationships quantitatively differed with a steeper slope for the operation span than the reading span. This difference suggested domain-specific resources for verbal and numerical activities, an interpretation supported by the correlational analyses between working memory spans and academic achievement. The two span tasks explained a large amount of shared variance in reading and arithmetic attainment, but reading span and operation span accounted also for unique variance in reading achievement, suggesting that these tasks do not only measure a domain-general ability, contrary to what Engle et al. (1992) or Turner and Engle (1989) argued. Finally, the task-switching model was tested by Towse et al. (2002) using a Brown-Peterson paradigm in which a distracting task is interpolated between presentation and recall of a list of memory items. Both the difficulty and the duration of the interpolated task were manipulated. For example, children ranging from 8 to 17 years of age had to solve either additions or multiplications considered as easy and difficult respectively. In a second experiment, 8- and 10-year olds had to perform a lexical decision task with non-words that consisted either of pseudohomophones (for example, 'werme') rendering the task difficult or in nonhomophones (for example, 'gled') that made it easy. In a third experiment, 10-year-old children performed either an easy two-choice (judging parity of numerals or their accuracy as a solution for a sum) or a more difficult four-choice processing task in which both tasks were considered in conjunction. Duration of the intervening task, and consequently retention intervals, varied from 4-6s to 14-16s across experiments. Contrary to any resource-sharing model, the difficulty of the intervening tasks had no effect on recall. By contrast, longer durations of the interpolated task resulted in poorer memory performance, supporting the task-switching model.

In summary, this series of studies that involved the main and most popular working memory span tasks converged towards the conclusion that spans depend on the retention interval, with longer delays of retention resulting in lower spans. Thus, the authors stated that 'from a theoretical perspective, the data emphasize the need to incorporate temporally based forgetting within models of working memory' (Towse et al. 1998, p. 215). A crucial problem was to identify the working memory system susceptible to underpin the observed phenomena. It seemed evident that the phonological loop, in which information was assumed to degrade within 2s, was not a plausible candidate. How could the phonological loop hold up to three items or more in tasks where the final processing episode lasted often more than 6s while discouraging verbal rehearsal? Towse et al. (1998) envisioned as a possible solution the intervention of the central executive. Though they acknowledged that the current conceptualisation of the multi-component model did not offer the theoretical framework for explaining the temporal dynamics of a central system in charge of processing and storage, they saw little reason why Baddeley's model could not accommodate such an approach. This is most probably because they were not yet aware of the last evolution of the multi-component model as it was introduced by Baddeley and Logie (1999) with a separation of the two functions, the central executive being exclusively devoted to processing while storage functions were relegated to slave systems. Quite surprisingly, although the results gathered by Towse and his colleagues directly contradicted this conception, this incompatibility actually ran unnoticed even when the main findings related to the task-switching model were extended to adults by Towse, Hitch, and Hutton (2000).

Though the precise working memory architecture that could account for the observed results remained unspecified, these results were at odds with the trade-off hypothesis and the idea that processing and storage share a limited pool of resource provided by some total processing space. Rather, it seemed that the mere hypothesis of a short-term memory in which memory traces decay, coupled with the idea that individuals switch from processing to storage activities, was sufficient to explain why memory spans depend on the duration of the interpolated task but not on its difficulty. Thus, when discussing the concept of central executive in light of their recent findings, Towse and Houston-Price (2001, p. 246) concluded: 'It is increasingly apparent that both theoretical and computational accounts make the idea of limited resource-sharing capacity superfluous'. This proposal constituted a complete upheaval of the current conceptions of working memory. Apart from the fact that several leading theories were based on the idea of a limited resource shared by processing and storage functions (Anderson *et al.* 1996; Baddeley and Hitch 1974; Case 1985; Daneman and Carpenter 1980; Just and Carpenter 1992), the tasks commonly used to measure working memory capacity such as the reading span (Daneman and Carpenter 1980) or the operation span tasks (Turner and Engle 1989) were based, and are still based, on this idea. Moreover, the hypothesis of a limited resource shared between cognitive functions lay at the heart of several theories of cognitive development (Case 1985, 1992; Halford 1993; Halford *et al.* 1998; Pascual-Leone 1970). Thus, the provocative assumptions of the task-switching model deserved a rigorous test. The next section presents our first attempt in this direction.

A preliminary test

Although Towse and his colleagues (Towse and Hitch 1995; Towse *et al.* 1998) demonstrated remarkable ingenuity in designing their experiments, we suggested that the series of experiments presented in these studies did not provide such strong evidence in favour of the task-switching model and its memory decay hypothesis as the authors assumed (Barrouillet and Camos 2001). Concerning Towse and Hitch (1995), we noted that the results support the memory decay hypothesis and rule out the trade-off hypothesis as long as it is admitted that increasing the number of targets to be counted only affects the duration and not the cognitive cost of counting. However, several factors could make counting a larger number of objects more demanding. The gradual learning during childhood of the number sequence from the smallest to the largest numbers could make increasingly demanding the production of larger numbers (Fuson and Hall 1983; Fuson *et al.* 1982). Moreover, a larger number of targets to be counted involves keeping track of an increasing number of objects already counted to avoid double counting and errors, something that could result in greater memory load (Engle *et al.* 1999). Accordingly, several developmental studies demonstrated that counting performance is affected by variations in the number of objects (Camos *et al.* 2001; Camos *et al.* 1999; Potter and Levy 1986). Thus, the hypothesis that counting larger arrays of dots affects only counting duration was not warranted. The same criticism applied to the method of manipulating the order of processing episodes used by Towse et al. (1998). The authors reasoned that manipulating this order would only affect the retention duration but not the overall difficulty of the task because the same arrays are to be counted. However, this is disputable. The counting span test introduced by Case et al. (1982) involves retaining the products of the successive counts. In doing so, the genuine working memory span task, that is the task requiring concurrent processing and storage, only begins at the end of the first count when obtaining its total (see Figure 2.3). Thus, when the first card is omitted, series ending either with a small or a large card actually differ in the size of the to-be-counted arrays and consequently could differ in overall cognitive cost. The same criticism holds for the operation span and the reading span tasks as manipulated by Towse et al. (1998). Longer sentences as well as longer arithmetic problems are likely to involve a higher cognitive cost that undermines the rationale of the comparison between the two orders of completion. Thus, we suggested that a more direct test of the impact of the cognitive cost of processing on concurrent maintenance was needed.

For this purpose, we proposed to reverse the logic of Towse et al.'s (1998) design and to manipulate the cognitive cost involved in the processing component of the task while keeping constant its duration. In a first part of our experiment, 8- and 11-year-old children completed a counting span task in which they had to count arrays of 6 to 10 red target dots displayed on cards along with green distracter dots. These cards were presented one at a time in series of ascending length, from 2 to 6 cards, with three cards for each length. Each dotted card was followed by a card with a letter, children being asked to recall these letters in correct order at the end of the series. The time taken by the children to count each card was measured from an audio record of their entire production. Three weeks afterward, the same groups of children were invited to complete a task we named the 'baba span task'. Its structure was exactly the same as the counting span task, except that children were required to say repeatedly 'baba' instead of counting dots. For this purpose, dotted cards were replaced by white cards that remained on screen for a duration equivalent to the time each child took to count the corresponding array. Thus, for each participant, the series of letters and retention intervals were exactly the same in both tasks, except that their processing component varied in cognitive cost (Figure 2.4). Indeed, it is usually argued that repeating the same syllable induces an articulatory suppression but involves a minimal cognitive cost. Baddeley et al. (1984) observed that a non-articulatory task inducing a comparable cognitive demand such as finger tapping had no effect on short-term memory performance, and Vallar and Baddeley (1984) reported the case of patient PV who did not seem to use verbal rehearsal in immediate serial recall tasks and who remained unaffected by suppression. Accordingly, Naveh-Benjamin and Jonides (1984) studied the cognitive cost associated with rehearsal and demonstrated that once an articulatory programme has been retrieved in a first demanding stage, the repetitive execution of this rehearsal programme is more automatic, demanding few processing capacities. Thus, we assumed that counting involved higher cognitive cost than saying 'baba'. Because the same children performed the counting span and the baba span tasks, and in order to control for an eventual

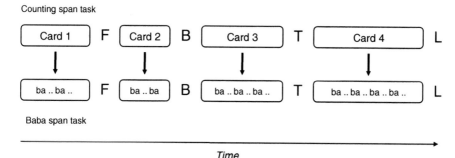

FIGURE 2.4 Design of the experiment by Barrouillet and Camos (2001) to disentangle time and cognitive load effects in working memory span tasks. In counting span, each to-be-remembered letter was preceded by a card with dots to be counted. The length of the different boxes (card 1, 2, 3, 4) reflects the duration of counting of each card. In the baba span task, empty cards were used and participants were asked to repeat 'ba, ba, ba' for the same duration as they took to count the dots on the corresponding card

practice effect, the experimental groups were compared with control groups who performed the baba span task twice (in these groups, the duration of each white card corresponded to the mean counting time of the dotted card it replaced).

The predictions of the two contrasted models were straightforward. Because counting is more demanding than repeating a syllable, the trade-off hypothesis predicted better performance in the baba span than in the counting span task. By contrast, the task-switching model and its memory decay hypothesis predicted no difference at all because processing times, and thus retention intervals, had been carefully equated.

Results were very clear. In the experimental groups performing first the counting span task and then, three weeks after, the baba span task, both age groups exhibited higher baba spans than counting spans. However, this difference was most probably imputable to a practice effect, the same increase in performance being observed in the control groups. Importantly, the statistical analyses did not reveal any interaction between groups and sessions. In fact, there was no difference between counting and baba spans, the former being even slightly higher in the first session when comparing the control with experimental groups (Table 2.1). These findings strongly supported the task-switching model. Variations in the cognitive cost of the secondary task had no effect on working memory spans when retention intervals were kept constant. This is not to say that counting or saying 'baba' had no effect on recall. A control experiment established that children who were allowed to remain silent when presented with the series of white cards used in the baba span task largely outperformed their peers (see the silent condition in Table 2.1). This suggested that the difficulty of the counting span and the baba span tasks was due to the articulatory suppression induced by counting aloud or repeating the syllable 'ba', but not to the cognitive demands of the tasks. Impressed and, we must admit, quite puzzled by these results, we wondered if the absence of difference between counting spans and baba spans was due to the possible high degree of automation reached by the counting activity in 11- or even 8-year olds. Towse and Hitch (1997) had shown that the coordination between pointing objects and saying the number sequence required by counting no longer involved cognitive cost from the age of 7 onward. Consequently, we decided to replicate the comparison between the counting span and the baba span in 6-year-old children, an age at which counting was supposed to remain a demanding task. Independent groups were assigned to the two tasks, the duration of presentation of each white card in the baba span condition corresponding to the mean counting time registered in the counting span group. Other changes consisted in presenting the letters before, and not after, each processing card to make possible the study of series of only one memory item, and in the experimenter reading aloud the letters at the same time children did. Once more, though there was a slight advantage for the latter, there was no significant difference between counting spans and baba spans (1.14 and 1.35 respectively). Power analyses indicated that a large pool of more than 150 participants per group would have been necessary to reach a level of .05.

It was clear from these two experiments that the comparison of the counting span and the baba span tasks confirmed the task-switching model. Provided that retention intervals were equal, varying the difficulty of the task to perform within these intervals had no effect. Of course, as Case *et al.* (1982), we observed a smooth increase in counting speed with age (536ms, 474ms, and 346ms per dot for 6-, 8- and 11-year-old children respectively) and the correlative increase in counting span (1.14 in 6-year olds with letters presented before the counting cards, 3.31 in 8-year-old children and 4.47 in 11-year olds with letters presented after the counting cards). However, this increase in spans could no longer be explained by an increase in processing efficiency that would have freed mental space for short-term storage. Towse and Houston-Price (2001) might have been right in their claim that the notion

TABLE 2.1 Mean spans (and standard deviations) as a function of the session and the task for children aged 8 and 11 in Barrouillet and Camos (2001)

	Age			
	8		11	
Session	First	Second	First	Second
Experimental group	Counting span 3.31 (0.81)	Baba span 3.75 (0.69)	Counting span 4.17 (.58)	Baba span 4.73 (.49)
Control group	Baba span 2.94 (0.78)	Baba span 3.56 (0.98)	Baba span 4.10 (.80)	Baba span 4.46 (.53)
Control experiment	Silent 4.31 (0.63)		Silent 5.29 (0.50)	

of limited resource-sharing capacity was superfluous! At the same time, we remained doubtful. A long and venerable tradition from the cognitive revolution had disseminated the view that controlled cognitive activities tap some limited cognitive resource, and the idea that varying the attentional demand of an activity could have no impact at all on the concurrent maintenance of information in working memory seemed counterintuitive. However, the notion of resource itself may turn out to be something like a theoretical soup stone, an 'excess baggage' that could be removed without any loss or damage from our theoretical panoply, as Navon (1984) claimed. Thus, as a last attempt, we decided to test the task-switching hypothesis by amplifying the contrast between the two activities under comparison.

Following Case *et al.*'s (1982) assumption, our as well as Towse and Hitch's (1995) experiments were based on the idea that counting is a demanding task for children. This is what a componential analysis of the task suggests, which requires pointing at objects, saying number words, and coordinating both activities while keeping track of already counted objects. However, counting is also one of the earliest and most extensively practiced numerical skills that could have reached a significant degree of automation, even in kindergartners. Various studies failed to find any cognitive cost associated with the coordination of pointing and enumeration, even in children as young as six years of age (Camos *et al.* 1999, 2001; Miller and Stigler 1987). Thus, it was still possible that the absence of difference between counting spans and baba spans was due to the insufficient cognitive cost associated with counting. Consequently, we decided to use a highly demanding task such as arithmetic problem solving. In a third experiment, 9- and 11-year-old children were required to perform either an operation span task or a baba span task. The operation span task consisted in series of consonants to be remembered that were displayed on screen for 1s. Each consonant was followed by a two- or a three-operand addition (for example, $9 + 8 = 18$? or $4 + 7 + 8 = 19$?). Children were asked to verify these operations and to respond ('true' or 'false') by pressing keys, their key press triggering the appearance of the next letter (or the word 'recall' at the end of the series). The baba span was designed in the same way except that each operation was replaced by a white screen for a duration equivalent to the mean solution time registered in the operation span group. The results were in sharp contrast to what we had previously observed. As in the previous experiments, older children outperformed younger children, but more importantly there was a significant effect of tasks. The operation span task elicited lower recall performance than the baba span task, an effect that did not interact with age (1.56 and 2.26 respectively in 9-year olds; 2.83 and 3.25 respectively in 11-year olds). These results remained unchanged when those participants who exhibited excessively short or excessively long mean solution times in the arithmetic task were removed from the analyses.

These latter results supported the hypothesis of a trade-off between processing and storage. Even when retention duration was kept constant, the more demanding task of solving arithmetic equations was associated with more forgetting and lower recall performance, as Case's theory would have predicted. However, we emphasised that these results did not rule out any impact of a potential memory decay phenomenon in working memory tasks, for at least two reasons. First, from a logical stance, the fact that an additional cognitive load results in more forgetting does not necessarily mean that memory traces do not suffer from a temporal decay during processing, but simply that any notion of cognitive load or resource cannot be jettisoned in explaining working memory functioning and performance. Second, arithmetic problem solving had a more detrimental effect on maintenance than a mere articulatory suppression, but the difference was smaller than we expected. After all, our experiment contrasted an activity presumed to involve no cognitive load with one of the most demanding activities, an activity so difficult that it is known to generate anxiety in many people (Ashcraft 2002). If a trade-off between operations and storage occurred as Case et al. (1982) assumed, we should have observed some dramatic effect. In fact, the effect was quite modest, the introduction of mental arithmetic resulting in a decrease of about 20 per cent of recall performance compared with the baba span, an effect that even failed to reach significance in 11-year olds. Once again, the cognitive system proved more robust than anticipated.

How to do two things at the same time: a rapid switching mechanism

These findings and the relatively modest effect of a highly demanding task on the concurrent maintenance of a series of consonants were reminiscent of the small impact that memory load had in solving reasoning problems in Baddeley and Hitch's (1974) study. In both cases, the presumed resource sharing that was expected to produce dramatic effects turned out to affect only slightly the component of the task under study. Reasoning was only slowed down by a near-span memory load with no impact on accuracy in Baddeley and Hitch (1974). Here, short-term storage capacity was only slightly reduced by the completion of a difficult task like mental arithmetic. In discussing their results, Towse and Hitch (1995) wondered what kind of memory store could underpin the performance they observed. They claimed that the phonological loop was definitely not the candidate, with three items or more surviving processing episodes that lasted often more than 6s while discouraging verbal rehearsal. The phonological loop model encountered the same difficulty in our study where verbal rehearsal was hindered by the repetition of 'baba' for more than 8s in 11-year-old children who were nonetheless able to recall more than three consonants in the correct order. In the same way, assuming some maintenance within the central executive was at odds with the multi-component model and its fractionation between processing and storage functions (Baddeley and Logie 1999). The multiple-component seemed unable to provide a convincing account for our results.

A far more preferable solution was to suppose, as Towse and Hitch (1995) did, some intervention of a long-term component. Several models of working memory assumed at the end of the 1990s that working memory is that part of long-term memory activated above threshold (Anderson 1993; Anderson and Lebière 1998; Anderson et al. 1996; Cantor and Engle 1993; Cowan 1995, 1999; Engle et al. 1999;

Engle and Oransky 1999; Lovett *et al.* 1999). This still prevalent theoretical view (Cowan 2005; Oberauer 2002) seemed able to account for both time and resource limitations in working memory. All these models assume that the items present in the focus of attention receive activation. Because of the limited size of the focus (Cowan 2005; Oberauer 2002) or the limitation in the amount of available attention (Anderson 1993), only a small number of items can receive activation from attention. Those items that have left the focus of attention are at risk of being lost, due either to the temporal decay of their activation (Anderson 1993; Cowan 1995; Lovett *et al.* 1999) or to interference (Oberauer 2002). Nonetheless, they could be reactivated by a process described by Cowan (1992; Cowan, Keller, *et al.* 1994) as a covert retrieval, some mental search that could bring back working memory items into the focus of attention for reactivation. Such a mechanism of reactivating decaying memory traces had the potential to account for our results.

The fact that solving arithmetic equations had a more detrimental effect on maintenance than a mere articulatory suppression while retention intervals were kept constant indisputably argued in favour of a trade-off hypothesis between processing and storage. However, if the two competing activities were run in parallel, with a continuous sharing of some limited resource, the effects we observed, as well as those reported by Baddeley and Hitch (1974) or Duff and Logie (2001), would have been far more dramatic. At the same time, there was something true in the task switching model and its idea of an alternation between storage and processing phases. Towse and Hitch (1995; Towse *et al.* 1998) observed that longer retention intervals filled with tasks preventing verbal rehearsal resulted in more forgetting, and we observed that when these intervals were kept constant, baba spans and counting spans did not significantly differ. A huge difference in cognitive demands seemed to be required to produce a moderate effect. This moderate effect of solving arithmetic equations suggested either that the decay of activation was rather slow even in young children, or that they managed to reactivate memory traces while performing the arithmetic task by switching their attention away from the calculation to the letters to be remembered. This switching could have occurred when reaching intermediary results for example. This idea was incompatible with the task switching model that assumed that individuals did not attempt to reactivate memory traces during processing, making retention interval the main determinant of spans, but it preserved the ideas of an alternation between functions and of temporally-based forgetting. Integrating a modified task switching model into the general framework provided by attention-based activation models of working memory provided us with a plausible explanation to the seemingly impressive performance of remembering letters while solving equations, or solving reasoning problems while remembering series of seven or eight digits. Instead of considering, like Baddeley and Hitch (1974) did, that the cognitive system is much more *robust* than anticipated, it could be more *flexible* than expected. We began to surmise that if human beings seem to be able to do two things at the same time, it is precisely because they are not doing the two things at the same time, but in alternation.

Conclusion

Temporal factors have always been taken into account in working memory theorising. From its first version onwards, the multi-component model has assumed that memory traces suffer from a temporal decay that has to be counteracted by rehearsal mechanisms to avoid their complete loss. Accordingly, short-term memory spans are a direct function of the rate at which verbal material can be articulated, a relationship that was advocated to account for developmental changes. Such a relationship received other explanations by defenders of unitary views of working memory who considered articulation rates as reflecting processing efficiency, with higher efficiency of processing leaving more room for storage purpose. This trade-off hypothesis accounted for complex span tasks like Case's counting span. Counting speed was assumed to predict counting span because faster counting reflects more efficient counting processes that are less demanding in cognitive resources. However, a simpler hypothesis was put forward by Towse and Hitch (1995) in their task switching model: faster counting is associated with higher counting spans simply because faster counting results in shorter delays of retention during which memory traces suffer from temporal decay.

Our own investigation of the relationships between cognitive cost, processing times and working memory spans revealed a more complex picture. When processing times were equated, demanding activities such as operation solving led to lower spans, but the effect was far from being dramatic, suggesting that children managed to refresh memory traces while solving operations. If this reintroduction of a temporal dynamics in working memory functioning along with the hypothesis of a time-based forgetting were correct, we surmised that a task that would require a continuous attentional focusing should have a highly detrimental effect on concurrent maintenance. This intuition was at the basis of the model of working memory we named the time-based resource-sharing model.

3
TIME-BASED RESOURCE SHARING

The studies reviewed in the previous chapters, which investigated the effects of storage on concurrent processing of incoming information or the effect of some demanding activity on the concurrent maintenance of lists of items for further recall, led to two main findings. First, a dual-task decrement is usually observed affecting both functions. Memory loads have an impact on reasoning, problem solving or comprehension (for example, Baddeley and Hitch 1974; Duff and Logie 2001) and, reciprocally, performing these tasks has a detrimental effect on short-term storage (Anderson *et al.* 1996; Barrouillet and Camos 2001; Duff and Logie 2001). This is in line with what Baddeley (1986) called the general model of working memory, which assumes that working memory is a system devoted to processing and storage. This impact of processing on storage, and *vice versa*, testifies for the existence of such a system and some trade-off between the two functions. The second finding is that these effects are generally small, or at least smaller than often anticipated (Baddeley and Hitch 1974; Barrouillet and Camos 2001; Duff and Logie 2001). We have argued in Chapter 1 that these anticipations seem to be based on the tacit assumption that both processing and storage draw continuously on a limited pool of resource in such a way that dramatic dual-task decrement should occur when performance on one task approaches its optimal level. The modest size of these effects is sufficient to rule out this hypothesis of a continuous sharing of a common limited resource. However, this does not mean that these effects can be ignored or dismissed as minimal or negligible, leading to the fractionation of working memory into a set of separate systems subserving specific functions, as Baddeley and Logie (1999) assumed.

As we suggested at the end of the previous chapter, an alternative possibility might be to assume that different functions alternate within a multi-purpose unitary system. This conception was often envisioned but never retained. Baddeley and Hitch (1974, p. 54) suggested *en passant* that their participants might have adopted a strategy of time-sharing between rehearsal of the memory letters and reasoning. They did not retain this idea, maybe because they observed an interaction between memory load and reasoning difficulty, while the time-sharing hypothesis would have predicted additive effects. Interestingly, this interaction vanished in further experiments (Baddeley and Lewis reported in Baddeley 1986), a phenomenon that Baddeley found difficult to interpret, but he did not mention any time-sharing option. When addressing the issue of the psychological basis for the trade-off they observed between speed and span, Case et al. (1982) evoked the possibility of a 'temporal interference' whereby the time spent to execute a difficult operation would decrease the number of memory items that a rehearsal loop could keep active. This eventuality was rejected on the basis of two pilot experiments using a counting span test in which counting times, but not counting difficulty, were equated between adults and 6-year-old children (for example, counting was made longer for adults by asking them to count additional dots or by colouring targets a similar shade to the distracters, making their discrimination more difficult[1]). Contrary to the temporal explanation, equating the time spent in counting between age groups did not narrow developmental differences, while equating counting difficulty did, something that supported Case's trade-off hypothesis. We will see in Chapter 7 that there exist ways of equating processing times that are more effective in reducing developmental differences than Case et al. (1982) surmised, but the result of their attempt was to reject the temporal explanation. In the same way, Daneman and Carpenter (1980) envisaged that a possible effect of increased efficiency, along with spared capacity, could be to speed up reading processing preventing the temporal decay of previously stored information, but they did not explicitly opt for one or the other of these accounts. Finally, we have seen that Towse and colleagues rejected the trade-off hypothesis to adopt a time-sharing account. However, the way they conceived the alternation, with attention switching to storage at the appearance of a memory item to switch back to processing at its offset, appeared to be an oversimplification. The surprisingly good memory performance of children, who were able to recall more than three letters while solving arithmetic problems over extended periods of time of more than 10 seconds in Barrouillet and Camos (2001), suggested that, contrary to Hitch and Towse's (1995) claim, they managed to reactivate memory traces during processing. It seems that attention is shared between processing and storage, but not continuously as in the traditional trade-off hypothesis nor following the stimulus-driven alternation supposed by the task-switching model. Instead, the limited resource of attention is probably rapidly alternated between processing and storage in something like a temporal resource-sharing mechanism that we undertook to describe in a new model of working memory, the time-based resource-sharing model.

Temporal decay and serial functioning

The time-based resource-sharing (TBRS) model is based on four main assumptions (Barrouillet et al. 2004). The first is that the two main functions of working memory, processing and storage, are fuelled by the same limited-capacity attentional resource. This resource is shared on a temporal basis because, and this is the second assumption, there is some bottleneck at the central level of cognition constraining the cognitive operations involved in both storage and processing to take place one at a time. Third, it is hypothesised that as soon as attention is switched away, memory items that are not anymore in the focus of attention suffer from time-related decay and interference. Finally, the complete loss of these memory traces can be avoided by a rapid switching of attention during short pauses that can be freed during processing in order to reactivate them. In the following sections we develop these four main tenets and the predictions they yield concerning working memory functioning.

Attention as the limited resource shared by processing and storage

In line with several other theories, we assume that working memory is concerned with those processes that require attention (Cowan 1999, 2005; Lovett *et al*. 1999). Note that we do not limit the attention involved in working memory to the controlled or executive attention described by Engle (Engle *et al*. 1999; Engle and Kane 2004), who suggested that working memory is mainly involved in those activities that need executive control to maintain goal-relevant information under conditions of interference or competition. Of course, working memory is important to maintain information in an active state and to solve the conflicts resulting from interference and activation of prepotent but inappropriate responses as Engle and Kane argue (see, for example, Bunting 2006; Kane and Engle 2003; Rosen and Engle 1998; or Unsworth *et al*. 2004, for compelling evidence). However, attention is also important for simple activations of knowledge from long-term memory, as supposed by theories like ACT-R (Anderson 1993). Thus, contrary to Engle and Kane (2004) who suggested, for example, that working memory capacity is not required in all circumstances for supposedly complex tasks such as reading, we assume that the goal-directed identification of material as simple as letters or digits necessarily requires working memory (see the next section and Barrouillet *et al*. 2008, for the involvement of working memory even in elementary cognitive processes).

In accordance with the first assumption of the TBRS model, the idea that attention is needed for the kind of goal-directed processing carried on in working memory is uncontroversial. For example, in Baddeley's (1986) model, the central executive in charge of the processing function of working memory is described as an attentional system. When considering the complex tasks used to assess working memory capacity such as the reading span, the operation span or the counting span tasks, there is no doubt that these activities involve attention. They require planning multi-step strategies, setting goals and subgoals, selecting relevant stimuli, transforming incoming information, maintaining intermediary results, selecting responses and monitoring outcomes, all activities that necessitate some allocation of attentional resources. Reading, solving arithmetic problems and counting also require retrieval of relevant knowledge from long-term memory. It has been assumed that even the simplest goal-directed memory retrievals require the allocation of source activations to retrieval cues in order to activate connected elements in long-term memory, these source activations being conceived of as attentional resources (Anderson 1993; Anderson et al. 2004; Anderson and Lebière 1998). Thus, processing information in working memory requires attention.

The hypothesis that this is the same for storage activities is less immediate. However, as Newell (1990) noted, working memory can be conceived as a kind of buffer necessary to get some temporal room for our cognitive system in its task to process the elements provided by an ever-changing and often unpredictable environment. Getting this temporal room involves the creation of memory traces able to survive until use, and Cowan (1999, 2005) has suggested that this is done by entering sensory memories into the focus of attention. There is indeed ample evidence that attention constrains the creation of memory traces and their content (Logan 1988, 1995, 1998; Logan and Etherton 1994). Accordingly, several theories assume that working memory traces consist in the activated part of long-term memory through attentional focusing (Cantor and Engle 1993; Cowan 1999, 2005; Engle et al. 1999; Engle and Kane 2004; Engle and Oransky 1999; Oberauer 2002). Thus, both processing and storage in working memory require attention, which is considered as a limited resource by all the theories evoked above.

Central bottleneck and serial functioning of working memory

The second assumption of the TBRS model is that a bottleneck constrains central processes to take place one at a time. The idea that central cognition is serial has often been expressed in general theories of cognition (Anderson 1993; Newell 1990). For example, in the ACT-R model (Anderson et al. 2004; Anderson and Lebière 1998), the atomic steps of cognition consist in firing productions. As we will see later in this book (Chapter 6), productions are 'If ... then' rules with a set of conditions (the 'If' part) that triggers some action (the 'Then' part) when they match the current content of working memory. What is relevant here is that it is assumed that production rules can only fire one at a time, creating an inherent serial functioning of central cognition. The same idea is captured by the concept of central bottleneck, first introduced by Welford (1967) from his work on the psychological refractory period (Welford 1952) and developed by Pashler (1998), according to which central processes like response selection can only take place one at a time in such a way that following processes are postponed. Another way to express the same idea is to assume that the size of the focus of attention is limited to only one element with the consequence that attention could only select one item of knowledge at a time for the next cognitive operation (Garavan 1998; McElree and Dosher 1989; Oberauer 2002, 2005). Thus, processing and storage activities could not take place in parallel, but alternate in occupying the central bottleneck. The most important consequence of this constraint is that processing incoming information postpones the activities related with the storage and reactivation of memory traces. This postponement is assumed to have detrimental effects because, and this is our third proposal, working memory traces suffer from temporal decay and interference when leaving the focus of attention.

Temporal decay and refreshing

Though the idea that working memory traces are subject to interference is commonly admitted, the existence of temporal decay is a matter of controversy (Brown and Lewandowsky 2010; Lewandowsky *et al.* 2009). Concerning interference, it has been largely demonstrated that phonologically similar items are more difficult to remember (Baddeley 1966; Conrad 1964; Lewandowsky and Farrell 2008) or that information maintained in short-term memory suffers from proactive interference (Keppel and Underwood 1962; Unsworth, Heitz, and Parks, 2008). However, following Baddeley (1986), Towse and Hitch (1995) or Cowan (2005), the TBRS model assumes that interference is not the unique source of forgetting in working memory and that memory traces fade away with time (Barrouillet and Camos 2009). This theoretical stance was primarily adopted for the sake of simplicity in accounting for the results of our first investigations that seemed to us difficult to explain only in terms of interference or temporal discriminability. The existence of a temporal decay of representations held in working memory is an intricate question, and we shall discuss evidence for and against this hypothesis in the next chapter. For the moment, let us assume that memory traces are subjected to decay, but that they can be reactivated by bringing them back into the focus of attention through a process that Cowan (1992; Cowan *et al.* 2002) describes as a covert retrieval. This process is akin to the refreshing described by Raye, Johnson, Mitchell, Greene, and Johnson (2007) as a minimal executive function distinct from verbal rehearsal and neurally located by these authors in the dorsolateral prefrontal cortex. Within our theoretical view, we regard this attentional refreshing mechanism, and more generally any active mechanism of maintenance, as especially important because it is the main feature that distinguishes working memory from long-term memory. Working memory would consist of representations that are created and actively maintained in an accessible state for further processing, whereas long-term memory is better described as the dormant information used to build transient (and hence to-be-maintained) working memory representations. This idea will be further elaborated in Chapter 6.

This refreshing process is so central for the TBRS model that, in its first version (Barrouillet *et al.*, 2004), we assumed that processing and storage functions mainly competed for a bottleneck that constrains memory retrievals to take place one at a time, as Rohrer, Pashler, and Etchegaray (1998) demonstrated. The process of refreshing memory traces through attentional focusing being assimilated to a covert retrieval, we reasoned that processing activities relying mainly on retrieval from long-term memory would have an especially detrimental effect on storage. Having explored the effects of a variety of tasks on concurrent maintenance, we later extended in Barrouillet *et al.* (2007) the central processes constrained to queue for occupying the bottleneck to all the executive functions as described by Miyake *et al.* (2000), including the minimal executive function of attentional refreshing described by Raye *et al.* (2007). For example, Liefooghe *et al.* (2008) verified that implementing task switching in working memory span tasks affected storage.

Recall performance decreased as a function of the number of task switches required by the processing component of the working memory tasks, from which we concluded that the switching process occupying the central bottleneck postponed attentional refreshing and disrupted maintenance.

Rapid switching

The decay of working memory traces during processing episodes makes time the main constraint of working memory functioning. Indeed, the two functions of working memory are in some sense adverse with each other. Processing consists in transforming representations while storage tries to maintain them intact, a duality reflected in physiologically-inspired models that describe working memory as a gating system alternating between the intact maintenance and the updating of its content (Badre 2012; O'Reilly 2006; O'Reilly and Franck 2006). However, while some working memory representation is transformed according to our current goal, memory traces storing information needed in further processing steps are subject to degradation. Avoiding the irreparable loss of these traces requires switching attention from processing to storage for their reactivation or refreshing. However, this switching would not occur as Hitch and Towse (1995) suggested, at stimulus onset and offset. Rather, it is assumed to be particularly fast, taking place during short pauses that can be freed while processing is running. As we stressed earlier in this book, this is possible because working memory is a memory. If all the information kept in working memory immediately disappeared as soon as attention is switched away to other contents, there would be no possible goal-directed cognitive activity or thinking. It is probably from our capacity to bring back to consciousness mental states that occurred some seconds before that our phenomenological experience of mental life takes the form of a continuous and coherent thread of thoughts instead of a chaos of unconnected perceptions and feelings. This capacity makes it possible to suspend the task in hand for a moment and resume it, switching back and forth between different thoughts. However, our intuition was that some cognitive tasks require a continuous attention to be completed and hardly suffer any interruption (for example, try to count backward by 67 starting at 1037), whereas others can be often interrupted and resumed without great damage. This led us to propose a new conception and a metric of the notion of cognitive load.

Cognitive load

According to the TBRS model, the deleterious effect of concurrent activities on the maintenance of information in working memory results from the fact that these activities occupy the central bottleneck and prevent refreshing activities taking place to counteract memory decay. This interplay between the decay of memory traces during the completion of concurrent activities and their refreshment during free times means that the amount of information that can be held in working memory depends on the balance between the duration of the two processes of decay and refreshment. We propose to define the cognitive load of a given activity as the impact that this activity has on other working memory functions such as storage: an activity that would impede any other activity taking place by a quasi-continuous occupation of the bottleneck would be considered as involving a high cognitive load, whereas an activity leaving room for other processes would have a low cognitive load. Note that, according to this view, the interplay between decay and refreshing means that cognitive load is not an intrinsic characteristic of the task but the result of the completion of this task within a temporal context. This is why time is so important for cognitive functioning. As Kahneman (1973) noted, the mental effort that a task demands cannot be entirely determined by the intuitive notion of task difficulty, because this demand is also obviously determined by the rate at which this task is completed. Of course, time pressure is inherent to some tasks (consider our example above of counting backward by 67 from 1037) because intermediary results are at risk of being lost if processing steps are too slow, and this is why these tasks appear so demanding. However, the demands of a poorly demanding task can strongly increase if performed under time constraints in such a way that it prevents any other process from taking place. Thus, the TBRS model defines the cognitive load of a task as the ratio between the time during which this task occupies attention (or the central bottleneck) to be completed and the time available to perform it. It should be noted that this definition sheds a new light on the intuitive relationships between cognitive load and mental effort. To say that cognitive load is the ratio between the time during which a task occupies attention and the time available to perform it amounts to saying that cognitive load corresponds to the ratio between the amount of work to be done and the time available to do it, which corresponds in physics to the notion of power. Cognitive load could be viewed as something like the mental power needed to perform a given amount of work in a given period of time. In the same way, cognitive capacity could be conceptualised as mental power, the amount of work that can be done per unit of time.

We noted above that, because attentional refreshing can be conceived as a retrieval process resulting in the reactivation of the retrieved memory items, a first version of the TBRS model emphasised the conflicting demands of storage and processing in terms of retrievals from memory. Within this view, Barrouillet et al. (2004) expressed cognitive load (CL) as

$$CL = \sum a_i n_i / T \qquad \text{(Equation 1)}$$

where n_i corresponds to the number of retrievals of the type i involved in the task, a_i to a parameter reflecting the time during which these retrievals occupy the bottleneck, and T to the total time allowed to perform the task. In the further elaborations of the TBRS model, the extension to any executive function of the processes susceptible to compete for occupying the bottleneck makes that n_i must be considered as the number of attention-demanding processing steps the task involves. In a highly simplified situation in which all these processing steps would occupy the bottleneck for the same duration, the cognitive load would correspond to

$$CL = aN/T \qquad \text{(Equation 2)}$$

where N is the number of processing steps and a their duration.

It appears from Equation 2 that there are several ways in which cognitive load can vary as illustrated in Figure 3.1. For example, any increase in the time during which each processing step occupies attention (parameter a in Equation 2), while the number of these processing steps and the time allowed to perform them are kept constant, should increase cognitive load (Figure 3.1 panel a). This could, for example, occur if these processing steps are made more demanding or if they are performed by younger individuals, as we will see in Chapter 7. However, a mere increase in the number of processing steps in a fixed period of time should have the same effect (Figure 3.1 panel b), as well reducing the time allowed to perform an unchanged

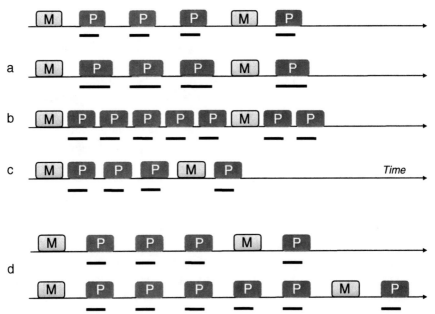

FIGURE 3.1 Diagram illustrating the different ways in which cognitive load (CL) can vary. The first row depicts successive screens on a computer-paced complex span task in which each memory item M is followed by a series of items to be processed P. Black lines beneath P items represent the time during which processing occupies attention. Panel a illustrates the increase in CL resulting from an increase in the duration of attentional capture (parameter a) while the number of processing steps N and the total time T allowed to perform them remain constant. Panel b illustrates the increase in CL resulting from an increase in the number of processing steps N while parameters a and T remain unchanged. Panel c illustrates the increase in cognitive load resulting from a reduction of T while N and a remain constant. By contrast, increasing the number of processing steps performed at a constant pace leaves CL unchanged (panel d)

number of steps (Figure 3.1 panel c). In each case, an increased cognitive load means that the proportion of time during which the task occupies the bottleneck increases, with the correlative decrease of the time available for other activities. Imagine that these processing steps are those required by the processing component of a complex span task. Increasing their cognitive load should result in lower spans, because in all the three cases the proportion of time during which memory traces suffer from temporal decay has increased whereas the proportion of time during which they can benefit from their refreshment is reduced. Note that this theoretical framework leads to two counterintuitive predictions. First, and contrary to the task switching model of Towse and Hitch (1995), shorter delays of retention could in some cases result in poorer recall performance. This is illustrated in Figure 3.1 panel c where the reduction of the time available to perform the intervening task results in a shorter delay of retention between encoding and recall, but also to a higher cognitive load that should have a deleterious effect on memory traces. Second, lengthening these delays of retention would not necessarily result in poorer recall performance. If the task to be performed remains unchanged, having more time to complete it should result of course in longer delays of retention but also in lower cognitive load, and thus in better, and not poorer, recall. However, more intriguingly, prolonging a task performed at a constant rate should have no effect at all on concurrent memory. Consider Figure 3.1 panel d, where more processing steps are performed at an unchanged pace. This constant pace means that the proportion of time during which the task occupies attention, and hence cognitive load, remains constant. Consequently, the amount of information that can be kept concurrently active remains unchanged because the balance between phases of decay and phases of refreshing remains unaffected. Thus, the critical variable in accounting for short-term memory for the TBRS model is not the time elapsed between encoding and recall, but the density of the concurrent activities performed during the retention interval, with a higher rate of concurrent processing resulting in more forgetting and poorer recall.

Considering the role of the temporal factors in the TBRS model, it became rapidly evident that testing the hypotheses issued from this model and the resulting notion of cognitive load necessitated working memory tasks allowing for a strict control of time. However, traditional complex span tasks such as the reading span, the operation span or the counting span are inappropriate for this purpose. Being self-paced in nature, these tasks leave the subjects free to process stimuli and refresh memoranda at their leisure, blurring the effects that could be expected from any manipulation of the processing component of the task. For example, subjects can slightly postpone their counting when presented with a new array in the counting span task, or the reading of a new sentence in the reading span task, and take advantage of this break to refresh and consolidate memory traces. In the same way, while solving an equation in an operation span task, they can delay some step of their calculation when reaching an intermediary result to surreptitiously turn their attention to the memoranda. If the TBRS model is correct and that temporal factors constitute the main constraint of working memory, its study requires experimental designs allowing for a strict control of temporal parameters. Several examples of such designs are presented in this book.

Testing the cognitive load hypothesis: empirical evidence

Varying parameter a

It is important to remember that the model we delineated above remains a resource-sharing model that predicts a trade-off between processing and storage, and even a perfect trade-off, any increase in the cognitive load of processing having an immediate and deleterious effect on storage. Among the factors susceptible to induce variations in cognitive load, the first we evoked in the previous section was the variations in parameter *a*, reflecting the demand of the task in terms of occupation of the central bottleneck. We have observed in children (see the study by Barrouillet and Camos 2001, reported in Chapter 2), and contrary to the predictions of the task switching model, that varying the attentional demand of the concurrent task while keeping its duration constant, and hence delays of retention, has an impact on short-term storage. The same hypothesis was tested in adults using a variety of tasks. We first verified that the difference between the operation span and the baba span while retention intervals are kept constant also held in adults, and this was the case (Barrouillet *et al.* 2004). However, arithmetic problem solving and concurrent articulation differ in many ways, making it difficult to identify the locus of the differences in spans that these two activities elicit. Thus, we designed a new task, which we called the 'continuous operation span task', aimed at allowing a finer level of analysis and the isolation of parameter *a*. The continuous operation span task is a kind of operation span task like that introduced by Turner and Engle (1989), but that allows for a strict control of time. It involves the maintenance of a series of letters presented successively on screen, each letter being followed not by a complex equation but by a very simple arithmetic problem (Figure 3.2). For example, instead of solving an equation like 4 + 7 + 8 =?, participants are presented with a one-digit number and a series of sign-operand pairs that appear successively on screen (for example, 4 / +1 / –2 / +1) and are asked to read aloud the operations and give their results while updating the running count. Following our example, participants are expected to say 'four, plus one, five, minus two, three, plus one, four'. The operations, the answer of which never exceeds 10, are deliberately simple to allow for their time-constrained completion. For example, the first number, which we call the root, may be presented for 1s and each sign-operand pair for 2s. Of course, letters are only displayed on screen for a fixed period of time (for example, 1s) and immediately followed by a root and its operations in such a way that participants have no leisure to postpone the arithmetic task and perform it at their convenience. In order to vary the attentional demand of the processing component of the task, we compared the continuous operation span task with a task we called the reading operation span task in which participants had to read, instead to solve, the successive operations. For example, the series '4 / +1 / –2 / +1' was replaced by '4 / +1 / 5 / –2 / 3 / +1 / 4' and participants were only asked to read aloud each successive screen. By presenting the sign-operand pair and its answer 1s each instead of the 2s allowed to perform the operation in the previous task, both tasks involve exactly the same total

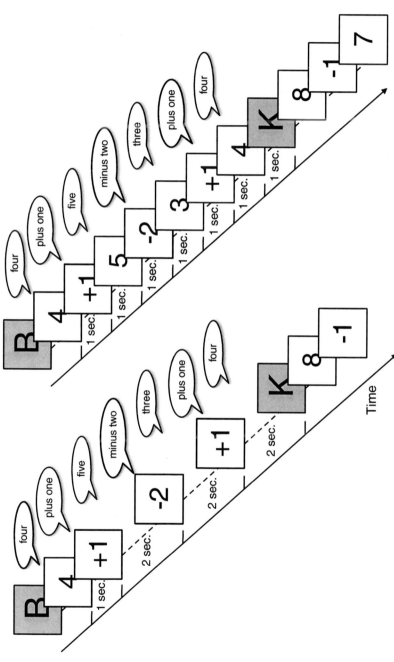

FIGURE 3.2 The continuous operation span task and the reading operation span task. On the left (continuous operation span task), participants are asked to read aloud each screen and solve the operations. On the right (reading operation span task), answers are provided, participants having just to read aloud the successive screens. Note that the time between two letters is the same in both tasks

duration of processing (i.e., the same inter-letter intervals), and thus the same delays of retention. Moreover, they involve the pronunciation of exactly the same words and the same process of retrieval from memory. It is usually assumed that small additions with sums that do not exceed 10 are solved through direct retrieval of their answer from memory (Ashcraft and Battaglia 1978; Siegler and Shrager 1984; Zbrodoff and Logan 2005), and reading digits involves retrieving the associated phonological codes (Dehaene 1992). However, they differ in parameter a. In the same way as Anderson *et al.* (1996) assumed that time and probability of retrieval reflect the amount of attention needed, we assume that differences in retrieval times reflect differences in the time during which the retrieval captures attention and occupies the bottleneck. Now, retrieving a one-digit number as the answer of an addition or subtraction takes longer than simply reading it (our own measures provide estimates of about 460ms and 700ms respectively, Barrouillet *et al.* 2008). Thus, we assumed that the continuous operation task involves a higher cognitive load than the reading operation task. These two tasks were compared with a baba span task, as we previously used in children (Barrouillet and Camos 2001). Here, a number of syllables 'ba', equivalent to the number of syllables that were uttered in the continuous and the reading operation span tasks, were successively displayed on screen at a constant pace within unchanged inter-letter intervals. This latter task involved the same retention interval and roughly the same level of articulatory suppression, but a lower attentional demand, than the other tasks, including the reading operation span task, because repeating 'ba' does not involve any retrieval from long-term memory as reading digits does. As we expected, working memory spans varied with the attentional demand of the concurrent task, the mean continuous operation span being lower than the reading operation span, which was in turn lower than the baba span (2.60, 3.15 and 4.22 respectively[2]). In line with the predictions of the TBRS hypothesis, whereas the number of processing steps and the total time available to perform them remained constant, increasing the attentional demand they involved resulted in more forgetting and lower spans.

We replicated this finding on several occasions. Imagine, for example, a task, which we call the reading digit span task, in which each of the screens following the to-be-remembered letters displays a digit to be read aloud. A way to vary the value of parameter a is to have the same task (i.e., reading numbers), with each interval between two letters filled with the same number of items to be processed at the same pace, except that their processing takes longer. This can be easily done by presenting the numbers as dice patterns instead of Arabic digits (for example, ∷ instead of 4). In a series of experiments about the effects of time and cognitive load in working memory, we first verified that it takes longer to identify numbers presented in dice-like patterns than in Arabic digits (507ms and 424ms respectively, Barrouillet *et al.* 2007). The range of the numbers used was limited to six to allow for an immediate recognition of the canonical dice pattern. Then, adult participants were presented with the reading digit span task involving either dots or Arabic digits, with series of 1 to 6 letters to be recalled, each letter being followed by four numbers at a rate of one number every 1500ms. As we expected, dice-like patterns took longer to be identified and elicited more forgetting and poorer recall of the letters (75 per cent and 82 per cent of letters recalled in correct serial position). The same phenomenon was observed with numbers displayed in their Roman form. Taking longer to be read, they also had a more detrimental effect on recall. The hypothesis that this difference was due to the time during which the numerical task occupied attention was confirmed by the fact that numbers presented in their word format (for example, 'four') elicited the same reading times as digits (425ms and 424ms respectively) and the same recall performance (82 per cent of correct recall in both conditions). Thus, all other things being equal, the amount of letters recalled depended on the time taken to process each stimulus in the intervening task, which most probably varied with parameter a, the time during which attention was occupied.

The previous examples concerned the deleterious effect of memory retrievals (reading digits, solving simple additions) on concurrent maintenance and working memory spans. However, we hypothesised that other executive functions compete with refreshing for occupying the central bottleneck. In a further experiment in Barrouillet et al. (2007), we varied the difficulty of response selection in a location judgement task. Digits to be read after each letter were replaced by a square appearing on screen in one of two possible locations, either in the upper or the lower part of the screen, with eight squares appearing successively after each letter. Participants were asked to decide where the square appeared by pressing keys. The difficulty of this task (i.e., the duration of each response selection) was manipulated by varying the distance between the two possible locations. Whereas this distance subtended a visual angle of 6.5° in a distant condition, this angle was reduced to 0.5° in a close condition. As we anticipated, the close condition elicited longer response times than the distant condition (377ms and 314ms respectively), and in line with the TBRS model, poorer recall performance (75 per cent and 83 per cent of letters recalled in correct position within series varying from 3 to 8 letters). These results confirmed that the deleterious effect of processing on concurrent maintenance varies with the duration of the attentional capture, validating the relevance of parameter a in the cognitive load equation.

Finally, we tested the critical hypothesis that activities that do not solicit central processes for a sizeable portion of time (i.e., when parameter a tends towards 0) should have no measurable impact on concurrent maintenance. For this purpose, we compared the effects on concurrent maintenance of a simple reaction time task with the effect of the square location task. Several studies have demonstrated that, contrary to choice reaction time tasks, simple reaction time tasks involve a minimal demand on executive control (for example, Schubert 1999) and do not interfere with serial recall (Vandierendonck et al. 1998). In line with our hypothesis, increasing the number of stimuli presented in a constant interval left recall performance unchanged when they required a simple response whereas recall decreased when a response selection was needed (Barrouillet et al. 2007, Exp. 4). This finding confirmed that not all activities have an effect on concurrent maintenance commensurate with their duration: attentional capture is needed.

Varying the number of processing steps N and the total time T

Although variations in parameter *a* proved effective in affecting forgetting and recall, strong variations in cognitive load should result from manipulating both the number of processing steps and the time allowed to perform them. In Barrouillet *et al.* (2004), we had adult participants performing a reading digit span task with either 6 or 10 digits to be read after each letter while the inter-letter intervals were kept constant at 6s. This resulted in a slow and a fast pace condition with one digit every 1000ms or 600ms respectively. This manipulation resulted in a dramatic difference in span, reading digits at a fast pace resulting in a lower mean span than reading them at a slow pace (2.77 and 4.28 respectively). The same contrast in paces was created in a further experiment by keeping constant the number of digits to be read in the inter-letter intervals while manipulating the time allowed to read them (either 1000ms or 600ms per digit). Once more, the concurrent task performed at a faster pace had a destructive effect on concurrent memory (mean spans of 3.01 and 4.67 for fast and slow pace, respectively). It is interesting to note here that a constant number of items processed at a faster pace corresponds to shorter delays of retention. However, contrary to the task switching model but in line with the TBRS predictions, this resulted in poorer recall performance. We replicated this finding using the continuous operation span task. Each root was followed by four sign-operand pairs that remained on screen either 2s as previously or 1.2s in a fast pace condition. While adult participants were able to reach a mean span of 2.88 in the slow pace condition, mean span dropped to 1.80 in the fast pace condition. The task was so difficult that several participants said they will never again participate in a working memory experiment!

It could have been argued that the effects related with reading digits or solving operations aloud were primarily due to the articulatory suppression these activities involve and not to the capture of attention as the TBRS assumes. Performing these tasks aloud at a faster pace involves a higher level of articulatory suppression that could have prevented verbal rehearsal of the letters, thus accounting for the effects we observed. To discard this hypothesis, we used a complex span task akin to the reading digit span task, except that participants remained silent (Lépine *et al.* 2005). Instead of reading the digits, participants were asked to judge their parity by pressing keys (there were between 4 and 8 digits displayed after each letter). The time allowed for each parity judgement was 800ms in a fast condition, and 1500ms in a slow condition. In line with the cognitive load hypothesis, the fast pace resulted in lower spans than the slow pace condition (3.81 and 5.10 respectively), making clear that the effects previously observed could not be simply accounted for by the well-known concurrent articulation effect.

Overall, these results make clear that increasing the pace at which the processing component is performed, either by increasing the amount of work to be done or by decreasing the time allowed to do it, has a dramatic effect on storage. Increasing cognitive load in these ways reduces the time available for refreshing memory traces to such an extent that it becomes difficult to counteract the effects of decay and interference, adult performance dropping to surprisingly low levels. This echoes Case et al. (1982) who reduced adults' counting spans to the level of six-year-old children. There is no doubt that counting with the unfamiliar and recently learned sequence strongly increased cognitive load. However, an important issue remained to be addressed. The experiments reviewed in this section contrasted two conditions of high and low cognitive load, without providing any hint about the form of the function relating cognitive load to working memory spans. To tackle this issue, we used a reading digit span task and created nine different conditions of cognitive load by combining in a factorial design three amounts of digits to be read in each inter-letter interval (either 4, 8 or 10 digits) with three durations of these intervals (either 6s, 8s or 10s). Nine groups of 16 undergraduate students were assigned to the resulting nine experimental conditions. We expected a smooth decline of recall performance with increased cognitive load, but the exact form of this function remained an open question. The results were very clear. Of course, as we previously observed, increasing the number of digits to be read as well as reducing the time available to read them had a significantly detrimental effect on recall performance, with no interaction between the two factors. Then, we plotted mean spans as a function of the cognitive load of the reading digit task expressed in terms of the number of digits to be read per second (Figure 3.3). It appeared that the function was linear. A regression analysis revealed an R^2 value of .93. We noted also that the intercepts of the regression line roughly corresponded to the levels of performance that could be expected if the two tasks (letters serial recall and reading digits) were performed in isolation. The intercept on the y-axis (5.62), which corresponds to a situation of short-term memory span with no concurrent task (cognitive load of 0), was close to the letter span reported by Dempster (1981) in adults (i.e., 6), whereas the intercept on the x-axis (3.80), which corresponds to a situation in which no letter would be recalled, was close to the maximum reading rate for digits reported by Naveh-Benjamin and Ayres (1986), that is 3.91 for languages with one-syllable digits, as it is the case for French. Moreover, performance in the reading digit span task was compared with a baba span task, a comparison we never made before. For the sake of simplicity, we only studied three values of pace. We reasoned that repeating 'ba' requires only little attention, resulting in a very small parameter *a* value. Consequently, we predicted that increasing the pace of this articulatory suppression should have a smaller effect than increasing the pace at which digits have to be read. This is exactly what occurred. It can be seen on Figure 3.3 that baba spans were higher than reading digit spans, and that increasing the rate at which 'ba' was uttered resulted in poorer recall performance, but this effect was smaller than that observed with digits.

This series of experiments was among the most informative that we have ever run about working memory functioning. First, cognitive load proved to be a strong determinant of working memory performance. Manipulating the number of items to be processed, the time allowed to process them, or the attentional demand of this processing produced the expected effects. Importantly, variations in cognitive load

56 Time-based resource sharing

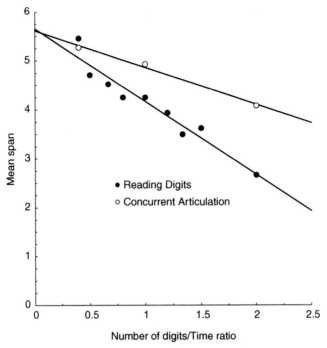

FIGURE 3.3 Mean working memory spans as a function of the number of digits to be read (reading digits) and the number of utterances of the syllable 'ba' (concurrent articulation) per second in the Barrouillet et al. (2004) study

induced dramatic differences in spans, with size effects that cannot be compared with any other known effect affecting working memory. The phonological similarity effect we evoked in the previous chapters cannot be compared with the size of the effects we observed in manipulating cognitive load. Even the detrimental effect of articulatory suppression is out of proportion with the cognitive load effect as Figure 3.3 illustrates. Increasing the rate of articulatory suppression generated by the repetition of the syllable 'ba' from one utterance every 2.5s to two utterances per second resulted in a decrease in span from 5.27 to 4.08. The same increase in the rate of reading digits resulted in a devastating effect, with a mean span dropping from 5.46 to 2.67, corresponding to a decrease in span of 51 per cent. Such a strong effect can only be compared to the word length effect reported by Baddeley et al. (1975) when comparing recall of one-syllable vs. five-syllable words (see, for example, their Experiment 7). However, it should be noted that Baddeley and colleagues compared immediate serial recall of memory items that strongly differed between conditions, whereas we observed our largest effects when keeping unchanged the memoranda and even the concurrent task, which only varied in its rate of completion. There is thus no doubt that the cognitive load effect is one of the main effects affecting working memory performance and a privileged access to understand its functioning.

On the (absence of) effect of lengthening concurrent tasks while keeping cognitive load constant

We have seen above that one of the most counterintuitive predictions of the TBRS model concerns the effect of lengthening a concurrent task without modifying its rate of completion. Such a manipulation that leaves unchanged the balance between periods of decay and periods of refreshing does not affect the cognitive load of the task (see Figure 3.1, panel d). Consequently, the TBRS model predicts that this manipulation should have no impact on concurrent maintenance and recall. This hypothesis was first tested in a developmental perspective. Gavens and Barrouillet (2004) compared a continuous operation span task and a baba span task in 9- and 11-year-old children. To test the prediction issued from the task switching model that recall performance in complex span tasks depends mainly on the duration of the intervening task and not on its difficulty, one of the critical manipulations of the experiment was to vary the duration of the tasks. Thus, a short duration condition involving continuous operations with 2 sign-operand pairs was compared with a long duration condition with 4 sign-operand pairs at a constant rate of one sign-operand pair every 2s. The baba span tasks were designed to involve the same durations of intervening tasks and the same number of syllables to be uttered as the continuous operation tasks (10 and 17 repetitions of the syllable 'ba' for the short and long duration conditions respectively). Apart from a trivial effect of age, the results revealed a strong effect of the nature of tasks that accounted for 73 per cent of the experimental variance, with higher baba spans than continuous operation spans, but also a small but significant effect of duration that accounted for 7 per cent of the experimental variance. Contrary to the predictions of the TBRS model, for both tasks and in each age, longer durations elicited slightly lower spans. Interestingly, Barrouillet et al. (2004) presented the same tasks in adults. Not surprisingly, this experiment replicated the difference between baba spans and continuous operation spans already observed, but more importantly the effect of duration totally disappeared (Table 3.1).

The fact that increasing the duration of the task does not lead to lower recall performance when cognitive load remains constant has been replicated in several

TABLE 3.1 Mean spans (and standard deviations) in the baba span (Baba) and continuous operation span (COS) task for long and short durations in children aged 9 and 11 as well as in adults

| | Age | | | | | |
| | 9 | | 11 | | Adults | |
Duration	Baba	COS	Baba	COS	Baba	COS
Short	2.44	1.40	3.06	2.06	3.97	2.49
	(0.64)	(0.53)	(0.85)	(0.64)	(0.83)	(0.86)
Long	2.21	1.13	2.79	1.50	4.01	2.50
	(0.63)	(0.34)	(0.89)	(0.67)	(0.98)	(1.11)

experiments. While testing an alternative account to the cognitive load effect proposed by Lewandowsky and Oberauer (2009), we designed a location judgement task in which the number of squares presented after each letter was systematically varied along with their pace of presentation (Barrouillet et al. 2011b). Either four or eight squares appeared at a slow, medium or fast pace (one square every 1180ms, 980ms or 780ms respectively) after each to-be-remembered letter of series of 7 letters. In line with the predictions of the TBRS model, recall performance decreased as the pace of the square location task increased, but there was no effect of the number of squares: the 8-square and 4-square conditions resulted in 69 per cent and 67 per cent of letters recalled in correct position respectively). More recently, Plancher and Barrouillet (2013) had adult participants remember series of 5 letters, each of these letters being followed by either two or four distractor words presented either at a slow or a fast pace. The task of the participants was in one experiment to read these words aloud, while in another experiment, they had to categorise them as animal nouns or not. The results were clear-cut. In both experiments, there was a significant effect of cognitive load, with words presented at a fast pace eliciting poorer recall of the letters. However, in both experiments, the number of words to be processed had no effect on recall (more will be said about these results and their implications for the question of forgetting in the next chapters).

These findings lend strong support to the prediction of the TBRS model that when cognitive load is kept constant, varying the number of items to be concurrently processed has no effect. More generally it indicates that, over and beyond both the duration of the retention interval and the number of events occurring within this interval, the main determinant of the amount of information that can be held in working memory is the cognitive load of the concurrent activities defined as the proportion of time during which this activity occupies the central bottleneck. When the pace of this concurrent activity remains constant, its lengthening has no effect. Although this has been repeatedly observed in adults, it should be remembered that prolonging processing induced a small but reliable decrease in children's span. We don't think that this is indicative of a qualitative difference in working memory functioning between children and adults, as Chapter 7 will make clear. Instead, it is probable that though cognitive load remains constant, children experience some fatigue and are less and less efficient in reactivating memory traces as the task goes on. This hypothesis, which suggests that the effect we observed in children should progressively disappear with age, remains to be investigated. In the same way, extending a complex span task even when cognitive load remains constant might in the long run induce some fatigue in adults and the degradation of their recall performance.

Cognitive load and the intuitive notion of difficulty

We evoked above Kahneman's (1973) remark that the mental effort a task requires cannot entirely be determined by its 'difficulty' but also by the rate at which it is performed. We use inverted commas to indicate that difficulty here refers to an intuitive notion rather than a theoretically grounded concept. We have seen in this chapter that seemingly elementary and easy tasks such as reading digits or adding and subtracting 1 to one-digit numbers can have a devastating effect on our capacity to concurrently store information, provided that they are performed under time pressure. We noted also that time pressure is often inherent to those cognitive tasks that are usually considered as 'difficult'. It seems that working memory researchers spontaneously choose this kind of task in designing working memory span tasks, which require participants to read sentences for comprehension or to solve complex arithmetic equations. The TBRS model assumes that the main determinant of the impact a task has on working memory is cognitive load. This means that elementary activities such as adding 1 or reading letters could have the same impact as complex activities like arithmetic problem solving or reading comprehension provided that they are performed at a sufficiently high rate. This is the hypothesis that Lépine et al. (2005b) tested in two experiments that compared the traditional self-paced operation span (Turner and Engle 1989) and reading span tasks (Daneman and Carpenter 1980) with computer-paced span tasks based on the TBRS approach. The first experiment compared the traditional operation span task and the continuous operation span task. In the former, participants were asked to remember series of letters followed by three-operand additions (for example, 8 + 6 + 9 = 24?). Each letter was displayed on screen for 1500ms, but participants solved the operations at their own pace. After having read the problem aloud, they gave their response ('true' or 'false') by a key press that removed the operation from the screen and triggered the apparition of the next letter. The continuous operation span task did not strongly differ from that already described, except that the operands were limited to +1 and −1, and that the number of sign-operand pairs varied in order to avoid an absolutely constant and predictable rhythm of presentation of the letters. These sign-operand pairs were presented either at a fast or a slow pace (every second or 2s, respectively). The second experiment compared a traditional reading span task with a computer-paced reading letter span task. In both tasks, participants were asked to maintain series of numbers (from 1 to 16) presented successively on screen. In the reading span task, each number was followed by a short sentence containing 4-11 words (for example, 'A cow lays eggs') that participants had to read aloud and evaluate. This sentence remained on screen without time limit until participants pressed a key for their response ('true' or 'false') that made the following number appear. In the reading letter span task, each number was followed by a series of 4-6 letters that were displayed on screen at either a fast (675ms per letter) or a slow pace (1300ms). Participants had to read these letters aloud.

The results were unambiguous. The tasks involving elementary activities (i.e., adding or subtracting 1 or reading letters) elicited higher spans than the traditional working memory tasks involving complex activities, but only when performed at a slow pace. When performed under time pressure, reading letters and adding or subtracting 1 proved as disruptive as reading sentences for comprehension or solving complex additions (Table 3.2). This suggests that what makes the difficulty of the working memory span task, that is the difficulty of maintaining the memoranda for further recall, is not the intuitive complexity of the activities involved, but their

TABLE 3.2 Mean spans (and standard deviations) as a function of the nature of the task involved in complex span tasks and the pace at which simple tasks were performed in Lépine, Bernardin, and Barrouillet (2005)

	Nature of the processing component		
	Simple computer-paced tasks		*Complex self-paced tasks*
	Slow	Fast	
Operation solving	3.65	2.30	2.30
	(0.92)	(0.78)	(0.81)
Reading	4.17	3.11	3.38
	(1.00)	(0.93)	(0.78)

cognitive load, which determines the opportunities offered to the subjects to turn their attention toward the decaying memory traces. It is thus not so surprising that the computer-paced tasks that we developed for studying time-based resource sharing proved at least as reliable as the traditional complex span tasks in measuring working memory capacity (see Chapter 7).

Time-based resource sharing in the visuospatial domain

For practical reasons owing to the facility of constructing and administrating tasks, the TBRS model was initially developed in the verbal domain. However, there was no theoretical reason for this restriction. Our theory assumes that temporal decay and interference affect any kind of representation stored in working memory and any activity requiring attention is assumed to occupy the central bottleneck. As a consequence, time-based resource sharing should also be observed in the visuospatial domain in which maintenance and recall of information should depend on cognitive load, as it is the case with verbal information. However, in apparent contradiction to the hypothesis of a central bottleneck, the occupation of which would impede maintenance and refreshment of any kind of memory traces, studies in the visuospatial domain led to its fractionation into separate visual and spatial sub-systems (Baddeley 2007; Baddeley and Logie 1999). Indeed, early studies not only reported that concurrent movements interfered with spatial maintenance (Baddeley and Lieberman 1980: Logie *et al.* 1990) and that viewing irrelevant pictures interfered with visual maintenance (Logie 1986; Quinn and McConnell 1996), but Logie and Marchetti (1991) established that concurrent movements interfered selectively with spatial maintenance whereas viewing irrelevant pictures selectively interfered with visual maintenance, a pattern that subsequent studies confirmed (Darling *et al.* 2006; Della Sala *et al.* 1999). More will be said in Chapter 5 about the pivotal role of the selective interference paradigm in the elaboration of the multi-component view of working memory, but we argued that the pattern of selective interference reported by Logie and Marchetti did not necessarily contradict the hypothesis of a resource-sharing at a central level for at least two reasons

(Vergauwe et al. 2009). First, the pattern of selective interference observed could be due to peripheral interference resulting from the similarity between the representations maintained and those produced by the concurrent stimulations, something that is not contradictory with the existence of more central interference. Second, according to the TBRS model, this central interference would result from the occupation of attention by the concurrent task, whereas the studies reporting the pattern of selective interference usually used passive spatial or visual tasks that did not solicit attentional control, such as simply viewing irrelevant stimuli without any processing on them (Darling et al. 2006; Della Sala et al. 1999; Logie and Marchetti 1991). Consequently, we explored the existence of a time-based resource sharing in the visuospatial domain with the same complex span task paradigm we used for studying the verbal domain, a paradigm in which memory items have to be maintained while performing a task requiring central processes like response selection.

Previous studies having concluded the existence of separate visual and spatial sub-systems, we designed four complex span tasks in which visual and spatial storage components were combined with visual and spatial processing components. These span tasks had the same structure as those previously described, with series of memory items successively displayed on screen, each of these items being followed by processing phases during which a succession of atomic processing steps are presented at a constant pace. Spatial storage consisted in remembering sequences of ball movements (selected between 16 possible movements within a square frame), a task proposed by Kane et al. (2004), whereas visual storage involved the maintenance of series of visual patterns constructed by filling in half of the cells of 2×3 matrices (a task inspired from Della Sala et al. 1999, see Figure 3.4 panel a). For spatial recall, participants were given squares with lines representing the 16 possible moves and asked to draw an arrow along one of the lines in each square to indicate the corresponding ball movement. For the visual recall, participants indicated the filled cells of each visual stimulus on blank matrices. Two types of tasks were used as the spatial processing component. The first, associated with spatial storage, consisted of judging the symmetry along the vertical axis of designs in 6×6 matrices (Kane et al. 2004). Because these stimuli could have interfered with the matrices used for visual storage, the symmetry task was replaced for the visual storage/spatial processing combination by a spatial fit task in which participants have to judge whether a line fits between two dots (Rybash and Hoyer 1992, see Figure 3.4 panel b). Visual processing consisted in a colour discrimination task. Monochromatic displays that filled the entire screen succeeded each other, participants being asked to judge whether the colour was more blue than red or more red than blue (Klauer and Zhao 2004). For each of the processing tasks, either three, five, or seven items were presented during a fixed 8500ms delay, resulting in a low, a medium and a high cognitive load condition respectively.

The TBRS model predicted that increased cognitive load should result in lower recall performance within and between visual and spatial domains. This is exactly what we observed. Memory spans for visual stimuli progressively decreased as the cognitive load of both the visual and the spatial tasks increased, with no effect on

62 Time-based resource sharing

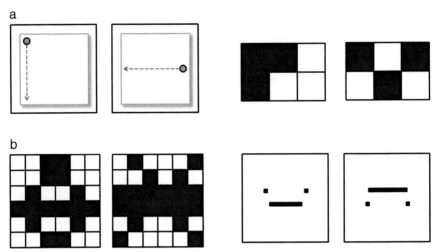

FIGURE 3.4 Material used by Vergauwe *et al.* (2009) for studying visuospatial working memory. In Panel a are displayed stimuli for spatial (ball movements) and visual (matrices) recall whereas Panel b shows stimuli used for spatial processing (matrices for symmetry judgements and displays for the spatial fit task)

the nature of the processing component and no interaction. The same pattern occurred for spatial storage. Increased cognitive load resulted in lower spans, with spatial and visual processing having the same effect on concurrent maintenance. The linear trend associated with cognitive load increase accounted for 99 per cent of the experimental variance in both storage conditions. The disruptive effects of spatial processing on visual maintenance and of visual processing on spatial maintenance clearly indicated central interference in the visuospatial domain, while the absence of any interaction between cognitive load and the nature of the intervening tasks was at odds with the pattern of selective interference so often reported. We thus decided to replicate one of the more recent, and according to Baddeley (2007), one of the most careful and thorough studies demonstrating a double dissociation between visual and spatial working memory, which is the study conducted by Klauer and Zhao (2004). They had adult participants maintain either one Chinese ideograph (visual storage) or the location of one dot (spatial storage) during a 10-s retention interval before recognition among eight Chinese ideographs or eight possible spatial locations respectively. The retention interval was filled either by a spatial or a visual task or remained empty (i.e., no intervening task). The spatial task consisted of finding and clicking on the sole asterisk that remained stationary among 11 other moving asterisks. This click (or non-response within a delay of 5s) made a new display appear. The visual task was the 'more red than blue' or 'more blue than red' binary choice presented above. The response (or a non-response within a delay of 3s) displayed the next colour. Klauer and Zhao observed the pattern of selective interference testifying, in their view, for a domain-based fractionation of visuospatial working memory. Recognition of the dot location was more impaired by discriminating movements than colours, whereas the reverse effect was obtained for the recognition of Chinese ideographs.

There is no doubt that Klauer and Zhao's (2004) study was cleverly designed and provided striking results, but we noted that three shortcomings might compromise their conclusions. First, the very important temporal aspects of the intervening tasks, which were self-paced, were poorly controlled. Second, the two intervening tasks probably differed in their attentional demand. Klauer and Zhao observed that their participants made almost twice as many colour discriminations than movement discriminations within the 10-s retention intervals, suggesting that the latter captured attention for longer periods of time. Third, the combination of the maintenance of a dot location and the search for a stationary asterisk involved probably more representation-based interference due to perceptive similarities than the combination of Chinese ideographs and monochromatic displays. Thus, we used the same recognition tasks and storage items (i.e., dot location and Chinese ideographs) as Klauer and Zhao (2004) but adapted their processing components to allow for temporal control. We used the same colour discrimination task, but we converted their movement discrimination task into a binary choice task by presenting displays of four asterisks where either all of them or all but one were moving, participants deciding between the two possibilities. Importantly, these tasks were not self- but computer-paced, with six items presented within the 10-s interval at a constant pace (i.e., 1666ms per item). Moreover, we assessed the attentional demand of these tasks in a pre-test that revealed longer response times for movement than colour discrimination (847ms and 472ms, respectively).

In line with the TBRS model, we made two main predictions. First, we expected visual and spatial maintenance to be disrupted by both processing tasks. In other words, for dot locations and Chinese ideographs, we predicted lower recognition accuracy and longer recognition times after a retention interval filled by an attention-demanding task, whatever its visual or spatial nature, than after an empty retention interval. Moreover, and in contradiction with any selective interference, these effects were predicted to depend primarily on the cognitive load involved by the intervening task. Because binary choices took longer for movement than colour discrimination, the former task was predicted to have a more detrimental effect than the latter for both visual and spatial storage. Figure 3.5, which displays the interference scores (i.e., the difference in performance relative to the empty retention interval condition), clearly indicates that these predictions were confirmed. Within- and between-domain interference was observed but no selective interference occurred. The task involving the higher cognitive load (i.e., the movement discrimination task) induced lower recognition accuracy and longer recognition times for both visual and spatial memoranda. Time-based resource sharing also governs visuospatial working memory.

The processing-storage function

Among the multiple constraints that shape mind, the first are, according to Newell (1990), the necessity to behave flexibly as a function of the environment, to exhibit

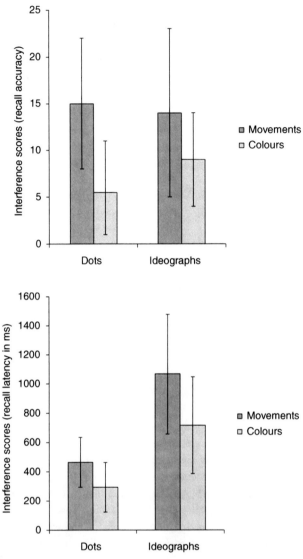

FIGURE 3.5 Mean interference scores (i.e., difference in performance relative to the experimental condition without interference) created by either a spatial (movement) or a visual (colour) intervening task on the maintenance of either spatial (dots) or visual (ideographs) information in Vergauwe et al. (2009, Exp. 2). Top panel: interference score in recall accuracy (difference in percentage of memory items correctly recognised). Bottom panel: interference scores in recall latency (difference in time needed for recognition, in ms)

adaptive behaviour, and to operate in real time. Operating in real time means that, because cognitive processes are biological phenomena that do not operate instantaneously in some temporal vacuum, a system is necessary to get temporal room to our cognitive system in its processing tasks, as Newell says. This system fulfils the contradictory objectives to maintain and protect from decay and interference reliable representations of the environment and, at the same time, to transform these representations for goal-oriented behaviour. Operating in real time also means that this system does probably not resemble the static assemblage of boxes by which our textbooks usually represent working memory, and in which no temporal dimension is mentioned. The studies reviewed in this chapter provides ample evidence that working memory achieves the optimal compromise between its contradictory functions through time sharing, by alternating between storage and processing. We have seen that the explanation offered by the TBRS model for this phenomenon is that the two functions compete for a central bottleneck that constrains executive processes to take place one at a time. This hypothesis leads to a prediction that has not yet been directly addressed, which is that what matters more is the time during which the bottleneck is occupied by processing activities than the nature of these activities. If the amount of information that can be maintained in working memory mainly depends on the balance between the periods of loss and those of refreshing, the duration of these periods should be more important than the nature of the task that impedes refreshing processes to operate. An experiment run by Barrouillet et al. (2007) sheds light on this question.

Two complex span tasks were compared that involved exactly the same memoranda (letters) and the same series of 4, 6 or 8 digits presented either in the upper or the lower part of the screen during processing phases of 6.4s. The sole difference was that one group of participants was asked to judge the parity of these digits, whereas the other judged their location on screen. Of course, recall performance decreased as the number of digits processed in the inter-letter interval increased, and in line with our predictions, the parity task elicited lower spans than the location task (4.48 and 5.23 respectively). This is easily explainable. Judging the parity of a digit requires a response selection but also a retrieval from long-term memory that the location task does not require (Dehaene et al. 1993). Accordingly, we verified that the former process took longer than the latter (mean response times of 554ms and 411ms respectively), an additional evidence of the impact of parameter a in working memory spans. However, our predictions went further. We reasoned that, if the TBRS model is correct in assuming that recall performance depends on cognitive load, then the effects on maintenance of the two tasks should not go beyond the time during which they occupy attention. Of course, there is yet no possibility to precisely assess this time, but we hypothesised that its variations should be reflected in the variations we observed in processing times. Thus, as a raw approximation, we assessed for each of the six experimental conditions the cognitive load it involved by calculating mean processing times (i.e., the mean total time devoted to process the stimuli in the inter-letter intervals, in other words the sum of the response times per string of stimuli). Dividing this total processing time by the duration of the processing phases (i.e., 6.9s³) provided us with the approximated cognitive load of the task. When mean spans were plotted on the resulting 'total processing time/total time' ratios, it appeared that the span values from the two tasks fell approximately on the same line. The slopes of the two functions were close (−7.82 and −7.68 for the parity task and the location tasks respectively), as well as their intercepts (8.04 and 7.84 respectively), confirming that recall performance was almost entirely determined by the time allocated to the processing component rather than by its nature.

These findings constituted a strong confirmation of the role of cognitive load as the main determinant of the relationship relating the two functions of working memory. Any variation in cognitive load δCL seems to result in a correlative variation $\delta Span$ in the amount of items that can be maintained active. This trade-off function between processing and storage and its exact nature necessarily reflects the structure and functioning of working memory. Several studies reported in this chapter revealed that the function between cognitive load and spans is linear (see Figure 3.3). Interestingly, a computational simulation mimicking the decay of memory traces during processing and their sequential refreshing in a cumulative fashion, starting from the first list item and proceeding forward until the end of the list, reproduces the linear function so often observed in experiments (Oberauer and Lewandowsky 2011). Thus, empirical and computational evidence converge in suggesting that the processing-storage function is linear in nature and can be expressed as

$$\text{Span} = a - b\,CL \qquad \text{(Equation 3)}$$

where CL refers to cognitive load. In a recent study, we reasoned that the TBRS model predicts the parameters of this linear function (Barrouillet *et al.* 2011a). Assuming that a task that would completely occupy the bottleneck for a prolonged period would prevent any maintenance activity taking place, a cognitive load of 1 should theoretically correspond to a complete working memory loss and a span of 0. This means that the function described by Equation 3 has the same slope and intercept and can be simplified in the following way

$$\text{Span} = k(1 - CL) \qquad \text{(Equation 4)}$$

The intercept k (which is also the slope of the function) corresponds in turn to a cognitive load of 0, which is a situation in which there is no concurrent task at all, all the working memory capacities being allocated to storage. This corresponds to the famous Miller's (1956) estimate of 7 plus or minus 2. Interestingly, we noted that the parameters we obtained when comparing the effects of parity and location judgements fitted these predicted values. The observed intercepts fell within the expected range (8.04 and 7.84), with slope values that did not greatly differ from these intercepts (−7.82 and −7.68 respectively).

We thus decided to further explore the parameters of the processing-storage function by analysing the impact on spans of variations in cognitive load. Because the

TBRS model explains the trade-off function by the fact that not only retrievals but all the executive functions involved in processing and storage compete for occupying the central bottleneck, we focused on the detrimental effect on span of processing components that varied in the involvement of identifiable executive functions. For example, in a first experiment, we used a complex span task in which the processing component consisted in a Stroop colour task. Participants maintained numbers for further recall, each number being followed by eight colour words or neutral words (adjectives not related to colours), the colour of which had to be named. Of course, these words were displayed on screen at a fixed and constant pace. As in a Stroop task, half of the words in the colour condition were incongruent trials. We reasoned that comparing the total processing times of the colour and neutral conditions would reveal the extra time needed to inhibit the prepotent responses consisting of reading the word instead of giving its colour. The difference in the resulting cognitive loads could be considered as a 'pure' δCL due only to the extra-involvement of inhibition in one condition. Thus, dividing the resulting difference in spans $\delta Span$ by this δCL would permit a precise assessment of the slope of the trade-off function. The same logic was used to compare the effects on storage of a Stroop digit task. The memoranda were words, each of them followed by a series of sets containing 1 to 4 items for an enumeration task. The need for inhibition was created by having a condition in which the to-be-enumerated items were digits, offering the possibility of 50 per cent of incongruent trials (for example, a set of three digits 4 requiring the response 'three'). This condition requiring inhibition was compared with a condition in which the to-be-enumerated items were letters that do not provide opportunity for conflicts.

In another experiment, the executive function under study was updating in a task inspired from Oberauer (2002). Letters to be remembered were followed by two frames appearing on screen that contained a digit. The following screens presented these frames, one of them containing a simple operand (i.e., either −2, −1, +1, +2). Participants were asked to update the content of the filled frame at a rate of one operand every 1500ms. In the control condition, the operands were replaced by a simple asterisk and participants asked to recall the digit that was at the beginning presented in the corresponding frame. Response time to each stimulus was registered using a vocal key. Both conditions required the retrieval of the content of the target frame from memory, but the former involved an additional activity of updating, the longer response times elicited by this condition being attributable to the involvement of this executive function. Finally, the necessity of updating working memory was manipulated using an N-back task. Participants had to maintain series of numbers followed by strings of 8 letters displayed at a rate of one letter every 1500ms. In one condition, participants were asked to perform a 2-back task on these letters. In another condition, participants were only asked to judge if each letter corresponded to one of the two first letters of the string. Thus, both conditions necessitated maintaining two letters in mind to perform the task, but the 2-back task had an additional requirement of continuously updating these two letters. Participants gave their responses by pressing keys, allowing for an easy measure of processing times. In each of these eight tasks (i.e., four tasks exploring inhibition and four tasks devoted to updating), cognitive load of the processing component was approximated by the ratio between total processing time and total time (i.e., the duration of the inter-memory item intervals).

In the inhibition experiments, cognitive load varied from .628 to .513, inducing variations in spans from 2.93 to 3.72. The regression of mean spans on cognitive load values revealed a linear trend accounting for 98 per cent of the observed variance in recall performance with a slope of − 6.78 and an intercept of 7.16. Manipulating the updating demand of the tasks resulted in variations in cognitive load from .247 to .454. For sake of comparison with the previous analyses, mean working memory spans in the updating experiments were increased by two units to take into account the fact that, in each condition of both experiments, the processing task involved the continuous maintenance of two items on top of the to-be-remembered items. When regressed on cognitive load, the resulting mean spans (ranging from 6.19 to 4.35) exhibited a linear trend that accounted for 99 per cent of the experimental variance with a slope of − 8.48 and an intercept of 8.18. In both studies, the observed intercepts were not so far from the slope values and fell in the expected range. These consistent results were included in a meta-analysis with the results provided by the study that compared parity and location judgements, which involved the executive functions of memory retrieval and response selection respectively. This meta-analysis thus regrouped 14 different experimental conditions. The different slopes ranged from − 6.78 to − 8.48 whereas the intercepts ranged from 7.16 to 8.18, confirming the predictions of the TBRS model. The observed values fell within the expected range, and the slope and intercept values never strongly differed, with slope/intercept ratios ranging from 0.95 to 1.04, all values very close to 1. The meta-analysis revealed a linear trend with an intercept of 8.13 and a slope of − 8.33. The linear regression accounted for 98 per cent of the variance (Figure 3.6).

These findings provide strong evidence that time is a crucial and most probably the main factor in working memory functioning. The amount of information that can be maintained in an active state depends primarily on the time during which concurrent activities prevent maintenance processes to counteract forgetting, beyond and above the nature of these concurrent activities and the processes they involve. Though these findings were in line with our expectations, we judged it necessary in Barrouillet *et al.* (2011a) to temper the conclusions that could be drawn from them and to emphasise the limitations of our study. We would like to restate here these reservations. First, the processing-storage function is not a working-memory-loss or a time-loss function. Indeed, Equation 4 says nothing about the rate at which forgetting occurs in working memory because cognitive load refers to a time ratio that cannot inform us about the effect of raw durations on forgetting. Second, the values of cognitive load we used in our analyses are coarse estimates that cannot be taken as precise measures. Processing times from which we estimated cognitive loads do not correspond to times of occupation of the central bottleneck and encompass cognitive steps that probably do not involve executive functions, such as the first steps of perceptual encoding or the realisation of motor responses. Finally, if Equation 4 has some validity, it is only under certain conditions. The notion

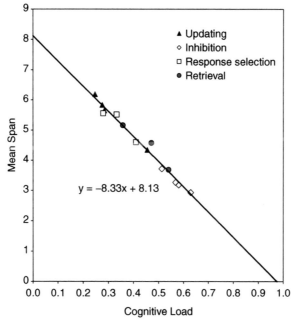

FIGURE 3.6 The processing-storage trade-off function. Mean working memory spans as a function of the approximate cognitive load induced by a variety of tasks involving different executive functions such as updating, inhibition of prepotent responses, response selection or retrieval from long-term memory. Data concerning response selection and retrieval are issued from Barrouillet *et al.* (2007). Data concerning updating and inhibition are from Barrouillet *et al.* (2011a)

of cognitive load makes sense only for sufficiently extended periods of time. Cognitive load reflects the balance between processing time during which working memory traces decay and the time available to restore them. Thus, cognitive load is related to spans because this balance determines the number of memory items that can be sufficiently refreshed during free time to survive decay and interference during processing time. No doubt a minimum number of these cycles is needed to reach the equilibrium reflected by the processing-storage function. Even a task involving a high cognitive load cannot be expected to be highly damaging if performed during very short periods of time (for example, 1s), because information probably does not totally vanish after so short a delay. Thus, the processing-storage function described by Equation 4 might be compared to those physical laws that only hold in an ideal world, such as those of thermodynamics that describe the behaviour of perfect gases that do not exist in nature. For example, a cognitive load of 1 is a theoretical abstraction with no psychological reality, as it is probably impossible to imagine a task that would continuously occupy our attention without any interruption. Everybody can verify that it is very difficult to continuously keep one's attention on something for a prolonged period without any diversion, and it is probably adaptive to be unable to do so. The capacity to totally protect our current thoughts from inner and outer stimulations could, in the long run, become damaging. We think that the rapid switching by which processing and storage alternate is the default mode of working memory functioning, and that overriding this default mode for prolonged attentional focusing requires mental effort.

Conclusion

These reservations having been made, the present chapter reviewed ample empirical evidence supporting the TBRS model and its fundamental assumption that the amount of information that working memory can hold depends on the cognitive load of the intervening activities, defined as the proportion of time during which these activities occupy attention and block the central bottleneck. Temporal factors appear then as the main determinant of working memory functioning. A simple way to explain these phenomena is to assume, as we did, that working memory performance results from the balance between the time during which processing occupies the central bottleneck, preventing any maintenance process to take place, and the time available for restoring the degraded memory traces still present in short-term memory. If we are correct in supposing that working memory functioning is sequential in nature and that only one item can be selected for the next operation, this means that working memory is a system characterised by a dynamic equilibrium between phases of memory loss and phases of memory reconstruction. The following chapters will focus in turn on these pivotal processes of human cognition.

Notes

1 It is interesting to note that Towse and Hitch (1995) considered the same manipulations as having different effects in counting difficulty, the former leaving difficulty unchanged while the latter was intended to increase it. Remember that, in order to increase difficulty, Case et al. (1982) asked adults to count using an unfamiliar sequence of nonsense numbers (see Chapter 2).
2 In this and the vast majority of our studies, spans are assessed following a procedure introduced by Daneman and Carpenter (1980) and used by Kemps et al. (2000) or Smith and Scholey (1992). Participants are presented with increasingly long series of memory items, with three series of each length, until they fail to recall in correct order the items of all three series at a particular length, testing terminating at this point. Each correctly recalled series counts as one third. The span corresponds to the addition of these thirds, reflecting the maximum number of items that can be reliably maintained and recalled while performing the concurrent processing task. For example, if the task begins at length 1 and a given participant correctly recalls all the series of one, two and three items, two series of four items and one series of five items, her span is $(3 + 3 + 3 + 2 + 1) \times 1/3 = 4$. When shortest lengths are not administered, the task beginning, for example, at length 3, the lengths not administered are credited with three thirds.
3 The processing phase of 6.4s was preceded by a delay of 500ms between the letter and the first digit, resulting in a total time of 6.9s.

4
WORKING MEMORY LOSS

As Crowder (1982) noted, the momentary distraction and subsequent loss of very recent information is a vivid real-life episode. Everybody has experienced it in reading long sentences, in losing the track of an intricate line of reasoning, or in trying to solve even moderately complex arithmetic problems without any recourse to pencil and paper. The studies reviewed in the previous chapter have led us to establish the law governing this memory loss. A reasonable hypothesis is to assume that memory traces tend to vanish when attention is diverted, and restored when attention is available anew. But why does recent information fade away under distraction? Surprisingly, despite its ubiquity, the causes of this phenomenon remain largely undecided and the subject of fierce debates, most of them focusing, as we will see, on the existence of a temporal decay in the short term (Barrouillet and Camos 2009; Brown and Lewandowsky 2010; Lewandowsky *et al.* 2009; Nairne 2002; Ricker *et al.* 2014). This chapter reviews the studies that have been dedicated to the sources of forgetting in short-term and working memory. Beginning with the first studies that aimed at differentiating short-term from long-term memory through the existence of distinct forgetting mechanisms and the role of temporal decay in the short term, the chapter reviews and assesses subsequent studies that have challenged the idea of temporal decay as well as those that endorsed it, before presenting alternative views that stress the role of event-based interference in short-term and working memory.

Short-term memory and rapid forgetting

The first studies

The advent of cognitivism and its conception of mind as an information-processing device turned the attention of psychologists to short-term memory as a system able to temporarily make recent information available for treatment. Within this framework, Brown (1958) noted that immediate memory usually operates under conditions that necessitate the retention of information while carrying over other activities, and surmised that forgetting might be extremely rapid under these circumstances. Though he acknowledged that the hypothesis of a decay of memory traces was unpopular at this time, probably because theories of forgetting had most often investigated forgetting over relatively long periods, Brown (1958) hypothesised that the memory trace resulting from the perception of a stimulus decays rapidly during the initial phase of its career. This hypothesis of rapid decay was tested through three experiments that have had an enduring importance in the study of memory and forgetting (see Ricker et al. 2014, for a thoughtful analysis of Brown's article and its continuing impact). In a first experiment, participants were asked to read out and attempt to remember one to four pairs of consonants immediately followed by five additional pairs of digits that participants were also asked to read out but not remember. In line with the decay hypothesis, this first experiment showed that when rehearsal was prevented by reading the digits, a delay of some seconds before recall could produce considerable forgetting in comparison with a control condition with no distracting stimuli to be read before recall. A second experiment investigated the effect of similarity between distractors and targets. Four pairs of consonants were presented for further recall, either immediately preceded or followed by three pairs of distractors, which were either other consonants or digits. When distractors were presented before, the target consonant pairs were followed by an empty delay in such a way that the delay of retention was the same in the four conditions. A control condition was added with no distractor but the same unfilled delay before recall. Results were striking. The similarity factor was of minor importance when compared with the position of the distractors. Although letters involved slightly more forgetting than digits, the effect of distractors on recall was moderate when they were presented before (59 per cent, 66 per cent, and 67 per cent of correct recall for the letter, digit and control conditions respectively) but huge when they were presented after the memory items (26 per cent and 31 per cent of correct recall for the letter and digit conditions respectively). These results were at odds with interference theories of the time that predicted larger retroactive interference from intervening stimuli similar to the target items. Moreover, and contrary to what it could have been expected, the rate of intrusions of the distractor consonants when presented before the targets was significantly *lower* than chance level, undermining the hypothesis that proactive interference (i.e., the deterioration of performance as a function of the material previously learned) is playing a major role in this task. The third experiment, less remarkable in its results, established that even when a delay of about 5s allowed for the consolidation of memory items, a distracting task preventing rehearsal still had damaging effect.

These findings favourable to the decay hypothesis were buttressed by a famous study by Peterson and Peterson (1959). Brown (1958) as well as Pillsbury and Sylvester (1940) reported decay over short intervals but none of these studies explored the course of retention over a variety of intervals. This was the question tackled by

Peterson and Peterson (1959). Participants memorised three consonants and counted backward by three or four from a three-digit number at a fixed rhythm given by a metronome (i.e., one number produced every second). The retention interval varied from 3s to 18s. The results are well known: the frequency of correct recall dramatically decreased as the retention interval increased, following an exponential curve. The presence of proactive interference was discarded by comparing performance within successive blocks of 12 presentations. Recall performance did not decrease but increased while going through the task, revealing no evidence for proactive interference. Several studies followed the same path, analysing the rapid loss of short-term memory and its conditions of occurrence. Watkins *et al.* (1973) established that forgetting of verbal material increases systematically with the retention interval even when it is filled with non-verbal distracting tasks, though to a lesser extent than with verbal distractors. They concluded that two main factors operate to reduce recall from short-term memory: the amount of attentional distraction induced by the intevening task and the similarity between distractors and memory items. More will be said about the role of similarity below. In the same vein, Reitman (1974) varied the similarity of the intervening tasks (either a tone or a syllable detection) with the memoranda (monosyllabic nouns). When participants were instructed to rehearse, they did not exhibit forgetting after 15s of delay, but avoiding rehearsal induced substantial drops in performance considered as clear evidence for decay. Moreover, the syllable detection task had a more detrimental effect, confirming the implication of similarity-based interference in forgetting.

Towards the demise of short-term memory

The research stream initiated by Brown (1958) and Peterson and Peterson (1959) studies aimed at establishing the existence of short-term memory as a valid memory system. Because it was admitted, since the arguments put forward by McGeoch (1942), that there is no time decay in long-term memory, the existence of an effect of time in short-term forgetting was a first step in this direction. Thus, it does not come as a surprise that the defenders of a unitary conception of memory, which assumes similar processes for short- and long-term remembering, tried to account for these seminal results through some well-known long-term memory phenomena. The critical study was run by Keppel and Underwood (1962) who argued that the typical effect observed with the distractor task paradigm can be accounted for by proactive interference resulting from the previous trials. Although Keppel and Underwood (1962) did not directly address this question, their study is recurrently described as having ruled out the decay hypothesis by demonstrating that, whatever the delay of retention, there is no forgetting at all in the first trial of a Brown-Peterson task and, therefore, no temporal decay in short-term memory (for example, Crowder 1982, 1993; Lewandowsky *et al.* 2009; Nairne 2002). Turvey *et al.* (1970) went further in reporting that performance in the Petersons' task was not affected by retention intervals varying from 5s to 25s when they were manipulated between, and not within, subjects as in the original study. In fact, rates of correct recall even slightly increased with the duration of these intervals. Moreover, a same retention interval of 15s proved to lead to very different recall performance depending on the duration of prior-item intervals, illustrating the role of proactive interference in short-term memory.

Along with the effects related to retention intervals introduced by Brown (1958) and Peterson and Peterson (1959), other phenomena considered as signatures of a separate short-term memory system were sharply discussed in the following decades. This is the case of the recency effect in free recall tasks, usually attributed to the retrieval of the last presented items from some short-term store (Glanzer and Cunitz 1966), a hypothesis that was undermined by the discovery of long-term recency effects (Baddeley and Hitch 1977; Bjork and Whitten 1974). This led Crowder (1982) to entitle his review of the literature 'The demise of short-term memory', a conclusion that still held in an update of this review published ten years later (Crowder, 1993). In the same way, the word length effect, initially attributed to more decay associated with the longer time needed to rehearse longer words, received alternative explanations (see Lewandowsky and Oberauer 2008 for a review). Overall, these reappraisals of phenomena initially considered as evidence for a short-term memory system in which memory traces would rapidly decay with time led to alternative accounts of forgetting in the short term in terms of interference (for example, Nairne 2002). However, is the evidence from which these sceptical conclusions were drawn so compelling? The next section focuses on the Brown-Peterson distracting task and the role of proactive interference. Some surprises are to be expected.

Proactive interference and decay

Keppel and Underwood (1962) reasoned that, if short-term memory was governed by the same laws and phenomena as long-term memory, a critical interaction should be observed between the number of potentially interfering associations (i.e., the number of prior trials), and the length of retention interval, with the hypothesis that the longer this interval, the greater the recovery of interfering associations and the poorer the recall performance. Consequently, no decrement should be observed as a function of the length of the retention interval when there are few or no prior trials. Something often overlooked is that, when strictly replicating Peterson and Peterson's experiment, Keppel and Underwood (1962) failed to verify these hypotheses. Admittedly, as they expected, they observed a large drop in the proportion of correct responses from trial 1 to trial 2 revealing proactive interference, but there was also, from the first trial onwards, an effect of same amplitude associated with longer retention intervals, and no interaction. Defenders of the unitary view of memory usually neglect this finding for retaining the following experiments. Indeed, Keppel and Underwood (1962) suggested that the absence of interaction could be due to a low degree of initial learning of the trigrams resulting in very low rates of correct responses at 9s and 18s of retention intervals in the second and third trial, the floor effect masking the expected interaction. Thus, they modified the original Peterson and Peterson task and abandoned the oral presentation of the to-be-remembered trigrams for their visual presentation during 2s. A second experiment following this procedure revealed no effect at all of retention interval at trial 1, recall being virtually perfect even after 18s. The expected interaction was now present (i.e., there was evidence for a build-up of proactive interference more pronounced with longer intervals), but this time probably due to a ceiling effect as the authors acknowledged. A third experiment using only two retention intervals (3s and 18s) for six trials revealed the expected interaction. The effect of retention interval, that was null at trial 1, increased progressively from trial to trial. However, with more than 90 per cent of correct responses at both retention intervals in trial 1, it can also be imagined that some ceiling effect contributed to this interaction.

The fact that the alleged absence of effect of the length of retention interval at trial 1 was actually due to ceiling effects did not run unnoticed. To avoid these ceiling effects as well as proactive interference, Baddeley and Scott (1971) tested subjects only once in their capacity to retain five-digit sequences instead of trigrams for various retention intervals. Forgetting occurred on this unique trial, indicating that proactive interference from prior trials is not essential for short-term forgetting. In subsequent experiments, Baddeley and Scott observed that this forgetting occurred mainly in the first moments, approaching asymptote within approximately six seconds. They consequently suggested that the Brown-Peterson distracting task comprises two components, a primary memory component, which rapidly decays within 6s, and a more stable long-term component from which memory traces can be retrieved using temporal retrieval cues. This dual-system account of Peterson's technique has been subsequently often advocated (for example, Baddeley 1997; Cowan 1988, 1995). The items to be remembered would lead to memory traces in both short-term and long-term memory. If short-term memory has decayed in such a way that recall is not possible, a search from long-term memory could take place based on temporal cues. However, proactive interference would make retrieval from the long-term store less and less likely as memory traces accumulate over successive trials. When there is only one trial, and provided that encoding was sufficiently strong (for example, as in Keppel and Underwood's Experiments 2 and 3, but not in their Experiment 1), the long-term memory trace can remain accessible even after long delays, creating the absence of effect of retention interval from which Crowder (1982, 1993) or Nairne (2002) conclude that there is no temporal decay. Interestingly, Baddeley and Scott's results were replicated by Nairne, Whiteman, and Kelley (1999) who studied forgetting for order using a reconstruction-order procedure. When proactive interference from prior trials was minimised, they found a small but reliable decrease in recall with longer retention intervals (from 2s to 96s), but a strong decrease in the first seconds when comparing immediate recall with a 2-sec interval. Thus, concluding that Keppel and Underwood (1962) proved that there is no temporal decay could be premature.

It could be argued at this point that Turvey *et al.* (1970) provided decisive evidence against temporal decay, longer retention intervals resulting in better recall in their experiment. However, it is probably important to note that, contrary to Peterson's method, the distracting task in Turvey *et al.*'s study was self-paced. We have seen in the previous chapter how the pace at which intervening tasks are performed is decisive in predicting recall. Without a strict control of this parameter, the results of Turvey and colleagues remain uninterpretable, undermining their explanation by Nairne (2002) in terms of temporal distinctiveness. This does not mean that a large part of the results related to the Peterson's method cannot be explained in terms of the relative discriminability of temporal cues as Baddeley (2007) assumes, but as Nairne (2003) acknowledged ten years ago, the dual-system account proposed by Baddeley and Scott (1971) had largely dominated the field for the past three decades.

A seemingly more promising avenue to account for Baddeley and Scott's (1971) results without any recourse to temporal decay is to assume the occurrence of some other kind of interference. Baddeley and Scott themselves evoked a possible intrasequence interference as Melton (1963) did. A modern, though slightly different, version of this account can be found in the idea that the rapid decay reaching asymptote after some seconds could be due to a loss of temporal distinctiveness between memory items as the retention interval increases. This hypothesis, mentioned *en passant* by Unsworth and Engle (2007b), was recently tested by Neath and Brown (2012) within the SIMPLE model (Brown *et al.* 2007). According to this model, memory is conceived as a discrimination task with items located along a temporal dimension, the zero point being the time at which the item is retrieved and each item having for value the time elapsed since presentation. The idea is that items with few close neighbours are more easily distinguished and recalled than items located in crowded temporal areas, discriminability decreasing as the memory items recede into the past. Neath and Brown (2012) showed that SIMPLE can produce the pattern observed by Baddeley and Scott (1971). The asymptote would result from a Weberian compression due to the logarithmic transformation of temporal values that condenses more large than small values. Thus, the distinctiveness of two items pertaining to the digit sequence to be remembered decreases more within the 30 first seconds of the retention interval than during the next 30 seconds.

While commenting on the SIMPLE model, Baddeley (2007) wondered if its complexity and large number of parameters would not lead to the danger that it may become a means of post hoc curve fitting instead of a heuristic conceptual tool. Indeed, Brown and Lewandowsky (2010) presented SIMPLE as a model producing forgetting curves appropriately described by a logarithmic function or a power law depending on small alterations in its parameters. There is no doubt that such a flexible model has the potential, provided the appropriate post hoc setting of its parameters, to fit any pattern characterised by a strong initial decline followed by an asymptote. Does this mean that temporal distinctiveness is the key for understanding what happens in the distracting task paradigm? This is possible, but not certain. As we will see later, it is quite easy to obtain results that contradict the predictions of a temporal distinctiveness model. Moreover, does the temporal distinctiveness hypothesis help us to understand how forgetting occurs in the short term? More than fifty years ago, Brown (1958) already argued that failure of discrimination cannot itself be a primary cause of forgetting, because it presupposes forgetting of that which determines which of the responses is correct. The metaphor of temporal distinctiveness is appealing as long as time is treated as space and memories compared to telephone poles receding into the distance, but all the memory traces are in our mind *hic et nun*, and not into some 'distance' or 'past'. So, what happens to these memory traces that makes them less and less discriminable as they get some seconds older?

A possible answer would be that the distracting material (for example, the numbers to be processed in the Petersons' task), which accumulates as the retention interval increases, has itself a damaging effect on memory traces through some retroactive interference. This is this explanation that is today favoured by those who deny any temporal decay in the short term. Consequently, providing evidence for or against decay has become more and more complex, the totally suitable procedure having to meet a set of almost incompatible conditions. On the one hand, recall performance must be assessed after various delays during which mechanisms that could counteract forgetting (rehearsal but also attentional refreshing) should be impeded.

On the other hand, the amount of interference created by the distracting tasks aimed at blocking maintenance activities should be kept as low as possible or at least constant through various retention intervals. In the last decade, several studies claimed to have met these requirements, leading to a renewal of this old problem.

Is there a temporal decay in working memory?

Meeting the challenge of demonstrating the existence or non-existence of temporal decay led to the proliferation of new paradigms that go further than the traditional Brown-Peterson method. This section reviews pros and cons studies, assessing to what extent they successfully met the methodological constraints needed to reach a reliable conclusion.

New evidence against temporal decay

Recently, a new series of studies challenged temporal decay as a source of forgetting in short-term memory, and Lewandowsky and colleagues argued that they had demonstrated that there is no temporal decay of memory traces in the short term (for review, Brown and Lewandowsky 2010; Lewandowsky *et al.* 2009). In a first study, Lewandowsky *et al.* (2004) investigated the effect of time on immediate serial recall of letters by asking participants either to recall letters at different rates (400, 800 or 1600 ms/item) or to repeat a suppressor ('super') either one, two or three times before the recall of each letter. Both manipulations aimed at increasing the delay between study and output. Contrary to the predictions of a model like SIMPLE, which accounts for forgetting through a time-based mechanism, serial positions never interacted with the manipulations of delay of retention. For the authors, this lack of interaction was strong evidence against any model that acknowledges a similar role for time in memory. However, this finding is weakened by four facts. First, the authors themselves acknowledged that this lack of interaction could result from poor statistical power due to a restricted sample of participants. Second, although the interaction with serial positions was non-significant, the main effect of manipulating the delay of retention was significant in both experiments. Whatever the type of manipulation used, longer delays resulted in poorer recall, something easily interpretable as evidence of temporal decay. Third, the critical and not observed interaction between delay of retention and serial position, which was considered in this study as the signature of time-based models, was subsequently presented by Oberauer and Lewandowsky (2008) as a prediction of SOB (for Serial Order in a Box), a model that denies any role for time in memory! As a matter of fact, this interaction was significant in their first experiment, which was similar to the experiments run by Lewandowsky et al. (2004). Thus, contrary to recurrent claims (for example, Lewandowsky et al. 2009), this first attempt to collect evidence against temporal decay was poorly convincing.

In the following study already mentioned, Oberauer and Lewandowsky (2008) extended this line of research in two ways. First, the suppressors were uttered at recall, as in Lewandowsky et al. (2004), but also at encoding as in a complex span procedure. Second, Oberauer and Lewandowsky (2008; Exp. 2) cogently noticed that utterance of the suppressor blocks any verbal rehearsal, but allows the attentional refreshing postulated by the TBRS model to take place, which could counteract the effect of decay. In order to block this mechanism of maintenance, they added a choice reaction time task to the utterance of the suppressor 'super', creating two different conditions. In a first condition referred to as AS-only (for articulatory suppression only), participants were asked to utter the word 'super' in response to a stimulus (an asterisk) that appeared either one or four times on screen. In a second condition referred to as AS + CRT (for articulatory suppression + choice reaction time task), the stimuli were either & or %. In response to these stimuli, participants had to say 'super' aloud and press the left or the right key respectively. These distractors were displayed either at encoding or at retrieval. As expected, recall performance was poorer in the AS + CRT than in the AS-only condition. Whereas increasing the number of distractors to be processed had no effect or even increased recall performance in the AS-only condition, recall diminished with increasing number of distractors in the AS + CRT condition[1]. However, it is rather difficult to draw a definite conclusion from these results, because both effects in AS-only condition and in AS + CRT condition were contradicted by other studies using similar designs. Indeed, the absence of an effect of delay in the AS-only condition is contradicted by the finding of such an effect at retrieval in Lewandowsky et al. (2004) and Oberauer and Lewandowsky (2008, Exp. 1), whereas Lewandowsky et al. (2008) observed no difference in recall between one and four distractors in the AS + CRT condition at retrieval. These contradictory results could be due to the fact that the tasks used by Lewandowsky and colleagues are self-paced. As Barrouillet et al. (2011b) argued, participants have enough time to perform intermittent refreshing in these self-paced tasks, making them inappropriate for assessing time-related effects.

It should be noted that these experiments acknowledged the fact that time-based forgetting cannot be assessed without taking into account the mechanisms described by the TBRS model. As a consequence, Oberauer and Lewandowsky (2013) designed a series of experiments inspired by the TBRS model to assess time decay, taking into account the attentional capture of a distracting task and the time allowed to refresh information. They asked participants to maintain letters in complex span paradigm, which involved either a visual search or a spatial fit task. In the inter-letter interval, the duration of attentional capture by the visual search was varied by increasing the number of objects in the visual display (1 *vs.* 4 or 2 *vs.* 6). For the spatial fit task, the attentional capture was increased by diminishing the difference in length between the gap and the horizontal bar that may fit in it. For both tasks, the free time between each display also varied (either 200 or 800ms). The results showed that neither the duration of the intervening task nor the free time affected significantly memory performance. According to Oberauer and Lewandowsky (2013), this failure to observe any effect on recall performance is new evidence against temporal decay. However, the authors admitted that their findings might result from the lack of time control. As noted by Ricker *et al.* (2014), intermittent refreshing could take place during the distracting task, explaining the absence of cognitive load effect. Moreover, it remains uncertain that the visual search task used by Oberauer and Lewandowsky (2013) as a distracter is appropriate for testing the effects related to attentional capture. In three experiments involving different visual search tasks, Kane, Poole, Tuholski, and Engle (2006) demonstrated that working memory capacity is irrelevant to performance in visual search with near-zero correlations with raw search RTs and slopes. Congruently, Drew *et al.* (2013) observed that neither RTs nor slopes are affected by working memory load, concluding that there is little overlap between resources involved in visual search and working memory tasks. Importantly, Woodman *et al.* (2001) showed that visual search tasks do not impair the maintenance of information in working memory, even within the visual domain. Finally, it should be noted that when introducing time control, the effects related to cognitive load reappeared in Oberauer and Lewandowsky (2013). The alternative account to the TBRS proposed by these authors in terms of representation-based interference resulting from time pressure will be discussed in Chapter 8. Overall, the empirical evidence against temporal decay in Oberauer and Lewandowsky (2013) is mixed, at best.

Another thought-provoking finding usually taken as evidence against decay has been recently reported by White (2012). In a Brown-Peterson paradigm, White had participants remembering a word pair during retention intervals of 2s, 4s, 8s, 16s or 32s filled either by an easy or a difficult task (every two seconds, adding two or three digits respectively). Not surprisingly, forgetting increased with the duration of the retention interval, and more for the difficult than the easy task. The critical condition consisted in switching from the difficult to the easy task after 8s. In this condition, recall accuracy at longer intervals recovered from the level consistent with the difficult condition to a level similar to the easy condition, memory performance being better after 16s or 32s than after 8s. Similar results were observed in a second experiment with a switch occurring after 16s. Increases in memory with increased retention-interval durations are usually taken as evidence against decay as a source of forgetting (Nairne 2002; Wheeler 1995; Roediger *et al.* 2010).

White noted that his findings are also at odds with the TBRS model because, once traces have decayed, it is intuitively implausible that memory strength would increase even if a lower cognitive load allows for more efficient refreshing. As a matter of fact, White (2012) failed to replicate, and was even totally opposite to, an ancient study by Dillon and Reid (1969) which he seemed to be unaware of. These authors basically ran the same experiment as White. Their participants memorised consonant trigrams for 15-s retention intervals divided into three 5-s segments filled with either an easy (read a pair of two-digit numbers aloud) or a difficult task (add two digits and judge the parity of the sum). All the eight possible combinations of easy and difficult segments were compared. When the difficult task was performed at the beginning of the retention interval, recall accuracy remained totally unaffected by the task performed in the remaining 10s, and lower than in all the conditions beginning by the easy task. Dillon and Reid (1969) concluded from this fact that the maximum amount of forgetting has already occurred after 5s. In two further experiments, they established that progressively increasing by 1-s increments the duration of the difficult task performed at the beginning of a 5-s retention interval resulted in poorer and poorer recall but, in any case, whatever the moment at which the switching to the easy task occurred, recall performance never recovered to the level observed when performing the easy task over the entire retention interval. Finally, and still contrary to White, they observed in a fourth experiment that adding an easy task performed after a difficult task resulted in recall decrements over and above those resulting from the difficult task alone. Anticipating Baddeley and Scott (1971), Dillon and Reid (1969) concluded that the rapid drop in recall during the first seconds certainly reflected forgetting from short-term memory related with the prevention of verbal rehearsal, whereas the steady level of recall following this initial phase most likely reflected recall from long-term memory. The phenomena observed by White (2012) after intervals of 8s or 16s filled with an arithmetic task that most probably prevented any type of rehearsal or refreshing could reflect long-term rather than short-term recovery and constitute less compelling evidence against temporal decay as it seems at the first glance.

New evidence in favour of temporal decay

In face of the renewal of studies searching for evidence against temporal decay, other studies have sought for evidence in favour of it. Many of these studies focus on the maintenance of visual or auditory non-verbal material, which reduces both the need to impede articulatory rehearsal and the risk to produce interference (McKeown and Mercer 2012; Ricker and Cowan 2010; Zhang and Luck 2009). Ricker and Cowan (2010) observed that the recognition of unconventional characters declined with time (from 1.5 to 6 seconds) whether participants had no concurrent task during the retention interval, or a task impeding either rehearsal (repeating digits auditorily presented) or both rehearsal and refreshing (subtracting one to each digit and giving the response aloud). McKeown and Mercer (2012) also provided evidence of time-based forgetting with non-verbal auditory material (the timbre of complex tones that cannot be verbally encoded) in a two-tone comparison procedure. A steady decrease in task accuracy emerged as the retention interval extended from 1 to 32 seconds. Many previous studies had reported a similar finding with tone comparisons (for example, Clément et al. 1999; Demany et al. 2008; Harris 1952; Kaernbach 2004; Kaernbach and Schlemmer 2008; Keller et al. 1995; Kinchla and Smyzer 1967; Moss et al. 1970). However, Cowan et al. (1997) suggested that proactive interference may account for this finding, because the gaps between trials were brief, and may influence the temporal distinctiveness at longer retention intervals. As a consequence, tones from previous trials may have influenced and distorted the representation on the current trial. To avoid such a possibility, McKeown and Mercer (2012) replicated the time-based decay they previously observed while controlling for distinctiveness by varying the inter-trial interval from 2 to 34 seconds. Whereas the performance was still poorer at long retention interval, the inter-trial interval had relatively little impact on performance. McKeown et al. (2014) found further evidence of time-based forgetting with abstract visual patterns. Other recent studies reported the loss of visual information after some seconds of an even unfilled delay (Morey and Bieler 2013; Pertzov et al. 2013). It should be noticed that these studies that report gradual decay of short-term memory were supported by Zhang and Luck's (2009) findings of time-based forgetting of memory for colours. However, items appeared to drop out of memory rather than gradually decay, a form of sudden forgetting or 'sudden death'.

Facing this evidence, even Oberauer and Lewandowsky (2013, p. 380) admitted 'that visual representations in working memory are affected by the passage of time in a different manner than verbal representations' and restricted their conclusions against temporal decay to verbal working memory. However, Cowan and AuBuchon (2008) provided evidence of time-based forgetting of verbal memory items. They noticed that, in Lewandowsky et al. (2004), a non-articulatory mechanism could maintain verbal information despite the concurrent articulation produced during the delay of retention. Following a similar rationale as Oberauer and Lewandowsky (2008) for whom both articulatory and non-articulatory maintenance mechanisms should be impeded to measure the impact of time-based forgetting, Cowan and AuBuchon (2008) developed an innovative approach that would not introduce interference, contrary to the addition of concurrent tasks. Participants were asked to maintain series of 7 digits, for which the pace of presentation was varied by introducing either a short (0.5s) or long (2s) delay between each digit. Moreover, the first and second halves of the digit lists could follow either the same or a different pace of presentation. Participants had to recall the digit lists in correct order either at a free- or paced-timing, i.e., reproducing at recall the pace of presentation of the lists. This latter condition allowed for testing the effect of temporal decay because the introduction of long rather than short delays in the first half of the list postponed recall of the last items. Moreover, the need to reproduce the pace of presentation occupies attention and adds an extra memory load, preventing the use of attentional maintenance mechanisms. As expected, in the paced-timing trials, evidence of memory loss over time emerged, a lengthy first half-list leading to a detrimental effect on recall. Thus, without introducing any further source of interference while mechanisms of maintenance were impeded, Cowan and AuBuchon (2008) provided evidence of time-based forgetting in verbal working memory.

Further evidence of temporal decay of verbal memory was provided by Portrat, Barrouillet, and Camos (2008) who slightly modified the square location task used by Barrouillet et al. (2007) already described in Chapter 3. Recall that increasing the difficulty of the response selection by reducing the distance between the two possible locations led to poorer recall performance, an effect that we accounted for by assuming that longer processing times in the close condition induce more decay. However, Oberauer and Kliegl (2006) noted that, in our paradigm, longer processing times result in shorter refreshing periods. Our finding could thus be compatible with an interference account of forgetting, shorter free times reducing the time available to repair degraded memory traces. To test this hypothesis, Portrat et al. (2008) replicated the location square experiment while keeping free time constant. In both the close and distant squares conditions, a constant delay of 650ms was introduced between the response and the occurrence of the next square. This manipulation did not impact the pattern of results, the close condition still eliciting poorer recall, from which we concluded that time-related decay during processing is the source of forgetting. However, reanalysing our results, Lewandowsky and Oberauer (2009) argued that this effect could be due to post-error processes susceptible to capture attention during free time, reducing the time available for refreshing. Indeed, it appeared that there were more errors in the close than the distant condition, and that when error rates were statistically controlled, there was no evidence for temporal decay. Nevertheless, Oberauer and Lewandowsky (2013) consistently failed to find an effect of proportion of errors on memory in three successive experiments. Although this result goes against the outcome of Lewandowsky and Oberauer's (2009) reanalysis, the authors concluded that distracter task errors *per se* do not disturb memory. Assuming a temporal decay of memory traces remains the simplest explanation of Portrat et al. (2008) findings.

Barrouillet et al. (2012) went further in showing comparable detrimental effects of time in the maintenance of verbal and visuospatial material, thus extending evidence that verbal as well as visuospatial working memory is sensitive to temporal decay. Using a complex span paradigm in which participants had to maintain either consonants or spatial locations followed by multiplications to be solved, Barrouillet et al. (2012) varied the duration of attentional capture by presenting the multiplications either in a digit ($3 \times 4 = 12$?) or word format (three $\times$ four = twelve?) while the free time after each operation was kept constant. The operations were simple enough to rely on retrieval from long-term memory, but multiplications in words involved longer solving times due to differences in encoding (Noël et al. 1997). Any increase in solving times increases the delay during which memory traces suffer from decay and should thus lead to poorer recall performance. As expected, while maintaining series of consonants, participants recalled fewer letters when the multiplications were presented in words than in digits. The same result was obtained while they maintained spatial locations. Observing the same effect for both verbal and visual-spatial information is difficult to reconcile with interference accounts of forgetting. Although it can be conceived that multiplications presented in words may interfere more with letters than the multiplications in digits, it is more difficult to imagine that they also involve more visuospatial interference. Thus, the simplest way to explain these findings seems to assume that memory traces decay with time when attention is not available for their maintenance. Further evidence in favour of temporal decay was provided by Barrouillet *et al.* (2011b; see Chapter 8 for discussion about this latter study).

Overall, the question of the existence of temporal decay remains a hotly debated issue that clearly needs more investigation. On the one hand, studies claiming to have provided evidence against decay often lead to contradictory results, the effects of time appearing and disappearing across experiments, leading to questionable conclusions. On the other hand, the need for avoiding the intervention of maintenance mechanisms makes that direct evidence for decay often concerns stimuli (tones, colours or unconventional characters) that do not correspond to what comes spontaneously to mind when referring to information-processing in working memory, and evidence concerning the temporal decay of symbolic information remains sparse. Nonetheless, whatever the final answer to this problem, a remaining and independent question concerns the other possible sources of forgetting that have been alleged, namely interference. What are the mechanisms by which representations interfere with each other, and what is the exact impact of this factor on forgetting?

Interference and forgetting

Different types of interference

The distractors interspersed between presentation and recall could interfere with the memoranda and impede their retrieval and recall in several ways. Lewandowsky *et al.* (2009) distinguish between process-based interference, representation-based interference and interference by retrieval confusion. Process-based interference would occur when processing activities disrupt the consolidation or refreshing of memory traces. It is worth noting that this kind of interference cannot in itself explain forgetting. If impeding consolidation or refreshing leads to forgetting, this only means that these mechanisms can counteract the effects of some source of forgetting that has to be found elsewhere. Consequently, we shall consider this kind of interference no further in this section. Interference by retrieval confusion does not necessarily involve the degradation of memory traces. As in the proactive interference account of the distracting task, too many memory traces would become associated with a given retrieval cue. As we have seen, this source of interference has been very popular in accounting for short-term forgetting. At the same time, its role should not be overestimated. As Ricker *et al.* (2014) note, proactive interference would predict a high rate of intrusions from previous trials, something that is disappointingly infrequent, as Brown (1958) observed[2]. The same source of forgetting could of course occur through retroactive interference, though it is frequent to use distractors that are not candidates for recall (for example, digits when letters are to be remembered).

More interesting for our purpose are those kinds of interference that produce genuine forgetting by degrading memory traces. They are usually assumed to result from the deleterious effect that the representations of distractors have on memory items, or from the effect that the representations of these memory items have on each other, hence their designation as representation-based interference. Some models assume that this interference could occur by feature overwriting (Nairne 1990) or feature overlap (Oberauer and Kliegl 2006). The idea here is that when several items in short-term memory share features, these features are at risk of being deleted, resulting in a selective degradation of memory traces. Note that, in this case, interference results from some similarity between representations. Other models using distributed item representations, like SOB (Farrell and Lewandowsky 2002) and its variants (for example, SOB-CS, Oberauer et al. 2012), assume that items interfere with each other by being superimposed in a composite memory, with more items encoded resulting in more blurred representations. Contrary to the former case, interference is not here conveyed by similarity but by novelty or dissimilarity with the content of short-term memory. Novel items would receive more encoding weight, creating more damaging effects on existing memory traces.

There is little doubt that representation-based interference occurs in short-term memory. More controversial is the idea that short-term forgetting could be entirely accounted for by the sole action of this type of interference. In the following, we review recent studies that assessed the effects related with either the similarity or dissimilarity of the distractors with the current content of working memory.

Interference resulting from similarity between representations

As we said when introducing this chapter, Brown (1958) observed that memory for consonants was more disrupted by a distracting task involving other consonants than digits, though the difference between the two conditions was moderate when compared with the effect related to the introduction of a distracting task, whatever its content. The same phenomenon of stimulus similarity effect has been subsequently observed in complex span tasks in several occasions, in adults (Duff and Logie 2001; Shah and Miyake 1996; Turner and Engle 1989) as well as in children (Bayliss et al. 2003; Conlin et al. 2005). Complex memory performance is generally lower when memoranda are from the same domain as the processing component of the task (for example, remembering numbers while solving arithmetic problems vs. reading sentences). These findings have been interpreted to reflect either the competition between processing and storage for some subsystem of working memory (for example, Bayliss et al. 2003; Duff and Logie 2001; Shah and Miyake 1996) or the intervention of similarity-based interference through representational overlap (Conlin et al. 2005; Saito and Miyake 2004). As Conlin et al. (2005) stressed, there is ample evidence that mechanisms mediating similarity decrements must be added to the attentional constraints of the intervening task that we described in the previous chapter in accounting for working memory performance. However, even if process-based interferences are set aside, these similarity effects could result from a variety of mechanisms such as the degradation of memory traces through representational overlap, but also response competition at retrieval or even during the recurrent reconstruction of degraded memory traces through attentional refreshing (see Chapter 6 for a mechanistic account of this process). A more fine-grained analysis of the impact of genuine representation-based interference, that is the degradation of memory traces provoked by their overlap with partially similar representations, is provided by studies that have manipulated the degree of this overlap.

The detrimental effect that similar representations concurrently held in short-term memory have on each other is nicely illustrated by the well-known phonological similarity effect by which recall performance is lower for phonologically similar (for example, 'mad', 'man', 'mat', 'cap', 'cad', 'can', 'cat', 'cap') than dissimilar items (for example, 'cow', 'day', 'bar', 'few', 'hot', 'pen', 'sup', 'pit'). This effect, largely documented within the immediate serial recall paradigm (Baddeley 1966; Conrad 1964; see Baddeley 2007 for a review), seemed to be less clear in complex span tasks, with some studies reporting the effect (Lobley *et al.* 2005) while others did not (Macnamara *et al.* 2011; Tehan *et al.* 2001). Re-analysing these studies, we noted that those experiments in which the effect did not appear involved concurrent tasks performed aloud, while the effect occurred when they were silent. This suggests that the phonological similarity effect in complex span tasks depends on the use of verbal rehearsal for the maintenance of the memoranda, a hypothesis that we verified in several experiments (Camos, Mora, and Barrouillet, 2013; Camos, Mora, Oberauer, 2011).

It is worth noting that the explanation given by Baddeley (2007) for the phonological similarity effect does not imply the supposition of the degradation of representations. It is assumed that memory traces are registered in the phonological store and associated with a series of contextual cues. Because items are stored as a series of phonological features, phonologically similar items share several of these features, increasing the likelihood of miscueing and confusion at retrieval. By contrast, the hypothesis of feature overwriting resulting from feature overlap (Nairne 1990; Oberauer and Kliegl 2006) supposes such degradation. This hypothesis differs from the former in that phoneme overlap is assumed to create interference even for low-confusable items (Oberauer 2009a). Camos *et al.* (2011) studied the recall of lists of phonologically similar words and high overlapping words in complex span tasks. For example, a list of phonologically similar words was 'ban', 'man', 'mass', 'gas', 'bag', 'match', whereas the list 'fight', 'ball', 'stone', 'male', 'side', 'term', which is made of words that cannot be confused with each other, presents a high degree of overlap. Camos and colleagues observed that the phonological similarity effect appeared when verbal rehearsal was used for maintenance, either spontaneously or through instruction, whereas the effect of phoneme overlap only occurred when participants were explicitly invited to rehearse. Moreover, this latter effect was small and less important than the phonological similarity effect.

Although the interference occurring between memory items is probably a non-negligible source of forgetting in working memory, the main question of interest since the pioneering works of Brown (1958) and Peterson and Peterson (1959) concerns the source of forgetting engendered by distracting tasks. Accordingly, several studies have investigated representation-based interference between memory items and distractors. For example, in a task akin to the first experiment in Brown (1958), Lange and Oberauer (2005) presented participants with three CVC-trigrams (i.e., Consonant-Vowel-Consonant non-words) for further recall, immediately followed by three distracting CVCs to be read. The critical manipulation was that one of the memory items, the target, had its constituent letters distributed among the three distractors, creating a large feature overlap, whereas the other memory items did not share letters with the distractors and were used as control. Feature overwriting interference was revealed by lower recall of the targets than controls, an effect that was replicated with words, all the phonemes of the target word being distributed among the distractor words. This feature overwriting phenomenon has to be distinguished from the phonological similarity, as Oberauer and Lange (2008) demonstrated. Using the same task of words followed by distractors, two types of targets were created: overlapping targets, which were memory items with their phonemes distributed among the distracting words, and similarity targets, which were phonological neighbours of one of the distracting words. In line with the feature overwriting hypothesis, the results revealed that both types of targets were less well recalled than control words, whereas the similarity-based confusion hypothesis would have only predicted lower recall of the similarity targets.

The critical study concerning interference between distractors and memory items was conducted by Oberauer (2009a). In eight experiments, he used a complex span task in which each of four words to be recalled were followed by four distracting words to be read at either a fast or a slow pace following the method we introduced in Barrouillet *et al.* (2004). The critical variables manipulated were the semantic similarity, the phonological similarity, and the degree of phonological overlap between distracting and memory words. For example, the phonologically similar distracting words following the memory item 'floor' were 'flair', 'for', 'lore', and 'flow', whereas the highly phonologically overlapping distractors for 'time' were 'tight', 'mind', 'fire', and 'foot'. Semantic similarity between distractors and memory words had a facilitative effect on a first experiment, an effect that disappeared when distractors related to a specific memory item were shuffled across the list. The effect of phonological similarity was far from being statistically significant and negligible in size (Cohen's d was −0.131). These results echoed previous findings by Oberauer *et al.* (2004) who observed that semantic or phonological similarity between memory items and distractors had little effect, though a small detrimental effect of semantic similarity sometimes occurred. Concerning the effect of phoneme overlap, which was investigated in two experiments, it was significant in the first experiment, but failed to reach significance in the second. More important are the sizes of these effects, which were disappointingly small. While the pace at which the distracting task was performed, which determines its cognitive load, had a systematic effect in every single experiment, with F values ranging from 10.52 to 56.72 and effect sizes ranging from $d = 0.78$ to $d = 1.22$, the effect of phoneme overlap yielded a maximum F value of 6.68 and d values of 0.59 and 0.27. Overall, these results indicate that the contribution of representation-based interference to forgetting is real, but moderate at best. Considering the effect sizes associated with phoneme overlap, it seems difficult to imagine that this type of representation-based interference could be the unique source of forgetting engendered by variations in the cognitive load of the distracting task.

In summary, representation-based interference resulting from the similarity between memory items and distractors has a surprisingly small effect in working memory. Of course, performance is generally lower when storage and processing involve information pertaining to the same domain, but this effect does not necessarily result from representation-based interference and could be due to process-based interference or response competition that do not constitute sources of forgetting *per se*. When specifically manipulating the similarity between memory items and distractors, increased semantic or phonological similarity does not seem to substantially impair recall. Concerning feature overwriting, it seems that a high degree of overlap between memory items and distractors is needed to produce effects that proved volatile (Oberauer 2009a). However, though intuitively appealing, similarity might not be the main vehicle of representation-based interference. Instead, it has been suggested that dissimilarity and novelty are main sources of interference.

Representation-based interference through novelty encoding

We evoked above the SOB model (Farrell and Lewandowsky 2002) and its variants SOB-CS (Oberauer *et al.* 2012), which assume that distractors are encoded onto working memory, interfering with the memory items. It is hypothesised that the amount of interference produced by a distractor is a function of its degree of dissimilarity with the current content of short-term memory, new items receiving stronger encoding weight and producing more interference. By contrast, repeated items would result in negligible encoding weight and add very little interference. These hypotheses have been tested in studies in which participants had to memorise lists of five letters, distracting words being interspersed either between retrievals in immediate serial recall (Lewandowsky *et al.* 2008) or between encodings as in a complex span task procedure (Lewandowsky *et al.* 2010). The rationale of these studies was to vary the number of either changing or repeated distractors with the hypothesis that increasing the number of repetitions of the same distractor (for example, 'office, office, office' *vs.* 'office') should not have damaging effects on memory because these repetitions do not result in additional interference. By contrast, any increase in the number of changing distractors (for example, 'office, question, yearly' *vs.* 'office') should result in lower recall performance because each novel distractor would receive strong encoding weight and produce additional interference. Overall, these predictions were verified, lending apparent support to the hypothesis that forgetting occurs through the encoding of distractors that are superimposed over memory items, the amount of interference and forgetting depending on the novelty of these distractors.

Although these findings could be considered as strong evidence for interference through novelty encoding, we have recently argued that they are less compelling than Lewandowsky and colleagues assume when methodological aspects are put under scrutiny (Plancher and Barrouillet 2013). Consider, for example, the procedure used by Lewandowsky *et al.* (2010). In most of their experiments, after each memory item, distractors to be read appeared rapidly on screen one after the other with short intervals of 200ms, that is almost simultaneously, and remained on screen until all distractors had been articulated. Because participants were informed of the nature of the forthcoming burst of distractors, it was possible to process the bursts made of three repeated distractors (called *simple* bursts, for example, 'office, office, office') by identifying their single word and repeating it without paying any further attention to distractors. By contrast, the *complex* bursts (for example, 'office, question, yearly') required participants to read three different words. Because reading words requires the retrieval of their phonological representation from long-term memory, a process involving attention, there was a confound in Lewandowsky *et al.*'s experiments between the nature of the bursts of distractors (simple *vs.* complex) and the amount of attention their processing required. Moreover, these intervening activities were self-paced, rendering hazardous any comparison between conditions. As we will see in the next chapter, the rate at which memory traces can be attentionally refreshed is so fast (about 50ms per item) that participants can take advantage of the shortest pauses to turn their attention towards the memoranda and refresh them, something that was amply illustrated in the previous chapter.

Consequently, Plancher and Barrouillet (2013) aimed at testing the main hypotheses issued from the SOB model while avoiding the confound between novelty and attention. They presented their participants with lists of five letters for further recall, each letter being followed by distracting words to be processed at various paces. However, instead of presenting these words simultaneously, they were presented successively on screen in such a way that the nature of the forthcoming word could not be anticipated, participants having to pay attention to each distractor. For example, the hypothesis that repeated distractors involve lower interference was tested by varying the number of dissimilar words in bursts of three distractors. Complex bursts containing three different words were compared with *mixed* bursts in which the same word was repeated, except in two unpredictable occasions where a change appeared. An experimental trial in this mixed condition could take the following form: C / 'slide slide fly' / N / 'attack attack attack' / J / 'chair chair adult' / R / 'century century century' / V / 'sorrow sorrow sorrow'. Overall, complex trials involved 15 different distractors whereas there were only seven different distractors in mixed trials. Participants were informed before each trial of its nature and of the fact that words were changing in the complex trials, but sometimes repeated in mixed trials. Results made clear that reading distractors induced forgetting, as a strong pace effect testified. In line with the predictions of the TBRS model, reading distractors at a fast pace (one word every 800ms) resulted in lower recall performance than reading them at a slower pace (one word every 1300ms). However, the degree of novelty of the distractors had no effect with no difference in recall between the complex- and mixed-burst conditions. The second SOB hypothesis, according to which increasing the number of changing distractors in complex bursts involves more interference and lower recall, was tested in comparing the effect on recall of changing bursts containing either two or four distractors. This manipulation had no effect at all, whereas the pace effect was strong. We replicated these findings in five successive experiments. The pace effect was significant in every single experiment, a meta-analysis revealing a strong effect with a mean d value of 1.17. By contrast, the effects related to the degree of novelty (i.e., the comparison between complex and mixed bursts) and the number of changing distractors were never significant and associated with negligible mean d values of 0.03 and -0.06 respectively. We concluded from these findings that forgetting in working memory is a multifactorial process that most probably involves representation-based interference, but no interference through novelty-sensitive encoding contributes to forgetting.

When do event-based and temporal factors have an effect?

Defenders of a unitised view of memory often argue against temporal decay, claiming that forgetting in the short term only results from interference (Brown and Lewandowsky 2010; Crowder 1982, 1993; Lewandowsky et al. 2009; Nairne 2002). More balanced views have recently been put forward. Altmann and Schunn's (2012) reanalysis of the classical Waugh and Norman (1965) study is a good example of this trend. Waugh and Norman asked their participants to study lists of digits in which the last digit was always the second occurrence of a probe that appeared somewhere before. The task consisted of recalling the digit that immediately followed this probe. The amount of interference was manipulated by varying the number of intervening digits between the target and the end of the list, whereas decay was manipulated by varying presentation rate (either 1 or 4 items/sec.). The authors reported a large effect of the number of interfering items, but no effect of the presentation rate, a result that has usually been considered as evidence for an interference-only view. However, Altman and Schunn noted that Waugh and Norman did not analyse the interaction, though it was reliable. A slower rate elicits better recalls when there are few interfering items, a trend that is reversed when their number increases. Altmann and Schunn argue that this is exactly what one would expect if interference and decay interacted in determining recall. Trials with many interfering items correspond to early occurrences of the probe and benefit from a fast presentation because items have less decayed and the target is easier to retrieve, whereas recent occurrences of the probe benefit from slow presentations because early items have more decayed and produce less proactive interference. They tested and confirmed this hypothesis with a simple formal model that provided a better fit of the data than a model in which presentation rate has no effect.

We obtained more direct evidence of the conjunction of interference and decay in a recent study using the same paradigm as Lewandowsky *et al.* (2008) in which distractors are interspersed between retrieval (Barrouillet *et al.* 2013). Though we used several types of distractors in this study, we will concentrate here on those experiments intended to directly confront sources of interference and decay. Lists of five consonants were presented for immediate recall, participants being asked to read digits successively displayed on screen before each retrieval. Sources of interference were varied by manipulating the number of these digits (either 1, 2, or 3), whereas temporal factors were introduced by varying their rate of presentation (one digit every 500ms, 1s, or 2s). Of course, in line with the TBRS model, we predicted better recall performance with slower paces of the reading digit task. However, we also surmised that interference and temporal factors could differently affect memory traces depending on their degree of consolidation. Superficial traces that have not yet been consolidated could be more prone to representation-based interference through feature overwriting than consolidated memory representations for which a number of phonological, visual or even semantic features could have been bound together. Thus, the time allowed to encode each to-be-remembered letter was fixed at either 0.5s, 1.5s, or 5s. Results are displayed in Figure 4.1. First, it appeared that letters benefiting from longer encoding times were better recalled. Moreover, as we expected, effects related to the number of distractors, intended to reflect the intervention of representation-based interference, were particularly clear on letters presented at a fast rate (panel a). Increasing the number of distractors impaired recall, an effect that interacted with the pace at which these distractors were processed. We reasoned that a fast rate of presentation prevents deep encoding and results in fragile memory traces, prone to degradation by interference, especially when a fast pace of the distracting task prevents any further consolidation by attentional refreshing. As a consequence, the effect of the number of digits was particularly clear when the distracting task was performed at a fast pace, with a release of this effect as the distracting task became less demanding. As we had imagined, the effects related to the number of distractors progressively disappeared as the rate of presentation of the letters became slower, allowing for their better encoding (Figure 4.1, panels b and c). By contrast, temporal factors still affected performance, the effect of the pace of the distracting task remaining highly significant.

The pattern described on panel c of Figure 4.1 deserves some comments. Whereas there is no effect of the number of distractors, the pace at which the concurrent task is performed still has an effect. This clearly indicates that the additional forgetting resulting from faster pace cannot be due to some additional interference. It is worth noting that these results are also totally contradictory with a temporal discriminability account. Indeed, all other things being equal, faster pace of the distracting task corresponds to a shorter delay between presentation and retrieval. Consequently, models based on temporal discriminability such as SIMPLE would predict a better recall performance (see above the analysis of Baddeley and Scott's results by Neath and Brown 2012). The exact opposite occurs. It seems that the

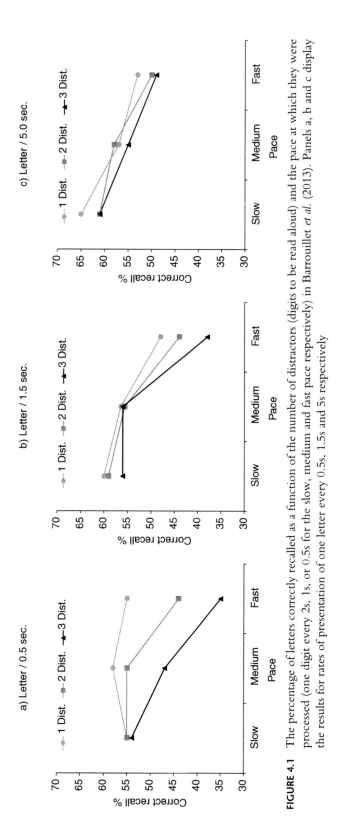

FIGURE 4.1 The percentage of letters correctly recalled as a function of the number of distractors (digits to be read aloud) and the pace at which they were processed (one digit every 2s, 1s, or 0.5s for the slow, medium and fast pace respectively) in Barrouillet *et al.* (2013). Panels a, b and c display the results for rates of presentation of one letter every 0.5s, 1.5s and 5s respectively

explanation given by the TBRS model in terms of temporal decay counteracted by refreshing processes is the simplest.

Overall, these findings suggest that event-based interference and decay could differently affect working memory. Interference seems to affect primarily superficial memory traces that have not been deeply encoded. This type of memory trace could be maintained in peripheral systems of working memory such as the phonological loop. Confirming this hypothesis, the same study revealed that a mere concurrent articulation (repeating a syllable) had the same effect as reading digits on poorly consolidated memory traces. However, when the encoding time of the letters increased, recall performance became more and more immune to concurrent articulation while the concurrent attentional demand induced by reading digits had still a strong effect (Figure 4.2). This indicates that consolidated memory traces tend to be less dependent on phonology, probably involving a multimodal coding at some central level of working memory like an episodic buffer. This distinction will be further elaborated in Chapter 6 when presenting the cognitive architecture of working memory. Suffice it to say here that interference-only as well as decay-only views of forgetting in the short term are probably dead ends, the description of forgetting as a multi-determined phenomenon being more promising.

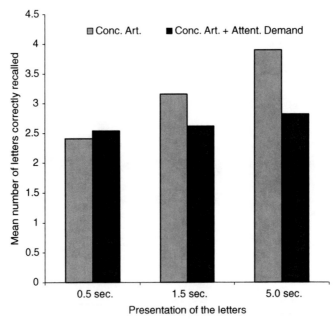

FIGURE 4.2 The mean number of letters correctly recalled as a function of their rate of presentation for concurrent tasks involving either a simple concurrent articulation (Conc. Art., i.e., repeating the same word 'two') or a concurrent articulation and an attentional demand (Conc. Art. + Attent. Demand, i.e., reading digits aloud). Data from Barrouillet et al. (2013)

Conclusion

As was evident throughout this chapter, the question of the sources of forgetting in the short term remains undecided, and more than 50 years of empirical enquiry have not yet been sufficient to decipher the puzzle. Even the apparently simple question of the existence of temporal decay proved more difficult to solve than expected. Baddeley (2007) concluded from his review on this issue that it remains unresolved, something always true nowadays. At the same time, the effects associated with retroactive representation-based interference proved disappointingly small when assessed. Moreover, despite the abundance of computational models for the sole task of immediate serial recall favouring the representation-based interference hypothesis, it seems that there is yet no metric for the amount of interference that a given distractor would produce on a given memory item. The recourse to proactive interference seemed more promising, but it remains unclear that this type of interference directly produces short-term forgetting. It could be that proactive interference mainly affect retrieval from long-term memory when short-term memory traces have been damaged to the point that they become useless for recall (Cowan 1988, 1995). Moreover, as Crowder (1982, p. 295) acknowledged, 'the source of proactive inhibition for the Brown-Peterson situation has clearly not been settled'. After all, one could wonder why proactive interference would be more pronounced for longer delays of retention. Keppel and Underwood (1962) explained this relationship by assuming that the longer the retention interval, the greater the recovery of interfering associations. But, what is the process in the Brown-Peterson task that would trigger the recovery of ancient associations during retention interval? Assuming that longer retention intervals result in greater decay of short-term memory traces and more frequent recourse to long-term memory would not it be a far simpler explanation? We will propose an elaboration of this explanation in Chapter 6. The same effect has been accounted for by invoking the loss of discriminability of memory traces with increased retention intervals (Baddeley 2007; Nairne 2002). However, we have seen that expectations based on temporal discriminability accounts are sometimes contradicted by facts.

Overall, it is likely that there is no unique cause for short-term forgetting, decay and interference jointly contributing to the degradation of memory traces, an idea that has been often proposed by the past (Massaro 1970; Reitman 1974; Wickelgren 1970). Moreover, we provided evidence that different factors could differently affect memory traces depending on their level of consolidation. The search for a definite and comprehensive account of working memory loss promises to be a long and arduous quest.

Notes

1 This effect just failed to reach significance at encoding, $p = .07$, but was highly significant at retrieval, $p = .001$.
2 It is interesting to note that, after convoluted explanations, Keppel and Underwood (1962) decided to not provide the data concerning intrusions by which they might have confirmed their hypothesis.

5
WORKING MEMORY RECONSTRUCTION

Within what Nairne (2002) called the 'standard' model is the idea that working memory traces undergo an inescapable decay of their activation that is counteracted by rehearsal in a continual trade-off. The TBRS model is close to this idea with its hypothesis of an alternation of phases of loss and reconstruction of memory traces. Nairne explained that this idea is intuitively appealing, probably because it can be expressed with concrete metaphors such as a juggler trying to maintain a set of plates, but endeavoured to discard it by accumulating arguments against the existence of both decay and rehearsal. The nature of his arguments made clear that Nairne's case against the standard model was actually a case against Baddeley's phonological loop model, with the main alleged evidence against rehearsal revolving around the sources of the word length effect and the relationship between articulation rate and span. However, the hypothesised mechanisms by which information would be maintained active in working memory go beyond the sole verbal rehearsal. Baddeley's multi-component model assumed the existence of a specialised system for reactivating visuospatial information (the inner scribe, Baddeley and Logie 1999; Logie 1995), and we have seen that earlier versions of this theory envisioned a possible storage function for the central executive (Baddeley and Hitch 1974). The modern idea of a reactivation of memory traces through covert retrieval (Cowan 1992; Cowan et al. 1994) or attentional refreshing (Raye et al. 2007) is not so far from this seminal supposition, and Repovs and Baddeley (2006) have assumed that attention would be involved in the maintenance of information in the episodic buffer. Thus, the question of the number and nature of the mechanisms of maintenance is embedded in a larger debate about the unitary *versus* non-unitary nature of working memory, a question that has been mainly addressed through the so-called selective interference paradigm. Are there different working memory sub-systems with their own domain-specific mechanism for maintaining information active and available for treatment, or is maintenance carried out by a unique domain-general system keeping up any kind of information, whatever its nature? In this chapter, we will argue and provide evidence for an intermediate view between unitary and non-unitary models of working memory. Along with a central mechanism maintaining working memory representations through attentional refreshing, there is evidence for a unique domain-specific mechanism devoted to the maintenance of verbal information through articulatory rehearsal. Importantly, we will provide direct evidence of the existence of these mechanisms by predicting and observing their effects on concurrent processing.

The selective interference paradigm

As nicely summarised in Shah and Miyake (1999), this issue of whether working memory is unitary or non-unitary has been a source of controversy for decades. Some researchers have emphasised the unitary nature of working memory (Anderson et al. 1996; Cowan 1995; Engle et al. 1992; Kyllonen and Christal 1990), whereas others favoured a non-unitary view (Baddeley 1986; Daneman and Tardif 1987; Martin 1993; Monsell 1984; Shah and Miyake 1996). When working memory is conceived as non-unitary, different ways to fractionate it have been proposed with no consensus on the number and nature of the subsystems (Shah and Miyake 1999). Baddeley's standard theory assumes that there are two systems of storage, one for the verbal information and the other for the visuospatial domain, with their own mechanism of maintenance fuelled by specific pools of resources (Baddeley 1986; Baddeley and Logie 1999). Several lines of research support the separability of these two systems of storage. Besides the study of brain-damaged patients who show selective impairment of either the spatial or verbal component of working memory (cf. Gathercole 1994, for a review), and brain imaging studies revealing the activation of different brain areas corresponding to the involvement of these two components (for example, Gruber and von Cramon 2003), the main supporting evidence for a multi-component view relies on the existence of selective interference.

Using dual tasks, and mostly the complex span paradigm, studies seeking selective interference require the maintenance of some information while additional information is being processed. Researchers have shown that dual-task performance depends on the particular combination of information involved in the two tasks. More specifically, interference between two concurrent tasks occurs when they involve information pertaining to the same domain (i.e., when they both involve verbal or spatial information), but no (or very little) interference would occur when the tasks involve information pertaining to different domains. For example, Farmer et al. (1986) asked adults to do some verbal or visuospatial reasoning tasks either alone or while performing a secondary task. The verbal reasoning task was similar to one used by Baddeley and Hitch (1974) in which participants judged if a sentence correctly describes the order of two letters (for example 'A is not followed by B – BA' which requires the response 'true'). In the visuospatial reasoning task, an upright or inverted manikin figure holding a circle in one hand and a square in the other was displayed on screen with one of these shapes appearing as a probe item below the figure.

Participants pressed the right or left response key, corresponding to the manikin's hand holding the probe. When performed with a secondary task, these two reasoning tasks were associated either with an articulatory suppression task, which required simply repeating the sequence '1, 2, 3, 4' continuously or with a sequential tapping task, in which participants tapped continuously some metal plates in turn with a stylus. Whereas articulatory suppression increased the rate of errors and the response times in the verbal reasoning task, it did not affect performance in the visuospatial reasoning task. Conversely, the continuous tapping induced longer response times in the visuospatial reasoning task but did not affect verbal reasoning. Thus, performance in the reasoning task was poorer when the secondary task belonged to the same domain.

Other studies using complex span tasks reported the correlative finding that recall performance is impeded by concurrent processing tasks when storage and processing involve information pertaining to the same domain (Logie 1986; Logie et al. 1990; Meiser and Klauer 1999; Salway and Logie 1995; Shah and Miyake 1996). Visuospatial recall performance is poorer when paired with visuospatial than verbal processing activities. Conversely, verbal recall performance is poorer when paired with verbal rather than visuospatial processing activities. For example, in Meiser and Klauer (1999), adults had to maintain either the order in which Corsi blocks were filled one at a time on screen or a series of consonants while they had to perform a secondary task either at encoding or during a 12-second retention interval. The secondary tasks, similar to those used by Farmer et al. (1986), consisted in articulatory suppression and tapping keys on a keyboard. The analysis of the decrement of recall resulting from the introduction of a concurrent task either at encoding or during retention showed reduced performance in any combinations of the tasks. More interestingly for the separability of the verbal and visuospatial systems in working memory, the decrement of recall for the Corsi blocks was stronger under concurrent tapping than under articulatory suppression. Although the size of this decrement differed, it was in the same direction whether the secondary task was performed during encoding or retention. For the verbal memory task, a reverse pattern was observed. The decrement in recall was larger under a concurrent articulation than under concurrent tapping, whether the secondary task was performed during encoding or retention. According to the authors, this crossover dissociation provides evidence for the fractionation of working memory into modality-specific systems as in Baddeley's standard model (Baddeley 1986; Baddeley and Logie 1999). Similarly, Shah and Miyake (1996) showed in complex span tasks that word spans were smaller when participants had to concurrently verify sentences (mean span of 3.14) than doing mental rotation (3.71). Conversely, span for the orientation of arrows was smaller when participants were doing mental rotation (2.67) than verifying the sentences (3.04). These observations are consistent with the non-unitary nature of working memory and its fractionation into two subsystems, the phonological loop and the visuospatial sketchpad. However, and as cogently noted by Kintsch et al. (1999), such empirical evidence does not permit one to distinguish between interpretations in terms of different storage buffers, different sets of procedures or different pools of resources. More importantly in our view, these studies cannot pinpoint the locus of the selective interference and their findings do not imply that two systems, verbal and visuospatial, are distinct and fully independent.

Patterns of selective interference clearly indicate some domain specificity, but they do not discard the existence of domain-general limited resources at a more central level of the information processing system. For example, it could be imagined that both verbal and visuospatial processing disrupt verbal maintenance because they all require a common process or rely on a common central pool of resources, but that verbal maintenance is more disrupted by a verbal than a visuospatial processing activity because verbal processing and verbal maintenance activities share a more peripheral domain-specific supply. Another reason could be that their concurrent completion creates more interference due to the similarity of the representations they involve. In accordance with this suggestion, in Meiser and Klauer's (1999) study, the predicted selective interference pattern occurred, but all the four combinations of verbal and visuospatial storage and processing tasks led to some decrement in recall performance (see also Logie *et al.* 1990, and Salway and Logie 1995, for similar findings). Thus, although selective interference is commonly used as evidence against the idea of domain-general limited resources, it only shows that at least part of the performance in working memory tasks relies on modality-specific systems. Moreover, some empirical evidence speaks in favour of the existence of domain-general resources.

While examining complex span performance, Bayliss *et al.* (2003) distinguished three main factors making a significant contribution and related to verbal storage, visuospatial storage and general processing. If this finding fits perfectly within Baddeley's framework, it also reminds us that domain-specific and domain-general factors jointly account for working memory performance. It was all the more remarkable for this study to distinguish between domain-specific aspects because no selective interference pattern between verbal and visuospatial domains was observed. Correlational studies also suggest the presence of a domain-general resource underlying both verbal and visuospatial mental processes. It has been shown that latent variables for recall on verbal complex span tasks and latent variables for recall on visuospatial complex span tasks were identical or shared 65 per cent or more of their variance (for example, Kane *et al.* 2004; Kyllonen 1993; Oberauer *et al.* 2003; but see Shah and Miyake 1996). However, the existence of domain-general limited resources remains to be established experimentally by demonstrating resource sharing between verbal and visuospatial activities.

Are there domain-specific mechanisms of maintenance?

Departing from the non-unitary conception, the TBRS model proposes a general-purpose pool of limited attentional resources that has to be shared across time between mental processes regardless of the nature of the information involved (Barrouillet and Camos 2010, 2012). In this view, verbal and visuospatial activities are assumed to compete for this common pool of domain-general limited resources, resulting in interference between such activities when they are performed concurrently. Although our model is not the only one to conceive working memory as unitary or as fuelled by a unique pool of resources, the TBRS model makes specific predictions that distinguish it from other models of working memory by going beyond the mere prediction of inter-domain interference. Observing the detrimental effect of a visuospatial task on the concurrent maintenance of verbal items is not sufficient to establish their common dependence on a unique pool of resources or supply. Such an effect could result from the demands inherently needed to deal with the dual task or to some conflict at the response level. What is needed is evidence for a resource sharing by which increasing the demand of one of the tasks affects the performance in the other in a predictable way. Specifically, our model not only predicts that any activity that occupies the bottleneck should have a detrimental effect on concurrent maintenance, whatever its nature, but it predicts that this effect should be commensurate with the cognitive load of this activity, that is the proportion of time during which it occupies the bottleneck. In other words, both verbal and visuospatial activities should have a detrimental effect on the maintenance of verbal items, but this effect is predicted to be proportionate to how long these activities require attention. A similar effect should be observed for the maintenance of visuospatial items.

To test this prediction, we used the same type of computer-paced complex span tasks we created to test the cognitive load effect and the processing/storage function. Four different span tasks were created by combining verbal and visuospatial storage with both verbal and visuospatial processing, each span task being performed by a different group of young adults (Vergauwe et al. 2010). For verbal storage, participants had to maintain series of consonants, whereas they memorised series of locations of a red square in 4 × 4 matrices for visuospatial storage. The processing tasks were both two-choice reaction time tasks. For verbal processing, participants judged whether a word presented on screen was an animal noun or not. The same visuospatial fit task used by Vergauwe et al. (2009; see Chapter 3 page 62), in which participants had to judge whether a horizontal line fits between two square dots, was introduced as a visuospatial processing task. It is important to note that our study departed from the usual selective interference design by systematically varying the demand of the processing component, something never done in previous studies.

For this purpose, three cognitive loads were created for each processing task by varying either the rate of presentation of the distracting items or their number. Thus, four words or four spatial displays (with two dots and the line) were presented either in 8000ms or 5172ms creating a low and a medium cognitive load for the verbal and visuospatial processing task, with a distracter every 2000ms or 1294ms respectively. To induce a high cognitive load, eight words or spatial displays were shown in a 8000-ms interval. At the end of each trial, participants recalled the consonants or the successive locations of the red square in their order of appearance by writing them down on response sheets. For the locations of the square, they crossed them on a series of unfilled matrices. The TBRS model predicts that recall performance should be affected by variations in cognitive load both within- and between-domain combinations.

As can be seen in Figure 5.1, and in line with the TBRS model, recall performance decreased linearly with increasing cognitive load for the four combinations of storage and processing tasks. Besides replicating once more the cognitive load effect, these findings suggest that verbal and visuospatial activities compete for the same pool of resources. To ascertain this conclusion, we replicated these experiments while minimising the possible implication of representation-based interference in these effects (Vergauwe et al. 2012). Indeed, in the previous experiments, domain-specific interference could have resulted from the visual presentation of both memoranda and items to be processed, or from the need to maintain spatial mappings in the task set of the verbal task (animal or not associated with different keys). Vergauwe et al. (2012) associated, in a first experiment, the maintenance of auditorily presented consonants with the spatial fit task requiring motor response and, in a second experiment, the maintenance of series of spatial locations visually presented with the animal task auditorily presented and requiring verbal responses (yes/no). These control experiments revealed the same level of recall performance and the same cognitive load effect, confirming the existence of a domain-general pool of resources in working memory.

These results are perfectly in line with some of our previous results in which the increased cognitive load of a visuospatial processing task (judging the location of a square on screen) led to a reduced verbal recall performance both in adults and children (cf. Chapters 3 and 7; Barrouillet et al. 2007; Portrat et al. 2008; Portrat et al. 2009). They are also congruent with other authors' findings. For example, Stevanovski and Jolicoeur (2007) showed that increasing the attentional demand of a pitch discrimination task resulted in poorer recall performance of visual stimuli. In a related vein, Morey and Cowan (2004, 2005; see also Saults and Cowan 2007) showed that visual and verbal storage compete for a shared limit. Thus, these results are in line with the TBRS model, but are also consistent with other theories proposing a unitary view of working memory (for example, Kahneman 1973, Kane et al. 2004; Kyllonen 1993). On the other hand, they are difficult to accommodate with non-unitary views of working memory in which verbal and visuospatial activities are supported by distinct subsystems (for example, Baddeley 1986; Duff and Logie 2001; Shah and Miyake 1996; Wickens 1984).

Nevertheless, one aspect of our results was in line with this latter view. When memory items were verbal, recall performance was poorer with the verbal than the visuospatial processing task (Figure 5.1, lower panel). Although recall decreased with the cognitive load for both processing tasks, the analysis of the individual data showed that the slopes of regression were on average significantly steeper for the verbal than for the visuospatial task. This domain-specific interference was observed only in the verbal domain, no such phenomenon occurring in the visuospatial domain in which both verbal and visuospatial processing tasks had very similar detrimental effects on recall, as testified by the absence of difference between the slopes for the maintenance of locations (Figure 5.1, upper panel). These findings are rather similar to Bayliss et al.'s (2003) results in which four complex span tasks were compared (i.e., the storage and processing component being either verbal or visuospatial).

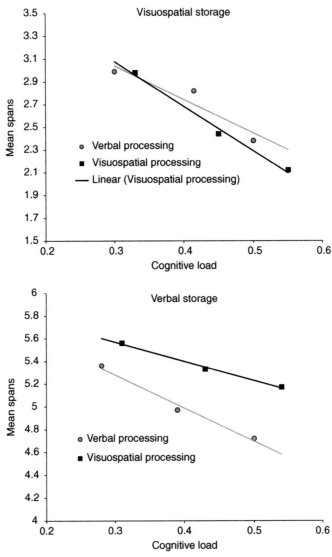

FIGURE 5.1 Mean spans for visuospatial and verbal memoranda as a function of the cognitive load involved by verbal and visuospatial processing tasks in Vergauwe et al. (2010)

The span for visuospatial items remained similar whether the processing component was verbal (mean span = 6.17) or visuospatial (6.00), whereas the verbal span was lower with a verbal (4.97) rather than a visuospatial (6.06) processing component. Both our and Bayliss et al.'s (2003) studies suggest that above and beyond a domain-general mechanism of maintenance, a domain-specific mechanism could be devoted to the maintenance of verbal information whereas, contrary to the assumptions of the multi-component model (Baddeley and Logie 1999; Logie 2005), visuospatial information would be devoid of a specialised mechanism of maintenance. The existence of two different mechanisms available for the maintenance of verbal information raised the question of their interaction. The next section focuses on studies that examine their relationships.

Attentional refreshing and articulatory rehearsal

The results from the study by Vergauwe et al. (2010) were twofold. First, they brought evidence for a domain-general mechanism relying on a limited pool of attentional resources. In the TBRS model, we named this mechanism 'attentional refreshing', a mechanism that could maintain representations either verbal or visuospatial in nature. Second, they also enlightened the existence of domain-specific interference in the verbal domain. What could be the source of this verbal interference?

In the multiple-component model of working memory, a large number of studies have shown the influential role of an articulatory rehearsal by the phonological loop (Baddeley 1986; Baddeley and Hitch 1974; Baddeley et al. 1984b; Baddeley and Logie 1999; Baddeley et al. 1975). This mechanism, responsible for the maintenance of verbal items, is modality-specific and relies on the overt or covert vocalisation of verbal information in a sequential manner by articulatory motor programmes. Thus, it could be suggested that the domain-specific verbal interference observed in Vergauwe et al. (2010) was due to the maintenance of at least part of the memory items by verbal rehearsal, a mechanism using articulatory processes that were probably also needed to identify the words in the verbal processing task (animal nouns or not?), hence the interference observed. Thus, verbal information would benefit from two mechanisms of maintenance, attentional refreshing and articulatory rehearsal.

Is attentional refreshing different from articulatory rehearsal?

Before presenting the evidence we collected that supports the existence of these two mechanisms of maintenance, we would like to recall a study by Hudjetz and Oberauer (2007) showing that the attentional refreshing mechanism we hypothesise in the TBRS model is not the articulatory rehearsal as defined by Baddeley. Hudjetz and Oberauer (2007) used a reading complex span task similar to that used by Saito and Miyake (2004). Sentences were presented in four segments of three words each. These segments appeared successively on screen, and the last word of the last segment had to be maintained for further recall. Moreover, the pace of presentation of the segments and the conditions of reading were varied independently. Each segment appeared on screen either for 1890ms in the slow pace or for 1323ms in the fast pace condition. In both paces, participants had to read the three words of each segment either at their own pace or continuously, a sequence of beeps giving the rhythm they had to follow (i.e., one beep every 610ms or 421ms on the slow and fast paces respectively). When participants had to read the segments continuously instead of at their own pace, the use of articulatory rehearsal was strongly impeded by this continuous utterance of words. The authors reasoned that if the maintenance of words relies on attentional refreshing, the conditions of reading should not affect recall, performance being poorer at a fast than a slow pace of presentation, as we observed in many experiments. By contrast, if the maintenance is achieved through articulatory rehearsal, the pace of presentation and the condition of reading should interact. Whereas a slow pace of presentation should permit participants to rehearse words more than a fast pace when they read at their own pace, the pace effect should disappear under continuous reading, due to the impediment of articulatory rehearsal. The results revealed a significant effect of both factors without any interaction.

This finding has several implications for different models or accounts of working memory. First, it contradicts the task-switching model proposed by Towse and Hitch. Remember that, according to this model, recall performance should decline with longer processing times. On the contrary, in Hudjetz and Oberauer (2007), recall performance was better with a slow pace of presentation resulting in longer presentation durations. Second, the authors noted that this finding cannot be accounted for by an interference account. The amount of material participants processed was the same whatever the presentation rate. Thus, the amount of representation-based interference was equivalent in both slow and fast paces, and could not thus explain the observed difference in recall. Third, the lack of interaction between presentation duration and reading instructions goes against the idea that maintenance relies on the articulatory rehearsal. Because the continuous reading leaves very little, if any, time for articulating the memory items, longer presentation durations should not be beneficial when reading is continuous, but only under the normal reading condition. To conclude, Hudjetz and Oberauer's (2007) findings clearly ruled out articulatory rehearsal as an explanatory account for the pace and cognitive load effects reported in Chapter 3 (Barrouillet *et al.* 2004, 2007). In a series of experiments, we tested the respective implication of the two mechanisms in the maintenance of verbal items.

Two independent mechanisms of maintenance

In two first experiments using complex span tasks, Camos *et al.* (2009) varied the opportunity of using one of the two maintenance mechanisms while the other was impeded. In Experiment 1, articulatory rehearsal was impeded while the availability of attention was manipulated. Participants had to maintain series of letters for further recall while solving arithmetic operations (for example, presented with '7 − 3 = ?', they had to say 'seven minus three equal four') or reading them aloud (for example, when presented with '7 − 3 = 4', they had to say 'seven minus three equal four'). Note that in both conditions, participants uttered the same words, which impeded articulatory rehearsal to the same extent whereas the two conditions affected differently the availability of attention for attentional refreshing, because solving operations requires more attention than simply reading them. Conversely, in Experiment 2, the attentional demand was kept constant while the availability of verbal rehearsal was manipulated. Participants were asked to maintain letters while their attention was occupied by judging the parity of digits presented successively on screen at a constant pace. The parity judgement task was performed either silently by pressing keys or aloud by saying 'odd' or 'even', which induces an additional articulatory suppression. If both the attentional refreshing and the articulatory rehearsal contribute to the maintenance of verbal information, reducing the availability of one mechanism when the other mechanism is impeded should reduce recall performance.

In both experiments, participants were able to recall a decent number of verbal items, although either attentional refreshing or articulatory rehearsal was impeded. As expected, the manipulation of the availability of one mechanism under the impediment of the other resulted in a reduction of recall performance. Under concurrent articulation, solving arithmetic operations led to poorer recall performance (mean span = 3.74) than just reading them (4.47). Performing the demanding parity task aloud led to a strong decrease in span compared with the silent condition (2.86 *vs.* 5.03 respectively). These findings confirmed the idea that both the attentional refreshing and the articulatory rehearsal are able to maintain verbal information in working memory. Two following experiments assessed the interplay of these two mechanisms through the orthogonal manipulation of their availability. In Experiment 3, participants performed either silently or aloud a processing task that varied in attentional demand. The low-demanding task was a simple reaction time task in which participants pressed a key or uttered a word when a square appeared on screen. The high-demanding task was the same parity judgement as used in Experiment 2 in which participants gave their responses either orally or silently by key press. Experiment 4 contrasted two tasks differing in their attentional demand. Each memory item was followed by a series of six digits successively displayed on screen. The low-demanding task consisted of a digit detection, participants pressing the space bar when '5' appeared on screen, whereas in the high-demanding task participants verified if the third and the sixth digits in the inter-items interval were the sum of the two previously presented digits. While performing either of these tasks, participants remained silent or read aloud all the digits successively presented on screen. Both experiments replicated the findings of the Experiments 1 and 2. Impeding one or the other of the maintenance mechanisms led to a reduction in recall performance. More interestingly, in Experiments 3 and 4 as in Hudjetz and Oberauer's (2007) study, the effect of the articulatory suppression was additive to the effect of the attentional demand involved by the processing component of the complex span tasks (Figure 5.2). This suggests that attentional refreshing and articulatory rehearsal are two independent mechanisms that concur to the maintenance of verbal information. The existence of a second maintenance mechanism, over and beyond verbal rehearsal, initially suggested by Baddeley and Hitch (1974), regularly reappeared to account for the fact that, under articulatory suppression, participants were still able to maintain a substantial number of verbal items (for example, Hitch *et al.* 1989, 1993; Salamé and Baddeley 1986; Towse *et al.* 1998; Vallar and Baddeley 1982). Although the idea of different mechanisms intervening in the maintenance of verbal information could be found before in the literature, Camos *et al.*'s (2009) study provided the first empirical evidence of the independence of attentional refreshing and articulatory rehearsal.

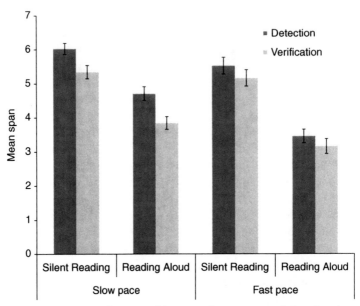

FIGURE 5.2 Mean spans as a function of the type of concurrent task (number detection *vs.* verification of additions), the level of articulatory suppression (silent reading *vs.* reading aloud), and the pace at which the concurrent task was performed in Camos *et al.* (2009, Exp. 4)

An adaptive choice of maintenance mechanisms

A logical consequence of the existence of two independent mechanisms is that adults should be able to favour one of them according to the constraints of the task or following instructions. To test the hypothesis that young adults can chose adaptively between articulatory rehearsal and attentional refreshing, we used the computer-paced complex span paradigm presented above in which the processing component was either a choice reaction time (CRT) task or a less demanding simple reaction time (SRT) task, the memoranda being lists of six phonologically similar or dissimilar words (Camos *et al.* 2011). We predicted that when the concurrent task is less demanding (i.e., SRT), attention is available for refreshing and then participants should favour this mechanism because it probably allows processing of non-phonological representations of the memory items. Such a mode of maintenance would reduce the confusability of the representations of the memoranda in the case of lists of phonologically similar words. By contrast, under a high attentional demand, participants should back up to articulatory rehearsal, which requires less attention (Naveh-Benjamin and Jonides 1984). As the use of articulatory rehearsal relies on the maintenance of phonological representations, recall performance should in this case suffer from the phonological similarity of some of the lists.

As depicted in Figure 5.3 for the 'no instruction' experiment, our results replicated the effect of the cognitive load of the processing component, the CRT task inducing lower recall performance. The most interesting results of this experiment concerned the occurrence of the phonological similarity effect. As we expected, when participants performed the CRT task, their recall was better for lists of phonologically dissimilar than similar words. However, when participants performed the SRT task as a concurrent task, the phonological similarity effect disappeared. Thus, the emergence of the phonological similarity effect in complex span tasks depends on the attentional demand of the concurrent activity. We suggested that varying this attentional demand led participants to make different choices in the type of maintenance mechanism. When the concurrent task left a large amount of attention available, participants favoured the attentional refreshing because it should reduce the risk of confusion between the representations of the phonologically similar words. However, when the amount of attention was much reduced, participants had to back up to a less demanding strategy of maintenance, i.e., the articulatory rehearsal. This was done at the cost of confusion between the phonological representations of similar words, which induced poorer recall performance for these lists.

To verify this assumption, in two further experiments, we directly instructed participants to use either articulatory rehearsal or attentional refreshing to maintain series of words in the same complex span task used in the previous experiment. The processing component was still either poorly or highly attention demanding (i.e., the same SRT and CRT tasks). The results of these two experiments were very clear (Figure 5.3). Whereas an increase in the attentional demand of the concurrent task led to reduced recall performance in both experiments, the occurrence of the phonological similarity effect depended on the instructions. When instructed to use articulatory rehearsal, and whatever the amount of attention available, recall was always poorer for lists of phonologically similar words. On the contrary, under the instruction to use attentional refreshing, the phonological characteristics of the lists to be maintained never affected recall performance. This study by Camos et al. (2011) showed that the use of the two maintenance mechanisms is adaptive and flexible, young adults being able to choose a strategy of maintenance according to its relative effectiveness or to follow instructions. Moreover, as proposed by Baddeley, the maintenance by articulatory rehearsal is sensitive to the phonological characteristics of the memory items. On the other hand, using attentional refreshing to maintain verbal information makes recall performance immune to the phonological similarity of the memoranda in the lists. This suggests that whereas articulatory rehearsal maintains verbal information under phonological representation, attentional refreshing acts on richer memory traces involving a variety of features.

The impact of the phonological characteristics of the memory lists

The studies presented above have made clear that there exist two mechanisms of maintenance for verbal information, the use of which leads to different effects on recall performance. Whereas any increase in cognitive load of the processing component reduces recall performance, the use of articulatory rehearsal makes recall sensible to the phonological similarity, a well-known effect specific to the phonological loop.

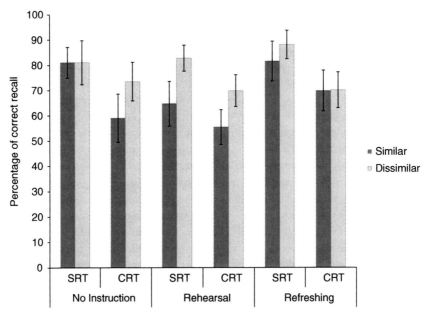

FIGURE 5.3 Variations of the phonological similarity effect (comparison of percent correct recall of phonologically similar and dissimilar words) as a function of the processing component of the complex span task (simple reaction time task, SRT, *vs.* choice reaction time task, CRT) and the type of maintenance strategy induced by instructing participants in Camos *et al.* (2011). Error bars refer to confidence intervals

The phonological loop, the structure responsible for the storage and maintenance of verbal information in Baddeley's (1986) model, has been extensively studied in the past 50 years or more. Maintenance within this structure is characterised by several phenomena, like the phonological similarity effect and the word length effect. We already recalled that the phonological similarity effect is characterised by poorer recall of phonologically similar (*vs.* dissimilar) lists of words. As we saw in Chapter 2, the word length effect is defined by poorer recall of series of long than short words, an effect that Baddeley, Thomson, and Buchanan (1975) attributed to the longer time it takes to rehearse long words. These effects characterise two aspects of the phonological loop model, the phonological nature of the stored representations and the functioning of the articulatory rehearsal. However, both effects depend on the use of the phonological loop. Following the idea that attentional refreshing and articulatory rehearsal are two independent mechanisms that maintain verbal information under different types of format (i.e., phonological and multi-modal respectively), we predicted that both the phonological similarity and the word length effects should disappear if articulatory rehearsal is impeded and the maintenance of verbal items must be achieved by attentional refreshing.

To test this hypothesis, and going further than Camos *et al.* (2011), we ran two studies in which we orthogonally manipulated the attentional demand of the concurrent task and the availability of verbal rehearsal. For this purpose, we compared four computer-paced complex span tasks in which participants maintained series of either phonologically similar or dissimilar words, or series of short or long words (Camos et al. 2013; Mora and Camos 2013). Participants had either to perform a concurrent location judgement task in the interval between two memory items or to do nothing, which allowed them to use this interval for reactivating the memory items. The availability of articulatory rehearsal was varied either by allowing participants to remain silent through the concurrent task or by asking them to repeat the word '*oui*' ('yes' in French). Our predictions were similar across the two studies. Hindering attentional refreshing and articulatory rehearsal should lead to poorer recall performance. However, if both phonological similarity and word length effects reflect the involvement of the phonological loop, impeding articulatory rehearsal should abolish both effects, whereas varying the availability of the attentional refreshing should leave them unaffected. Both studies confirmed these predictions. The addition of a concurrent task in the inter-item interval and the concurrent articulation of '*oui*' resulted in reduced recall performance in both studies. These studies also replicated the well-known phonological similarity effect with dissimilar word lists being better recalled than the similar word lists, as well as the word length effect with better recall performance for short than long words. However, whereas these effects did not interact with the presence *vs.* absence of a concurrent task, they both disappeared under articulatory suppression (Figure 5.4). The disappearance of these effects has already been observed in simple span tasks when the memory items were visually presented, as was the case in our studies, and when a concurrent articulation occurred during the encoding of the memoranda (for example, Baddeley and Larsen 2007; Coltheart 1999; Fallon et al. 1999). The present studies showed that there is no need to block articulatory processes during encoding to affect the phonological similarity and the word length effects. Concurrent articulation can also reduce strongly these two effects when it hinders subvocal rehearsal during maintenance. Thus, the impact of the phonological characteristics of the memory items depended on the use of the verbal-specific system, whereas recall performance was immune from these effects under the use of attentional refreshing.

In summary, attentional refreshing and articulatory rehearsal are two distinct mechanisms that can be jointly used to maintain verbal information with additive effects (Camos et al. 2009). Because of this independence, adults can chose to favour the use of one or the other either intentionally when instructed to do so or adaptively because attentional refreshing reduces the occurrence of confusion for phonologically similar material (Camos et al. 2011). Finally, each of these mechanisms of maintenance induces a different pattern of recall performance. The use of articulatory rehearsal makes recall sensitive to the phonological characteristics of the material to be maintained, which do not affect recall performance when attentional refreshing is used (Camos et al. 2013; Mora and Camos 2013). This does not imply that attentional refreshing is a 'better' mechanism of maintenance that should always be favoured. Attentional refreshing is more attention demanding than articulatory rehearsal

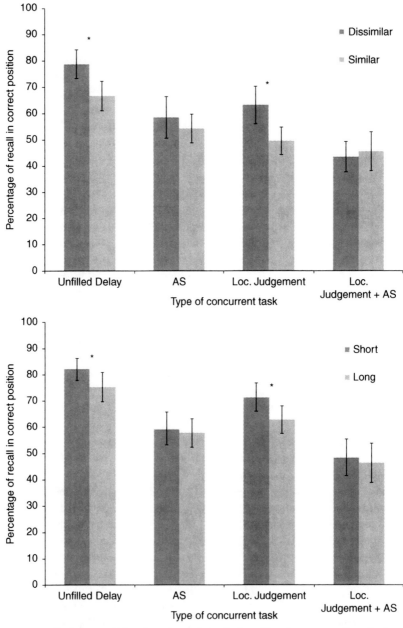

FIGURE 5.4 Variations of the phonological similarity effect (upper panel) and of word length effect (lower panel) in the four experimental conditions used by Camos *et al.* (2013) and Mora and Camos (2013) respectively, in which each memory item was followed either by an unfilled delay, an articulatory suppression (AS), a location judgement task or the combination of this task with articulatory suppression

and, as a consequence, very sensitive to the availability of attention. When it is used, variations of the attentional demand directly impact recall performance.

Distinct brain networks support the two mechanisms of maintenance

We collected a vast amount of behavioural evidence that supports the distinction between a general mechanism of attentional refreshing and a specialised mechanism of articulatory rehearsal. Examining the literature about the neural implementation of these two mechanisms brings further support to this distinction. Lesions studies as well as functional neuroimaging bring convergent evidence in favour of two distinct neural networks underlying verbal short-term memory (for a review see Martin 2005). For example, Hanten and Martin (2000) distinguished one network involving the superior temporal lobe and the supramarginal gyrus that would subserve the retention of phonological information from another network constituted by the inferior and middle temporal lobe and the inferior frontal lobe that would maintain semantic information. Accordingly, patients with damage to left inferior and middle frontal gyri present deficits in semantic short-term memory, while damage to inferior parietal areas is associated with deficits in phonological short-term memory (Hamilton et al. 2009). While further studies are needed to exactly delineate these two networks, phonological and semantic short-term memory appear to be related to different patterns of brain damage and neural activation. A simplistic dichotomy would map the verbal-specific and the attention-based systems we hypothesised in the TBRS model onto phonological and semantic networks respectively. Although the attention-based system is probably not restricted to semantic code but acts on multimodal representations, this neurological evidence strongly supports the use of a verbal specific system through which verbal information would be phonologically encoded and maintained in this format. Accordingly, we have already shown that both the word length effect and the phonological similarity effect appear when the verbal-specific system is available and disappear when it is not.

While some similarities can be seen between the distinct networks described in verbal short-term memory and the two mechanisms we differentiate in the maintenance of verbal information in working memory, other studies directly explore the brain networks associated with these two mechanisms. Using brain imagery techniques, Raye et al. (2002, 2007) showed that articulatory rehearsal and attentional refreshing are neurally distinguishable processes. In several experiments, these authors showed an increased activation of the dorsolateral prefrontal cortex (DLPFC, Brodmann's area (BA) 9) when healthy young adults were instructed to think briefly of words (i.e., to refresh) compared to when they had to repeat or read them silently, or to simply press a button. Moreover, studies aiming to distinguish attentional refreshing from articulatory rehearsal revealed that Broca's area (ventrolateral prefrontal cortex, VLPFC, BA 44) was selectively activated in articulatory rehearsal condition whereas attentional refreshing condition selectively involved activation of the DLPFC (Raye et al. 2007, Experiment 2). Similarly, Smith and

Jonides (1999) have linked the activation of the VLPFC to the use of articulatory rehearsal strategy. Raye *et al.* (2007) concluded that VLPFC reflects a subvocal articulatory rehearsal of phonological information, while DLPFC is assumed to reflect attention to various types of activated information (for example, its activation did not differ between verbal and non-verbal information, Johnson *et al.* 2005). Whereas Broca's area is a specialised structure dedicated to language, the DLPFC is more broadly involved in executive control (D'Esposito *et al.* 1995). This neurological distinction between a specialised peripheral and an executive central structure echoes nicely in turn the differentiation we introduce in the next chapter between the phonological loop and what we call the executive loop.

The effect of maintenance on processing

The studies reviewed so far in this chapter mainly addressed the question of the mechanisms of maintenance by exploring the effects of a variety of processing activities on the recall of concurrently held memory items, from which the nature of the mechanisms subserving this maintenance were deduced. However, the other way round, analysing the effects that the maintenance of a variety of memory items have on concurrent processing activities could shed light on the mechanisms involved in this maintenance. In working memory functioning, the impact of processing on storage has been extensively studied, whereas the impact of maintenance on processing has been relatively neglected. We review here a series of our studies that addressed this problem. Apart from confirming the sequential functioning of working memory postulated by the TBRS model, the results shed light on the structure of working memory, confirming that though there is no domain-specific mechanism for reactivating visuospatial memory traces that are consequently maintained through the domain-general attentional system, there exists a mechanism for verbal memory that corresponds to the phonological loop in Baddeley's theory.

The TBRS model predicts the effect of processing on concurrent maintenance activities: recall performance is a linear function of the cognitive load of the concurrent task (see Chapter 3). Conversely, our model also makes predictions on how the maintenance activities can affect the processing of incoming information. Like the predictions concerning the effect of processing on storage, this new set of predictions derives from the hypothesis of a central bottleneck and the resulting sequential functioning of working memory. In such a functioning, when processing and storage are performed concurrently, processing episodes are postponed by maintenance activities in the same way as maintenance activities are postponed by processing. Whereas the postponement of maintenance activities results in memory loss due to the temporal decay of memory traces, the postponement of processing by maintenance activities should have a negligible effect on processing accuracy provided that the stimuli to be processed remain available in the environment. However, this postponement should appear through processing times. Because attentional maintenance proceeds in a cumulative fashion, starting from the first list item and proceeding in forward order until the end (McCabe 2008), this postponement should linearly increase with the number of items to be maintained. Moreover, the slope of this predicted linear function should be indicative of the time it takes to refresh one item through attentional focusing. As already mentioned above, because the resource shared between processing and storage is assumed to be domain-general, this memory load effect on the postponement of the processing task should be observed regardless of the domain involved.

To test this new set of predictions, we developed a new paradigm. When examining the impact of processing on storage, the most appropriate paradigm is the complex span task. The rationale of this paradigm is to evaluate the amount of information that can be stored and recalled while participants are asked to give priority to a concurrent task, the variable of interest being the amount of recalled items under theoretically perfect performance on this concurrent task. Investigating the effect of maintenance on processing requires the reversal of this logic (Vergauwe *et al.* 2014). The performance of the processing component becomes the dependent variable, while the demand in storage is manipulated. For this purpose, we used a Brown-Peterson paradigm in which participants had to maintain a list of items for further recall and to perform an intervening task over a fixed retention interval prior to recall. However, participants were instructed to perform this intervening activity in such a way that, while trying to achieve the best performance in this task, they should not forget the memoranda. For example, in one experiment, participants were presented with series of 0 to 7 letters to be remembered, and asked during a 12-sec retention interval to judge the parity of as many numbers as they can by pressing keys, each key press displaying a new number on screen. To minimise the risk of forgetting and achieve a perfect recall of the memoranda, participants should refresh all of them before each processing episode. As a consequence, the hypothesis of sequentiality predicts that processing times (i.e., the duration between the onset of a number to be judged and the key press response) should increase linearly with the number of memory items to refresh. Using this paradigm, we tested our predictions in a series of experiments in which we varied the nature, either verbal or visuospatial, of the memory items and the stimuli to be processed in the intervening task.

In the first two experiments, participants had to maintain visuospatial memory items while they performed a visuospatial or verbal task during a 12-sec interval before recall. The visuospatial memoranda were series of 0 to 5 locations of a coloured square. Sixteen squares were randomly displayed on screen and one of them was coloured in blue at a rate of one location per second. The last location of the series was followed by the retention interval during which participants had to perform the same spatial fit task as used by Vergauwe *et al.* (2009) and described above or a parity judgement task on digits appearing successively on screen. These two first experiments led to convergent findings (Figure 5.5; Exp. 1 and 2). Maintaining an increasing amount of memory items led to slower responses in the intervening task. This postponement increased linearly with the number of items to be maintained, and this did not depend on the nature, verbal or visuospatial, of the concurrent activity. These findings echoed nicely the results by Vergauwe *et al.* (2010).

Contrary to the selective interference pattern, the effect of visuospatial memory load on the visuospatial task (slope of 54ms per memory item) was similar and even slightly smaller than its effect on the parity task (slope of 63ms).

In a further experiment, we examined the effect of a verbal memory load on the same parity task. Participants had to maintain series of 0 to 7 letters presented successively on screen for 1 second each before performing the parity judgement task for 12 seconds. In the previous section we showed that, besides attentional refreshing, another mechanism, articulatory rehearsal, is available for maintaining verbal information. However, the aim of this first series of experiments was to examine the sharing of attention between processing and storage, and more precisely how the use of attention for maintenance purpose leads to the postponement of a concurrent task. Thus, to be sure that verbal information was maintained through attentional refreshing only, we asked participants to repeat 'badibu' during the retention interval while completing the parity judgement task by pressing keys. Experiment 3 provided congruent results with the two first experiments, as can be seen in Figure 5.5. As for spatial storage, maintaining an increasing amount of verbal memoranda under concurrent articulation slowed the responses in the concurrent task. In this combination of verbal storage with numerical processing, the postponement of the intervening task increased also linearly with the number of

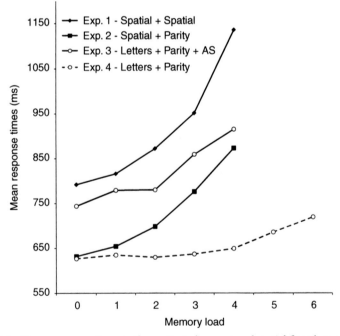

FIGURE 5.5 Mean response times in the parity judgement and spatial fit task as a function of the verbal or spatial memory load in Vergauwe et al. (2014)

memory items, and the slope (42ms) reached similar values as for the combinations of visuospatial storage with either visuospatial or numerical processing. Thus, whatever the nature of both the memoranda and the intervening task, refreshing memory items postpones concurrent processing activities, indicating that the two activities compete for a general-purpose mechanism. Moreover, the observed linear increase in processing times revealed similar slope values of around 50ms across experiments, which reflects the time needed to refresh one item. Such a value is close to the time estimated by Cowan, Saults and Elliott (2002) to reactivate a verbal item by covert retrieval (around 40ms). This is also very close to the rate of serial memory scanning (38ms) suggested by Sternberg (1966).

Contrary to attentional refreshing, the maintenance of verbal items through articulatory rehearsal requires very little attentional demand. Releasing the constraint to repeat 'badibu' during the retention interval should allow participants to maintain as many verbal items as they can through articulatory rehearsal. As a consequence, attention would be available for performing the concurrent task without any postponement. This was the aim of Experiment 4, in which participants had to maintain series of 0 to 7 letters while performing the parity judgement task but, contrary to Experiment 3, without any concurrent articulation. As illustrated in Figure 5.5, this experiment led to a very different pattern of results compared with Experiment 3. Whereas the processing times steadily increased with the memory load under articulatory suppression, no such increase was observed in Experiment 4 till a load of four letters. As we predicted, the slope remained nearly flat, processing times increasing only 22ms from 0 to 4 letters. This absence of postponement contrasted also with the increase in response times observed when memory load overcame four letters. From 4 to 6 letters to be maintained, the slope was 35ms, which was akin to the slope observed under articulatory suppression. These findings support our proposal of two distinct systems of verbal maintenance, with a verbal-specific system able to maintain up to four letters without any interference with a concurrent attention-demanding task. This echoes also one of the first proposals put forward by Baddeley and Hitch (1974) who suggested that the central executive would have some storage capacity that could be used when the capacity of the phonological loop is exhausted (cf. Chapter 1).

According to the description of the phonological loop made by Baddeley, the number of verbal items that it can maintain should vary with articulation demands as, for example, is observed in the case of long words resulting in the word length effect. Consequently, a further experiment examined whether the limit of the verbal-specific system to four letters resulted from the functioning of an articulatory loop. According to this model, this capacity limit should vary as a function of the articulatory demand of the memoranda, with higher demand resulting in fewer items maintained in the verbal-specific system without any implication of attention. This new experiment used the same paradigm as the Experiment 4, except that participants had to maintain series of monosyllabic or bisyllabic words, instead of series of letters, while performing the parity judgement task.

These monosyllabic words involved a slightly higher articulatory demand with a mean of 2.74 phonemes per monosyllabic word compared with 2.11 for letters. The articulatory demand was even higher for the bisyllabic words with a mean of 4.53 phonemes per word. As we expected, whereas four letters could be stored without any postponement of the parity judgement task, only three monosyllabic words were maintained without interference with the concurrent processing, with a small increase in responses times of 35ms from 0 to 3 monosyllabic words. Mimicking the pattern observed with the maintenance of letters, the slope of the response times was much steeper when the number of monosyllabic words exceeded 3, response times increasing more than 100ms between 3 and 4 monosyllabic words. When the articulatory demand was strongly increased by asking participants to maintain bisyllabic words, maintenance seemed to rely on at least some sporadic interventions of the attentional refreshing even with 3 items. Indeed, the processing times from 0 to 3 words presented a moderate but not negligible slope of 20ms per memory item.

To conclude our investigation of the impact of memory load on processing, we examined this relationship for memoranda that cannot be maintained attentionally. In that case, the TBRS model predicts that the relationship between memory load and processing time observed in the previous experiments for verbal and visuospatial items should no longer be observed[1]. We evoked in the previous chapter the study by Ricker and Cowan (2010) that asked young adults to maintain unconventional visual characters and observed the loss of this information within seconds, even when attention was available. This forgetting observed even across an unfilled retention interval indicates that some features are non-refreshable and thus decay inescapably with time. Following this idea, we verified in a pre-test that fonts of letters (for example, Arial, Courier New, Bauhaus 93) undergo the same time-related decay as unconventional characters, even when attention is available for refreshing. Thus, in a final series of experiments, we used such non-refreshable information as memoranda in the same paradigm as the one used in Experiments 1 to 5. In two experiments, participants had to maintain series of 0 to 5 different fonts while performing a numerical or a visuospatial task while repeating 'badibou'. The addition of a concurrent articulation for both concurrent tasks assured us that participants would not maintain the fonts using some verbal code. The numerical concurrent task was the parity judgement task, and the visuospatial task was the colour discrimination task used by Vergauwe et al. (2009; cf. Chapter 3) in which participants had to decide if monochromatic displays were more red than blue or more blue than red. Each display was presented one at a time and remained on screen until a response was given. The results revealed that, for both experiments, processing times did not vary as a function of the number of to-be-maintained fonts, with no significant linear trend. Thus, contrary to what we observed for the maintenance of letters, words or locations, increasing the number of non-refreshable memory items did not postpone concurrent processing. This trend occurred whether the concurrent task was a parity judgement task or a visual discrimination task. This gives strong support to our idea that the postponement is only observed insofar as maintenance actually relies on attention, that is when it is achieved through attentional refreshing.

Conclusion

Overall, the findings reported in this chapter reveal a clear structure concerning the systems of maintenance of information in working memory. First of all, as the TBRS model predicts, it seems that there is a general-purpose mechanism involved in the storage and maintenance of both verbal and visuospatial information. This system relies on attention, as testified by the detrimental effect that attention-demanding concurrent activities of any nature have on the maintenance of both verbal and visuospatial information, and by the postponement of these activities by the active maintenance of verbal or visuospatial information. These systematic trade-offs between processing and storage suggest that some central system of working memory is in charge of both functions. Our estimates of the time taken by this system to refresh a single memory item (i.e., between 40ms and 60ms) are close to those obtained by Cowan *et al.* (2002) when measuring the time needed to reactivate a verbal item by covert retrieval or to the rate of serial memory scanning suggested by Sternberg (1966). Interestingly, all these estimates fall into the range of tens of milliseconds, which corresponds according to Newell (1990) to the level of memory access. This level would be the lowest of what he calls the 'cognitive band' that he defines as the 'apparatus necessary to go from neural circuits to general cognition' (Newell 1990, p. 142). Thus, the speed of this general mechanism at the lowest level of the cognitive system along with the variety of its operations (from maintenance to processing of any type of representations) designate it as the central mechanism of working memory and cognition. We describe in the next chapter this mechanism as an 'executive loop'.

However, along with this central mechanism, another system of maintenance is available for verbal information. Empirical findings clearly indicate that it is independent from the central system and does not depend on attention for its operations. Maintaining phonological representations through articulatory rehearsal, it may correspond to the phonological loop described by Baddeley (1986) in the multi-component model. When available, this mechanism works as an auxiliary system able to hold a limited amount of phonological information. Behavioural and neural evidence strongly suggest that it is closely linked to the mechanisms of reception and production of language, something that could explain its relative independence from the central attentional system. This could also explain why this system seems to be an exception in the cognitive architecture, and probably the unique peripheral system able to maintain information in an active state. Indeed, contrary to what the multi-component model assumes, there is no evidence that such a specialised mechanism exists for visuospatial information. Contrary to what we observed with verbal memory, the maintenance of visuospatial items is disrupted to the same extent by concurrent verbal and visuospatial activities, and the maintenance of only one of these items is sufficient to postpone concurrent attention-demanding activities.

These findings clearly indicate that visuospatial information entirely relies on the central attentional system for its maintenance, creating an asymmetry between verbal and visuospatial working memory. The conclusions that can be drawn from the results reviewed in this chapter along with those that emerged from the study of cognitive load and time sharing point toward a working memory architecture that we describe in the next chapter.

Note

1 We have seen in Chapter 3 that a concurrent activity that involves little attention, such as an SRT task, did not affect concurrent maintenance. Correlatively, we expected here that when storage does not require attention, it remains innocuous for concurrent processing.

6
A WORKING MEMORY ARCHITECTURE

The previous chapters presented the functional aspects of the TBRS model and reviewed the studies that tested its main predictions. Their results delineate a coherent picture in which the two functions of working memory, processing and storage, compete on a temporal basis for a common supply. Processing activities postpone the processes in charge of the maintenance of memory traces, leading to their forgetting, while these maintenance activities postpone further processing steps. The study of the interaction between the two functions permitted us to identify the main mechanisms by which working memory traces are maintained in an active state, while the linear functions relating working memory spans to cognitive load on the one hand, and processing times to memory load on the other, corroborate the sequential functioning hypothesised by the TBRS model. Overall, these findings point towards a new working memory architecture.

Overview of the model

In the following section, we describe a working memory architecture in which a central system is in charge of both the maintenance and the transformation of working memory representations by modulating activation of information in peripheral sensory buffers and declarative long-term memory through attentional focusing (Figure 6.1). These working memory representations are transient mental models integrating elements provided by the peripheral sensory systems and elements retrieved from declarative long-term memory. Their integrative and heterogeneous nature make them akin to the representations held in the episodic buffer described by Baddeley (2000). Though about four working memory representations can be maintained in an active state in the episodic buffer, it is assumed that, at any point in time, there is only one representation directly available for treatment. From a phenomenological point of view, this representation constitutes

118 A working memory architecture

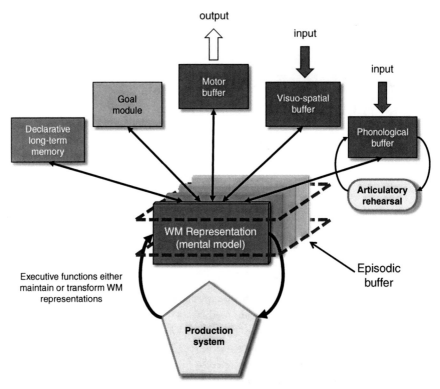

FIGURE 6.1 The working memory architecture. The episodic buffer maintains working memory representations integrating information from peripheral buffers. These representations are read by a production system and either modified or reconstructed depending on the goal at hand (i.e., processing or storage). This continuous interaction between the episodic buffer and the procedural system creates an executive loop. Among the peripheral buffers, an articulatory rehearsal system can maintain a limited number of phonological representations, whereas the visuospatial buffer is devoid of such a maintenance mechanism

the current content of consciousness. In Oberauer's (2002) hierarchical model, this representation would correspond to the single representation held in the focus of attention, whereas the other representations held in the episodic buffer would correspond to the region of direct access. A procedural system reads this representation and, depending on the goal currently active, maintains or updates its content through production firing. The current goal can also command a switch to another of the working memory representations held in the episodic buffer. Within this architecture, what is known as the central executive in current theories of working memory corresponds to a self-regulated loop made of the episodic buffer and the production system. This loop, which is in charge of both processing and maintenance activities, would be better described as an 'executive loop'. Because productions fire one at a time, the functioning of the executive loop is sequential in nature, alternating processing, which requires the transformation of some working memory representation, and storage activities, which require their upholding or reconstruction when degraded. Indeed, due to both their transient nature and the sequential functioning of the executive loop, working memory representations suffer from time-related decay and interference during processing episodes, which have in turn to be postponed when the executive loop is occupied by the necessary operations of refreshment of memory traces before their complete loss.

These functional characteristics impose severe constraints on working memory functioning, with a number of working memory representations retrievable from the episodic buffer that seems to be limited to about four and the need for frequent interruptions of processing for maintenance purposes. Rather than being 'the most significant achievement of human mental evolution' as Goldman-Rakic (1992, p. 111) claimed, working memory seems to be the result of a makeshift assembly of structures aiming at providing our cognitive system with the temporal room needed for processing ongoing information in an ever changing and often unpredictable environment (Newell 1990). As the studies reviewed in this book made clear, one of the main limitations of working memory is its slowness. It is because processing is slow that working memory representations are at risk of being lost, and it might be because their reconstruction, which involves some processing activity, takes time that only a limited amount of information can be held in a state appropriate for its use in cognitive operations.

As we noted above, working memory representations integrate information activated from declarative long-term memory but also from perceptual memories that constitute peripheral buffers. The information held in these buffers can remain active only for a short period of time without the support from ongoing sensory activity or attentional focusing directed by the central system, this attentional focusing resulting in the integration of this information into a working memory representation (Cowan 1995, 1999). These peripheral modules are passive stores, with the exception of the phonological buffer in which verbal information can be maintained in an active state without the support of the central system by an articulatory loop through overt or covert verbal rehearsal. We have seen in the previous chapter that this peculiarity creates an asymmetry between verbal and visuospatial working memory. Whereas maintenance of visuospatial information is exclusively carried out by the executive loop, maintenance of verbal information can be carried out by both the executive loop and the articulatory loop. However, as with the episodic buffer, the phonological buffer is also capacity limited. As we saw in the previous chapter, the articulatory loop can only maintain in the phonological buffer about four letters and probably an even smaller number of words without any attentional involvement. When this capacity is exhausted, or when the articulatory loop is unavailable (for example, when occupied by concurrent articulation), maintenance activities of verbal information are taken in charge by the central system. In the following, we detail the structure and functioning of the different components of this working memory architecture, beginning by the peripheral systems.

Peripheral systems

Several models share the assumption that a set of modules with their associated buffers maintains a limited amount of modality specific information (Anderson *et al.* 2004; Baddeley 1986; Hazy *et al.* 2006). These buffers were referred to as slave systems by Baddeley (1986) who described a phonological loop for verbal information and a sketchpad for visuospatial information. Anderson *et al.* (2004) do not give an exhaustive list of the buffers in their ACT-R model but assume that they have similarities with the slave systems in Baddeley's theory, suggesting that there is also a goal buffer linked to an intentional module, a retrieval buffer related to a declarative module, and a motor buffer. The existence of these peripheral buffers is supported by brain imaging techniques that have made possible the identification of the corresponding cerebral structures. Recent reviews of the literature conclude that phonological short-term memory emerges from the integrated action of the neural systems involved in the perception and production of speech in which the left posterior *planum temporale* has an important role (Buchsbaum and D'Esposito 2008). The storage of visuospatial information in working memory would be supported by posterior regions of the dorsal and ventral visual processing streams involving posterior cortical regions (Postle and D'Esposito 1999). Anderson *et al.* (2004) assume that the declarative module involves the hippocampus and medial temporal cortex regions, while the motor buffer is supported by the motor cortex and the cerebellum.

Thus, we will assume that there is a series of peripheral buffers in the cognitive system, each maintaining a limited amount of modality specific information that can be used for further processing. These specialised buffers would constitute the peripheral level of working memory. Following Anderson *et al.*'s (2004) and Baddeley's (1986) approaches, we retain as peripheral systems in our model a declarative module providing information stored in long-term memory, a goal module, and a motor, a visuospatial and a phonological buffer (Figure 6.1). There are probably several other buffers for other types of input (for example, musical, tactile or olfactory), but their relations with working memory have not yet been extensively explored (but see Andrade and Donaldson 2007; Berz 1995; Gilson and Baddeley 1969; Miles and Borthwick 1996; Williamson *et al.* 2010 for some studies on these domains).

Visuospatial and verbal buffers

The visuospatial and the phonological buffers are described in Baddeley's (1986; Baddeley and Logie 1999) theory as the storage systems of working memory, which are coordinated by a central executive exclusively in charge of the processing activities. This conception led Baddeley (1986; Baddeley and Logie 1999) to assume that each slave system is equipped with its own mechanism of maintenance. Contrary to this view, the studies reviewed in Chapter 5 indicate that there is no mechanism specifically dedicated to the maintenance of visuospatial information, which is taken in charge by the central system, whereas a limited amount of verbal information can be maintained in an active state through verbal rehearsal in an articulatory loop. As Baddeley and Hitch (1974) cogently surmised before abandoning this idea (see Baddeley 1986), when the storage capacity of the phonological loop is exhausted, the central system can supplement this peripheral buffer in maintenance activities. We have seen that the two systems are independent but work jointly to maintain verbal information active (Camos et al. 2009). The precise way these two systems interact and coordinate their activities remains an open question.

Declarative long-term memory

The other main constituent providing information to the central system is declarative long-term memory. Assuming that declarative long-term memory pertains to the peripheral systems of working memory implies that, contrary to previous versions of the TBRS model (Barrouillet et al. 2004a, 2007) and other approaches of working memory such as Cowan (1995), Engle et al. (1999), or Oberauer (2002), but in line with Baddeley's (2007) conceptions, we do not consider working memory as that part of long-term memory activated above threshold. In the next section devoted to the structure and functioning of the central system, we develop the reasons for this theoretical option. Nonetheless, even if we reject the idea that working memory representations are merely representations stored in long-term memory that are activated above threshold, information stored in long-term memory is the main constituent of the ephemeral constructions that working memory representations are. In the other way round, working memory representations constructed at the central level leave footprints in long-term memory, thus resulting in a learning process (Cowan 2005; Logan 1988; Perruchet and Vinter 2002; see also the ADAPT architecture, Barrouillet et al. 2004b). Thus, though working memory is more than the activated part of long-term memory, there is an incessant flow of information between the two systems that will be described in greater detail below.

The goal buffer

A point particularly important in this architecture concerns the production of goals, which play a crucial role at the functional level. We assume that goals correspond either to the encoding of task instructions as declarative knowledge (for example, 'read and remember the letters presented on screen') or to the representations of internal or external states considered as valuable, pleasant or useful. These representations could in turn result either from envisioning the future by constructing hypothetical events or from retrieving memory traces of past experiences. It is interesting to note that, according to Buckner et al. (2008), both activities of mental simulation and remembering the past involve the same cortical structures (mainly the hippocampal formation and the medial temporal cortex), which have been described by Anderson et al. (2004) as supporting the declarative module structures. Thus, we suggest that goals are representations either produced by this declarative module or constructed from task instructions (i.e., task sets). This conception is akin to Case (1985) who described goals (more precisely 'objectives' in his theorising) as one of the three parts of the executive control structures that govern behaviour. Executive control structures are structured representations that link environmental features relevant for the task at hand, goals and sub-goals associated with these features and strategies to reach these goals. In this view, goals are representations closely associated with the representation of the task. However, it remains unclear whether it is always necessary to actively maintain task goals as a working memory representation. For example, in the working memory span tasks we use, it would be surprising to have to continuously refresh a task set like 'remember the letters and add one to each digit'. It is probably simpler to assume that each occurrence of a letter triggers the same productions previously activated when processing the other letters, while each digit automatically reactivates a select-next-item-in-number-line procedural rule. However, this goal maintenance seems to be more problematic in highly interfering environments. Engle and Kane (2004; Kane and Engle 2003) report several studies in which low span individuals seem more prone than the others to lose the goal at hand and read the words in Stroop tasks or attend the signal in anti-saccade tasks. Despite commendable efforts to clarify the functioning of the central executive (Baddeley 1996), the precise mechanisms by which working memory controls behaviour still remain impenetrable, the reason why Baddeley (1986) described the central executive as an homunculus, a useful sleight of hand that has not yet been overridden (Baddeley 2007).

The central system

The executive loop

We assume that the peripheral systems described above are linked to a central system in charge of maintaining and processing working memory representations that combine information provided by these peripheral systems. Accordingly, several neuroscientific studies show that the prefrontal cortex (PFC) maintains working memory representations in an active state through bidirectional excitatory connections with posterior cortical areas sustaining the peripheral buffers (Brass et al. 2005; Hazy et al. 2006; Ruchkin et al. 2003; Smith and Jonides 1999). This idea is akin to Kane and Engle's (2002) proposal of an executive-attention domain-general system residing in the dorsolateral PFC that is networked to different more posterior domain-specific regions. The PFC has itself strong connections with the basal ganglia, a subcortical structure that sends output primarily to the frontal cortex and which is known to be implicated in motor behaviour but also in learning stimulus-response associations and habits (Packard and Knowlton 2002). It has been suggested that this subcortical structure provides the PFC with the adaptive gating mechanism able to rapidly update certain information while simultaneously maintaining other information remaining relevant for the task at hand (Braver and Cohen 2000; Frank et al. 2001; O'Reilly 2006; O'Reilly and Frank 2006; Jilk et al. 2008). The basal ganglia system would thus house the procedural memory described by ACT-R (Anderson 1993).

Following the ACT-R theoretical framework (Anderson 1993; Anderson *et al.* 2004), we assume that procedural memory contains production rules that produce behaviour by reading information from working memory and writing information to working memory, leading to the transformation or reconstruction of working memory representations. The studies reviewed in this book made clear that any type of attention-demanding task, whatever its nature, has the potential to disrupt the concurrent maintenance of any kind of representation, either verbal or visuospatial. This suggests that the procedural system interferes with a domain-general storage system akin to the episodic buffer hypothesised by Baddeley (2000; Repovs and Baddeley 2006), i.e., a limited capacity store for episodic representations binding information in a multi-modal code. In a recent study, we provided direct empirical evidence for the existence of such a system and its interactions with concurrent processing by investigating the effect of the cognitive load induced by a variety of tasks on the maintenance of cross-domain information like letters in location (Langerock *et al.* 2014). We observed that the maintenance of this type of multi-modal information was affected in the same way by a verbal (semantic judgement), a spatial (spatial fit) and a neutral task (tone discrimination), providing evidence that domain-specific (verbal or spatial) resources are not involved in the maintenance of cross-domain information. This reveals a clear distinction between the episodic buffer and peripheral systems.

The procedural system, along with the episodic buffer in which working memory representations are maintained, form an executive loop that constitutes the central system of working memory (Figure 6.1). At each point in time, only one representation among those maintained in the episodic buffer is available for ongoing treatment. In line with the ACT-R framework (Anderson 1993; Anderson *et al.* 2004), the procedural system would recognise the pattern of activation that constitutes this representation and fire the most appropriate production rule to achieve the current goal. This executive loop would be responsible for the construction, the maintenance and the transformation of working memory representations. In the following, we describe in turn each of these three functions.

Constructing and consolidating working memory representations

Following a distinction introduced by Jolicoeur and Dell'Acqua (1998), we have assumed that peripheral buffers such as the phonological store or the visuospatial sketchpad constitute perceptual memories, a memory state also described as 'very short-term conceptual memory' by Potter (1993). These representations can remain active only for a short time without the support from ongoing sensory activity and are thus unfit for the sustained use required by multi-step goal-directed cognition. A working memory with a sequential functioning requires representations able to resist time-related decay and interference while attention is dedicated to the processing of another representation. For this purpose, perceptual memories must be strengthened through a process named consolidation by Jolicoeur and Dell'Acqua (1998). Consolidation would transfer representations produced by perceptual encoding into a more durable form of memory called durable storage. These latter representations can maintain information over a long time and constitute a form of short-term memory that corresponds in our model to the working memory representations maintained by the PFC. Accordingly, Ricker and Cowan (2014) showed that greater amounts of time for consolidation of visuospatial information lead to slower rates of forgetting in the short term. Recent studies in our laboratory led to the same conclusion concerning verbal memory traces (Dirix 2014). We observed that increasing the time allowed for encoding the memoranda in a complex span task (i.e., the time each to-be-remembered letter is presented before the processing episode begins) leads to a logarithmic increase in recall performance, memory traces becoming more and more immune to variations in cognitive load of the concurrent task. The hypothesis that durable storage is related to the central level of working memory is supported by Jolicoeur and Dell'Acqua (1998; Stevanovski and Jolicoeur 2007) who have demonstrated that the process of short-term consolidation requires central processing mechanisms. For example, encoding items for further recall causes interference with concurrent central processes such as response selection, a phenomenon that does not occur when items have to be ignored.

The study by Vergauwe et al. (2014) reported in the previous chapter allowed us to assess the time course of this consolidation process. Remember that participants were presented with series of memory items of varying length followed by a 12-sec retention interval during which they had to process as many items as possible while maintaining the memoranda. Interestingly, processing times were far longer on the first than on the following items to be processed. We interpreted these longer processing times as reflecting a consolidation of the memory traces before entering the processing activity. In all the experiments, these consolidation times increased linearly with the number of memory items. Regression analyses revealed consolidation RTs of 236ms for the letters, and 222ms and 294ms for the spatial locations. These values are close to the time needed to consolidate a memory target in the imaginal module postulated by Taatgen et al. (2009), which can be seen as the equivalent within the ACT-R framework of Baddeley's (2000) episodic buffer. The authors estimate that this consolidation takes 250ms on average (see Shapiro et al. 1994, for a similar estimate).

The fact that consolidation involves central processes leads us to suppose that perceptual memories are consolidated through attentional focusing that strengthens memory traces by increasing their activation level, but also by enriching these representations with features from other peripheral buffers and long-term memory through a binding process. Indeed, as suggested by Logan and Etherton (1994), representations are not mere snapshots of perceptual events but result from a goal-oriented selection of features (see also Cowan 2005, for similar ideas). This selection would be achieved by the procedural system that modulates allocation of attention to the content of the various peripheral systems. For example, when a letter is encoded for further recall, the sensory memory resulting from the visual presentation of this letter could be consolidated by linking its visual representation with its phonological label, a given name beginning by this letter, and information related to the encoding context. One specific type of contextual information that could also be integrated through this binding process is the information related to order in serial recall tasks as in working memory span tasks. It has often been assumed that, in serial recall, items are linked to temporal or positional context cues (Burgess and Hitch 1999; Oberauer and Kliegl 2006; Oberauer et al. 2012). Thus, coding order information necessitates episodic buffer representations binding a variety of features provided by different peripheral systems. Interestingly, in the same way as Jolicoeur and Dell'Acqua (1998) demonstrated that consolidation involves central processes, Elsley and Parmentier (2009) provided evidence that binding information from different modalities (for example, verbal and spatial) recruits attentional resource. Thus, we assume that the consolidation of perceptual memories and the construction of integrated working memory representations through the modulation of attention by the procedural system is the primary function of the central system.

As we suggested above, these working memory representations should not be seen as the part of long-term memory activated above threshold. Rather, they are functional goal-oriented constructions that link together tokens retrieved from long-term memory with elements pointing to both the internal and the external context. As a consequence, the working memory representation for a letter in a list to be remembered would strongly differ from the representation of the same letter constructed to judge its vowel or consonant nature when involved in a choice reaction time task. Contrary to the information stored in long-term memory, the functional and contextualised nature of these *ad hoc* constructions makes them inherently ephemeral. Of course, representing contextual elements can also involve permanent knowledge stored in long-term memory (for example, tagging an item as the last one in a series requires something like a concept of 'last' involving knowledge stored in long-term memory), but the resulting working memory representation constitutes an original arrangement of tokens that is not retrieved but constructed. Thus, working memory representations would be better described as mental models (Johnson-Laird 1983, 2006), making our conception akin to the self-organising consciousness theory presented by Perruchet and Vinter (2002) who assume, following Dulany (1991, 1997), that the only representations people create and manipulate are those that form the momentary phenomenal experience (i.e., the working memory representations in the present theory).

Maintaining and transforming working memory representations

The central system that constructs working memory representations is also in charge of their maintenance or transformation, depending on the current goal. Following the ACT-R theory (Anderson 1993), we assume that when the goal is to transform the current representation (for example, when the task is to add 2 to the digit presented on screen), the production rule providing the best match with the pattern of activation that constitutes the current working memory representation fires and modifies its content (for example, by retrieving in declarative memory the answer of the addition of 2 with the presented digit). This results in a new pattern of activation (i.e., a new representation) that matches the conditions of activation of another production rule that fires, and so on. This cyclic functioning is depicted in Figure 6.2. Successive states of the episodic buffer content are represented, including the current goal and a restricted number of tokens. This content activates productions through a process of pattern matching as described by Anderson (1993), the most relevant production for the goal at hand and the current state of working memory being fired. This production contains, in its action part, instructions to modify the content of the working memory representation. According to Anderson et al. (2004), the critical cycle of pattern-recognition by the production system, firing of the relevant production, and updating working memory representation for another cycle is fairly fast and takes about 50ms to complete. Such a speed would be compatible with the TBRS hypothesis of a rapid switching between processing and maintenance activities.

We assume that production rules achieve this updating of working memory representations by triggering executive functions that can shift attention from a completed goal to the next one, select relevant information within the environment,

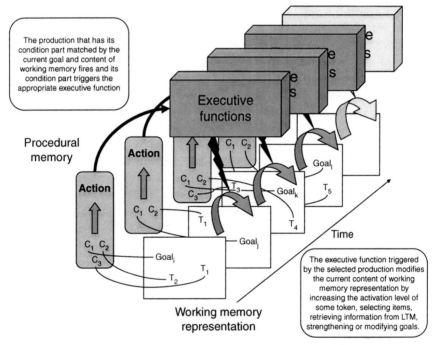

FIGURE 6.2 The functioning of the executive loop inspired by Anderson (1993). The figure represents successive contents of the episodic buffer, in which some representations *Ri* and the current goal *Goali* are matched to the condition part (condition *Ci*) of the selected production within the procedural memory. The action part of the production triggers an executive function that modifies the content of the episodic buffer that is matched in turn to another production

retrieve an item of knowledge from declarative memory, select a response and then trigger the appropriate motor programme for overt behaviour if necessary. Among these executive functions, refreshing, that is foregrounding information by thinking briefly of a just-constructed representation, is of particular importance. Raye *et al.* (2007) demonstrated that this minimal executive function that involves left dorsolateral PFC can be neurally distinguished from articulatory rehearsal and most probably plays a major role in the active maintenance of working memory representations. Thus, goal-directed productions can either modify working memory representations or actively maintain their content. We suggest that maintenance is achieved through a refreshing process that takes the form of a reconstruction of the representation, as if this representation was brought back into the focus of attention[1]. This reconstruction is made necessary by the fact that, because productions fire sequentially, there is only one active representation at a time, the representations previously constructed suffering from temporal decay and interference that provoke the deactivation of their constituents and the loss of the bounds between them. Because the executive loop can only refresh one representation at a time, maintenance would be achieved by a rapid rotation of the representations and their reconstruction one after another in a rapidly repeating cycle. We have seen at the end of the previous chapter that the time necessary to refresh a single memory item (i.e., between 40ms and 60ms) falls within the range estimated by Anderson *et al.* (2004) for running a production (i.e., about 50ms). This convergence supports the idea that the same procedural system is in charge of both processing and maintenance functions[2].

This reconstruction of working memory representations has some similarity with the redintegration process assumed to underpin cue-based retrieval in cue-driven accounts of immediate retention (for example, Hulme *et al.* 1997; Nairne 2002). Remaining features of degraded working memory representations would be used as cues for retrieving potentially relevant information in long-term memory. This process will be further discussed and illustrated in the final section of Chapter 8. The permanent construction and reconstruction of representations is a mechanism by which these representations could, at the same time, be enriched by the adjunction of new features that were not part of the initial encoding, but also polluted by irrelevant information. This mechanism would explain the well-known long-term memory effects on short-term recall (for example, word frequency, lexicality, concreteness; Baddeley 2012; Gathercole *et al.* 2001). It could also account for several phenomena related to proactive interference in working memory, such as their increase with the retention interval in Brown-Peterson task (Keppel and Underwood 1962), or with the accumulation of trials in complex span tasks (Lustig *et al.* 2001; May *et al.* 1999). In the Brown-Peterson task, longer intervals involve more reconstructive episodes during which irrelevant features from prior trials could be recruited in reconstructing current representations. In the complex span tasks, previous trials stored in long-term memory could induce the distortion of subsequent working memory representations when reconstructed.

Executive functions within the executive loop

It is worth noting that within this architecture, executive functions do no longer play the role of the homunculus who takes important decisions, but are subordinate processes involved in goal-directed cognition[3]. They are central because they operate across modalities and process representations whatever their nature and content, but they are not executive because they do not make any decision: they are simple and 'unintelligent' processes monitored by goals. Thus, the central executive can no longer be conceived, as in Baddeley's theory, but also in Cowan's or Engle's models, as an assembly of smart executive functions that control attention and supervise the cognitive system. Within our theory, the central executive consists in the loop constituted by the episodic buffer and the procedural system that either maintains or modifies working memory representations. Thus, and contrary to Baddeley's current model, this executive loop is in charge of both functions of working memory, processing and maintenance, which are the two faces of the same coin. As a consequence, the functioning of the executive loop results in a trade-off between the two functions: any processing step of a controlled activity requires the modification of the working memory representation, something conflicting with its maintenance and, in the other way round, maintaining this content actively or refreshing previously constructed working memory representations blocks any other processing requiring the executive loop.

Neurological evidence for a time-based resource-sharing mechanism

The executive loop model assumes that working memory functioning is characterised by a time-based resource-sharing mechanism by which processing and maintenance episodes alternate through a process of rapid switching. We recently began to explore the neural bases of this time-based resource-sharing mechanism, looking for brain areas where activity varies as a direct function of cognitive load. Indeed, cognitive load not only affects recall performance through the balance between loss and reconstruction, but is also related to the involvement of the rapid switching mechanism that permits sharing resources over time. Recall that cognitive load increases with both the number of processing steps per unit of time and the attentional demand of each of these steps. Increasing cognitive load by increasing the number of steps leads to the fragmentation of the maintenance activities that have to be more often interrupted and resumed. Making each of these steps more attention demanding renders subsequent switching more difficult as it has been observed that switching costs are higher when switching from more difficult tasks (Allport, Styles, and Hsieh, 1994). In both cases, higher cognitive load poses increased demand for the switching mechanism. Thus, Vergauwe, Hartstra, Barrouillet, and Brass (2014) used fMRI to examine whether there are brain regions that are sensitive to variations in the cognitive load induced by both verbal and spatial concurrent tasks, assuming that these areas should be found in regions typically involved in switching-related processes. One of the regions that have been most consistently associated with task switching in neuroimaging studies is the Inferior Frontal Junction (IFJ), situated at the junction of the precentral sulcus and the inferior frontal sulcus, and located at the border of the premotor and prefrontal cortices. Several studies have shown that this region is implicated in task switching in a domain-general way (see Kim *et al.* 2012, for a meta-analysis). Accordingly, the analyses of Vergauwe *et al.* (2014) revealed that the right IFJ is recruited as a direct function of increased cognitive load whatever the domain involved (verbal or spatial), whereas this was only true for the verbal task in the left IFJ.

Overall, the Vergauwe *et al.* (2014) study confirmed the conclusion reached by Chein *et al.* (2011) that there are cerebral regions making domain general contributions to working memory performance. However, our study goes further in suggesting that the IFJ might be the neural basis of the key process by which working memory alternates between its two functions of processing and storage. Accordingly, the IFJ has not only been identified as central in task switching, but several studies have suggested its involvement in common operations of cognitive control such as interference control, task set reconfiguration and updating of task representations (Brass *et al.* 2005; Derfuss *et al.* 2004; de Fockert *et al.* 2004; Kim *et al.* 2012). Importantly, and in line with the executive loop hypothesis, Dux *et al.* (2006) have suggested that the IFJ corresponds to the neural basis of the central amodal bottleneck that is found in PRP experiments and assumed to constrain working memory activities to take place one at a time within the executive loop. Thus, a body of empirical evidence converges to designate the IFJ as the cerebral area subserving the rapid switching mechanism that underpins time-based resource sharing. This is only a first, but promising, step towards an integrative approach that would relate the cognitive architecture of the time-based resource-sharing model with its neural substrates. At the very least, this first investigation supported the hypothesis of a general-domain mechanism sensitive to cognitive load as the main constraint on working memory performance.

Working memory and long-term memory

All the current theories of working memory have addressed the question of the relationships between working memory and long-term memory, some of them arguing that working memory is that part of long-term memory activated above threshold (Cowan 2005; Engle *et al.* 1999; Lovett *et al.* 1999; Oberauer 2002). In contrast with this latter proposal, we assumed above that working memory representations are *ad hoc* ephemeral constructions that differ from the information passively stored in long-term memory. More precisely, we propose to define working memory (or short-term memory[4]) as the assembly of systems devoted to the active maintenance of information within the cognitive system. The number of these systems is limited to two: an executive loop at the central level of working memory and the phonological loop described by Baddeley (1986) at a more peripheral level. Apart from the short-living information present in sensory memories, all the information stored by the cognitive system that is not maintained in an active state by these systems corresponds to long-term memory. According to this functional definition, working memory is neither defined by the relative recency with which information has been encoded, nor by the amount of information that has been recently encoded. Rose *et al.* (2014) have demonstrated that even a single item cannot be reliably held in working memory and must be retrieved from long term memory after a sufficiently distracting task. What matters is not the delay between encoding and test or the amount of information presented, but whether cognitive activities intervene or not to preserve information in a state suitable for treatment. Consequently, the difference between long-term memory and working memory is better defined by the state of the information held in these systems. Whereas working memory holds representations that correspond to mental states producing behaviour, long-term memory passively stores footprints of these mental states that have lost their representational nature. Thus, while working memory representations are transient and tend to fade away, suffering from temporal decay and interference as soon as they leave the focus of attention, long-term memory traces do not suffer from decay but from the interference created by the incessant accumulation of traces resulting from construction and reconstruction of working memory representations within the executive loop.

Long-term memory traces of transient working memory representations

The accumulation of long-term memory traces resulting from the construction and reconstruction of working memory representations is attested to by a study by McCabe (2008), though he favoured a slightly different theoretical framework from ours. Following a widespread conception, McCabe assumed that working memory is that part of long-term memory activated above threshold with a more highly activated part that corresponds to the focus of attention. McCabe reasoned that, during complex span tasks, the processing component temporarily occupies the focus of attention. Thus, memory items would be displaced towards long-term memory from which they could be retrieved for refreshment purposes, repeated covert retrievals progressively strengthening these long-term memory traces (see Unsworth and Engle 2007b for a similar conception and see below for its discussion). This would not happen in simple span task in which memory items can be maintained in the focus of attention, at least when their number remains limited to four. This conception led to a quite counterintuitive prediction. When considering immediate recall, a simple span task like a word span should result in better performance than an operation span task in which the maintenance of words is impeded by intervening calculations. However, this effect should be reversed in delayed recall because the memory items in the operation span task are subject to repeated retrieval from long-term memory, whereas items maintained for word span are not. This is exactly what McCabe (2008) observed. However, although this result is in line with McCabe's hypothesis, there is no need to suppose that memory traces are repeatedly retrieved from long-term memory to account for it. The hypothesis of a recurrent process of reconstruction of working memory representations within the executive loop that leaves traces in long-term memory is sufficient to explain that complex span tasks elicit better delayed recall. Due to the degradation of memory traces during processing episodes, complex span tasks require more active refreshing activities over longer periods of time than simple span tasks that allow for an immediate recall. This sustained activity of reconstructing working memory representations in complex span tasks results in more long-term memory traces that can be retrieved for delayed recall.

This hypothesis is reinforced by two subsequent studies by Loaiza and McCabe (2012, 2013). In the first study, they manipulated the number of refreshing opportunities in tasks requiring the maintenance of series of four words while solving arithmetic operations. The critical factor was the format of presentation of these words that were either spaced or massed. The spaced condition consisted in a complex span task in which each word was preceded by an operation to be solved. When massed, the four words appeared in immediate succession either after solving the four operations or just before this processing period, mimicking a Brown-Peterson task. Such a manipulation allowed the varying of the number of refreshing opportunities. In the spaced presentation, and because attentional refreshing acts in a cumulative way, starting always with the first presented item, the number of refreshing opportunities depended on the serial position of the memory item. For example, the first word could be refreshed after each operation and could benefit from three refreshing periods, whereas there was no refreshing opportunity for the last word that was immediately followed by the recall phase. In the massed presentation, each word had the same number of refreshing opportunities, either none if words were presented after the operations and just before recall, or three if presented before the processing period, each word having the opportunity to be refreshed after each operation[5]. As in McCabe's (2008) study, participants were asked to perform an unexpected delayed recall task after having performed four trials of each of the three span tasks. Loaiza and McCabe's (2012) results were very informative. The proportion of words recalled at delay decreased linearly with their serial position in the spaced presentation. Words that benefitted from more refreshing opportunities were better recalled, just as if each refreshing period strengthened the episodic trace of the memoranda. Accordingly, in the massed presentation, the proportion of correct recall did not vary with serial position. Moreover, when words were presented just before recall and did not benefit from any refreshing opportunity, their rate of recall was akin to that of the last word in the complex span task, for which there was no opportunity of refreshing. In parallel, when items were massed before the processing period, with three refreshing opportunities, their rate of recall was similar to the first word in the spaced condition, which benefitted from the same number of opportunities. Loaiza and McCabe (2013) replicated these findings in young and old adults. In both age groups, performance in delayed recall increased linearly with the number of refreshing opportunities, the increase being steeper in young adults.

These studies strongly suggest that the active maintenance of information in working memory leaves footprints in long-term memory that can be subsequently retrieved, with more refreshing opportunities increasing the probability of retrieval[6]. However, and in line with our hypothesis, it seems that the reconstruction of memory traces at the central level of working memory through attentional refreshing is the condition for leaving traces in long-term memory, while more peripheral mechanisms of maintenance such as verbal rehearsal remain ineffective. Past and recent studies reviewed below converge towards this conclusion.

Long-term memory and the mechanisms of maintenance in working memory

It should not be concluded from the findings reported above that any maintenance of information in working memory results in its storage in long-term memory. The study of Loaiza and McCabe (2013) evoked above illustrates this point. Using modified operation span tasks, Loaiza and McCabe investigated the effects on episodic memory of variations in the opportunity to either attentionally refresh or verbally rehearse items held in working memory. One of their experiments used the same operation span task as previously described in which participants were asked to maintain words for immediate recall while solving arithmetic operations. The number of opportunities for refreshing was manipulated by varying the number of operations presented before each word (either 0, 1 or 2 operations). Note that in the 0-operation condition, the task corresponded to a word span task, while the addition of intervening arithmetic problems in the other conditions turned the task into a complex operation span task. Whereas the word span elicited better immediate recall than the complex operation span tasks, the proportion of words recalled at delay increased with the number of operations to be solved which was also, according to the authors, the number of opportunities of refreshing, a finding that replicated Loaiza and McCabe (2012).

However, in another experiment, the authors manipulated the opportunity to verbally rehearse the memoranda. They used for this purpose a method previously used by Hudjetz and Oberauer (2007), a study we have already described in the previous chapter. In a modified operation span task, each word was preceded by an arithmetic problem to be read aloud and solved within 6500ms, this operation being displayed on screen either in a 'simultaneous' or a 'continuous' reading condition. In the former condition, the operation was presented in its entirety for 6500ms (for example, $6 \times 4 = 24$), whereas in the latter, each part of the problem was individually presented for 900ms (i.e., 6, $6 \times$, 6×4, $6 \times 4 =$, and so on), requiring the participant to read each part of the problem as it appeared on screen, thus resulting in a continuous reading that reduced the opportunities of verbal rehearsal. In line with several previous observations (Camos et al. 2009, 2011, 2013; Hudjetz and Oberauer 2007; Mora and Camos 2013), reducing the possibility of verbal rehearsal in the complex span task resulted in poorer immediate recall. However, and more interestingly, there was no difference between the two conditions at delayed recall, suggesting that verbal rehearsal is important for working memory but not for episodic long-term memory.

A recent study by Camos and Portrat (submitted) shed light on the mechanisms underlying these phenomena. Loaiza and McCabe analysed their interesting findings in terms of the number of opportunities for refreshing (for example, in Loaiza and McCabe 2012, either one, two or three opportunities). However, if attentional refreshing proceeds, as we assumed above, through a cyclic rapid rotation of representations within the executive loop at a rate of 50ms per representation, estimating the exact number of opportunities for refreshing becomes pointless. A more appropriate estimate could be the time during which the executive loop is available for refreshing representations in working memory, longer refreshing times allowing for more refreshing cycles and resulting in more traces left in long-term memory. In a first experiment using complex span tasks, Camos and Portrat asked participants to maintain series of five words while performing concurrently either a low or a high demanding task. The high demanding task consisted in judging the parity of six digits successively displayed on screen after each word at a rate of one digit per second. In the low demanding task, the digits were replaced by dots and participants asked to press a key when a dot appeared on screen. The opportunities for verbal rehearsal were manipulated by asking participants to perform these tasks either silently by pressing keys, or aloud by responding to each digit with 'odd' or 'even' (in the dot task, participants uttered alternatively the words 'odd' and 'even'). In line with the studies reported in Chapter 5, increasing concurrent attentional demand or introducing a concurrent articulation led to a reduction of recall performance in immediate recall test. More interestingly, delayed recall was reduced when the attentional demand of the concurrent task increased, but remained immune from the addition of a concurrent articulation. These findings confirmed that delayed recall critically depends on the availability of attentional refreshing whereas verbal rehearsal does not impact long-term memory. A second experiment went further in investigating the effect of time. The availability of attentional refreshing was manipulated by varying the pace at which the parity task had to be performed. Each word was always followed by six digits, but the time available to process each digit was either 800ms in a fast pace condition or 1500ms in a slow pace condition. Moreover, these tasks were performed either silently or aloud. Note that in terms of the number of opportunities for refreshing as defined by Loaiza and McCabe (2012), the fast and slow pace conditions offered the same number of opportunities (i.e., six). However, the time available for refreshing was longer in the slow pace condition. Not surprisingly, this slow pace condition elicited better immediate recall, as we have so often observed, and the articulatory suppression involved by performing the parity task aloud resulted in poorer recall. More interesting are the results of the delayed recall. Whereas impeding verbal rehearsal had no effect, the slow pace condition allowing for longer periods of refreshing involved better delayed recall.

It could be concluded from these findings that both immediate and delayed recalls depend on the cognitive load of the concurrent task: the lower cognitive load involved by the slow pace condition facilitates both types of recall. This is not the case. Immediate and delayed recall depend on different memory systems and distinct memory traces. While immediate recall depends on the integrity of working memory representations maintained in an active state by attentional refreshing and verbal rehearsal, delayed recall depends on the number of long-term memory traces resulting from every reconstruction of working memory representations within the executive loop. Whereas the critical factor for working memory is cognitive load (i.e., a proportion of time), what matters for long-term memory is the absolute time during which a given representation is recirculated within the executive loop, leaving a footprint at each refreshing cycle. This difference between working and long-term memory is illustrated by Loaiza and McCabe's (2013) experiment already evoked above in which the authors manipulated the number of opportunities of refreshing by varying the number of operations presented before each to-be-remembered word (either 0, 1 or 2 operations). Interestingly, each operation was presented for a constant duration of 5250ms in such a way that presenting one or two operations at this constant pace resulted in the same cognitive load. In conformity with the law relating processing to storage, there was no difference in immediate recall between the two conditions (see Chapter 3, pages 57-58 for similar findings and their explanation). However, though one or two operations involved the same cognitive load, the absolute time available for refreshing working memory representations was longer in the latter condition, and as it could be expected, this resulted in a higher rate of delayed recall. These findings suggest that immediate and delayed recall rely on different memory traces affected by different factors. Whereas working memory depends on the availability of attentional refreshing and verbal rehearsal to counteract the deleterious effects of decay and interference, long-term memory traces of working memory representations depend on the iterative refreshment of these representations in the executive loop, but not on their recirculation in the phonological loop through verbal rehearsal.

Memory systems, mechanisms of maintenance and levels of processing

The idea that the formation of long-term memory traces depends on the nature of the mechanisms used to maintain information in short-term (working) memory is not new in psychology. It echoes research in the 1970s, in which studies distinguished between 'Type I' and 'Type II' processing (Craik and Lockhart 1972), 'Type I' and 'Type II' articulatory rehearsals (Glernberg, Smith, and Green, 1977), or 'maintenance' and 'coding' articulatory rehearsals (Rundus 1977). These studies occurred before Baddeley's work on the multi-component model, when multistore models of memory distinguished stores in terms of duration of retention (short *vs.* long term retention) and aimed at accounting for how information was transferred from one store to the other. This distinction between two types of maintenance derived from the alternative framework proposed in the famous paper by Craik and Lockhart (1972) who introduced the idea of different levels of processing to account for memory phenomena. Similar to our distinction between articulatory rehearsal and attentional refreshing, Type I or maintenance articulatory rehearsal was assumed to process information at a structural level and to have only transitory but no long-term effects. This type of articulatory rehearsal was also described as a rote repetition or a recirculation of information at a phonemic level (Mazuryk and Lockhart 1974). In contrast, Type II or coding articulatory rehearsal was assumed to involve a deeper and more elaborative processing of information, which influences long-term retention. It was shown that increasing the total study time improves delayed recall when the added time is used for Type II processing (Craik and Watkins 1973). As summarised by Rundus (1977), the two mechanisms were assumed to differ in codes and levels of processing.

When considering the studies reviewed above and in Chapter 5, the distinction we introduced between articulatory rehearsal and attentional refreshing in working memory maps nicely the distinction proposed at the time between Type I and Type II mechanisms. On the one hand, the well-known phonological nature of the articulatory rehearsal and its absence of long-term effect replicated the findings related to Type I mechanism. On the other hand, we have shown that attentional refreshing induces long-term effects on the retention of the items, and we suggested that this maintenance relies on more elaborated and deeply processed representations, which is akin to the description of the Type II mechanism. Interestingly, if studies in the 1970s showed that the time during which Type II is used improves long-term retention, we specified this relationship by showing that it is the time during which attention is free for maintenance that predicts delayed recall.

Comparison with other models

We have presented a theory of working memory in which a sequential executive loop can construct and maintain a limited number of transient representations that fade away as soon as they leave the focus of attention. Because this executive loop is in charge of both processing and maintenance activities, working memory representations decay during processing episodes, and their necessary reconstruction for refreshing purposes postpones further processing. These phenomena occur whatever the verbal or visuospatial nature of the representations. Whereas constructing enduring working memory representations is a relatively time-consuming process, their refreshment is fairly fast and achieved at a rate of about 50ms per item. This central system can be supplemented by a phonological loop that can maintain some verbal items without interfering with the executive loop functioning, whereas it seems that there is no such a system for visuospatial information. When leaving the central system, information loses its representational nature and is no longer directly accessible to consciousness. Being inactive and dormant, the resulting long-term memories are no longer prone to decay, but they can become inaccessible due to interference. In this section, we examine the relationships between our theory and other current theories of working memory. We will in turn address the multi-component model proposed by Baddeley (1986) and its more recent developments, theories that conceive working memory as that part of long-term memory activated above threshold such as Cowan's (2005) embedded-process and Oberauer's (2002) hierarchical models, and the primary-secondary memory approach developed by Unsworth and Engle (2007b). Finally, we address Anderson's ACT-R theory (Anderson et al. 2004).

The multi-component model

Several aspects of the present theory were inspired by Baddeley's theory (1986, 2000; Baddeley and Logie 1999). As in the multi-component model of working memory, we distinguished between a central system in charge of processing activities connected with peripheral stores for verbal and visuospatial information, with an episodic buffer in which cross-domain representations are constructed. In line with Baddeley et al. (2010) who envision the episodic buffer as 'analogous to the screen of a computer', we have emphasised the unique representational nature of the information maintained in working memory. Following this theory, we have also assumed that information is maintained in the phonological store by verbal rehearsal through an articulatory loop. Nonetheless, our theory departs from the multi-component approach in several ways.

First, as we noted in the introduction, the structure and functioning of the central executive remains underspecified in Baddeley's theory as an assembly of executive functions triggered by some homunculus, while we have suggested that it can be conceived of as an executive loop connecting the episodic buffer with a procedural system. Thus, and contrary to Baddeley's approach, the central system in our theory is in charge of both processing and storage activities that compete for a common supply. Moreover, we have specified the main constraints of this central system that are due to the sequential functioning of the executive loop and the ephemeral nature of working memory representations.

Second, the episodic buffer in Baddeley's theory was initially conceived as a system for binding features from different peripheral systems (Baddeley 2000). Because it appeared that this binding process does not depend upon executive resources (Allen et al. 2006; Allen et al. 2009; Baddeley et al. 2011), the idea of an episodic buffer that would actively bind information into chunks was subsequently abandoned. It is now described as acting as a passive store holding multidimensional representations that are created elsewhere within the cognitive system (Baddeley et al. 2010). We suggested a different conception according to which, far from being a passive store, the episodic buffer is involved in an executive loop in charge of the construction and reconstruction of working memory representations. It seems that the negative conclusions reached by Baddeley et al. (2010) derive from an exclusive focusing on the binding process. As suggested by Cowan (1995, 1999), it is possible that binding is the by-product of the simultaneous coding of a few features, hence its undemanding nature. We have already evoked the study by Langerock et al. (2014) in which we observed that the maintenance of cross-domain information made of letters in locations relies on attentional resources and is similarly affected by the cognitive load of verbal, visuospatial or neutral intervening tasks, confirming the supra-modal nature of representation held in the episodic buffer. However, this effect was not stronger for cross-domain information than for its domain-specific constituents, suggesting that the maintenance of binding *per se* does not add any attentional demand. Thus, even if the binding process does not involve executive resources as Baddeley (2000) surmised, the episodic buffer appears as the core of the cognitive system.

Third, our theory also departs from the multi-component view concerning the slave systems. Baddeley and Logie (1999) assumed a clear distinction between processing and storage, the latter function being underpinned by the slave systems in which information would be maintained by specific refreshing mechanisms. We have shown that this is true for the phonological buffer only, whereas the visuospatial sketchpad does not seem to have a specific maintenance mechanism like an inner scribe. Moreover, our results indicate, as Baddeley and Hitch (1974) initially surmised before abandoning this idea, that the phonological loop is not the sole mechanism for maintaining verbal information. Storage functions are taken in charge by the central system when the phonological loop capacity is exhausted or when it is unavailable. Thus, working memory structure and functioning appears more complex than the multi-component view assumes.

Working memory as the activated part of long-term memory

Several models (Cowan 1999, 2005; Engle *et al.* 1999; Oberauer 2002, 2009b) have assumed that what is described by Baddeley (1986) as discrete buffers can be conceived of as the temporarily activated portion of long-term memory, with a subset of items in a higher level of activation making them available for treatment. This subset that would be limited to three to five chunks of information is described as the focus of attention in Cowan's embedded-processes model or as the region of direct access by Oberauer (2002), who limits the focus of attention to a single item. In Cowan's approach, the focus of attention is controlled by automatic orienting responses to changes in the environment but also by voluntary effort directed by the central executive towards current goals. Because the focus of attention is involved in both the retention of data and in processing activities, there is a conflict between processing and storage. The problem of the relationships between processing and storage is resolved by Oberauer (2009b) by suggesting the existence of a procedural working memory that would be isomorphic in structure to the declarative working memory and devoted to the representation and selection of the cognitive operations. Among the subset of procedures activated at any time by representations of goals or by stimuli to which they have been applied by the past, a central component corresponding to the region of direct access and called 'the bridge' would hold the currently operative task set in control of thought and action. Within the bridge, a unique procedure could fire at a time to process the item selected in the focus of attention. In this conception, procedural and declarative working memories are assumed to be separated and independent, with their own capacities.

There are several convergences between these approaches and our theory. The focus of attention described by Cowan (2005) corresponds in our theory to the working memory representations maintained in an active state by the executive loop, which is also in charge of processing. Cowan stresses that the capacity of this focus of attention appears clearly when verbal rehearsal is prevented, suggesting as we did that maintenance of verbal information through attentional focusing and verbal rehearsal must be distinguished. The single-item focus of attention described by Oberauer (2002) would correspond to the representation currently processed by the executive loop. The diverging conceptions about the size of the focus of attention (i.e., either one or four items) can be reconciled by considering that the rapidly rotating executive loop means that several representations are almost simultaneously present to the mind.

However, there are also strong differences between our theory and these approaches. Of course, all our studies on the relationship between processing and storage contradict Oberauer's (2009b) hypothesis of independence between procedural and declarative working memories that interact in our theory through the executive loop. Moreover, and more importantly, we have assumed that working memory differs from the activated part of long-term memory. Of course, Cowan (1995) emphasises the fact that working memory goes beyond the activated portion of long-term memory in that it includes new episodic links between items presented concurrently. This corresponds to what we described as working memory representations within the episodic buffer. In the same way, Cowan assumes as we did that these new links are entered into long-term memory as new records. However, our theory assumes that working memory representations are more than the activated part of long-term memory in which new links are created. We have suggested that there is a difference in nature between the content of the episodic buffer, which holds representations, and long-term memory that stores information in a resting state, resulting in different forgetting mechanisms. Indeed, what is known about how memory traces decay in working memory does not fit with the idea that these memory traces correspond to long-term memory information activated above threshold.

McKone (1995, 1998, 2001) ran a series of studies that illustrate this latter point. For example, McKone (1995, Exp. 4) presented participants with an old-new recognition task involving lists of words or pseudowords in continuous sequences of 250-300 trials with 35 per cent of the target trials that were a repeat of an item seen earlier in the list. The critical manipulation concerned the lag between two occurrences of the same item, that is the number of intervening items that varied from 0 (immediate repetition) to 23. The dependent variable was the RT to respond 'old' on targets. The results were particularly clear. Immediate repetitions elicited the fastest RTs that linearly increased up to lag 3 and then remained unchanged whatever the number of intervening items (Figure 6.3). McKone (2001) analysed these results as compatible with a capacity limit of four as hypothesised by Cowan (2001). Because the very long lists most probably discouraged active verbal rehearsal, the maximum number of items that could be held in working memory was limited to four. Assuming that an 'old' response was facilitated when a representation of the target item was still present in working memory, this leaves room for only two additional intervening items. Accordingly, repeats at two intervening items were still facilitative, whereas RTs no longer varied from lag 3 upwards. It should be noted that, contrary to theories that assume an equal activation of the items within the focus of attention (for example, Cowan 2005) but in line with our hypothesis of

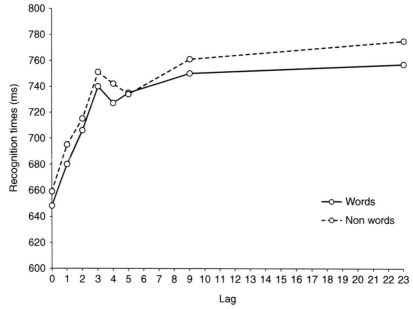

FIGURE 6.3 Recognition times for words and non-words as a function of the lag (i.e., the number of intervening items between the probe and its previous occurrence) in the old-new recognition task used by McKone (1995)

sequential construction of working memory representations suffering from temporal decay, RTs progressively increased from lag 0 to lag 3. As the previous occurrence of the target recedes into the past, its working memory representation fades away, resulting in longer 'old' responses. Most importantly, the results indicated that when the capacity of the executive loop is exhausted (i.e., at lag 3), RTs no longer vary with the number of intervening items.

Similar findings were observed by McKone (1995) with a lexical-decision instead of an old-new recognition task. In the lexical-decision task, repeats produce a repetition priming effect known to speed up responses (Scarborough et al. 1977). For low frequency words, repetition priming was strong at lag 0 (about 145ms) and progressively decreased with increasing lags. By lag 4, priming reached a stable value reflecting the long-term component of repetition priming, no further decay taking place beyond this point. McKone (1998) further explored this phenomenon by examining the contribution of time delay and number of intervening items in repetition priming decay. For this purpose, she compared an interference condition in which trials were presented at a rate of one every 2 sec with either 0, 1, 2, 3, 4 or 7 intervening trials between repeats, with a no-interference condition in which the time delays between repeats were the same (i. e. either 2, 4, 6, 8, 10 or 16 sec) but without inserting intervening items that were replaced by blanks. The results of the interference condition replicated the decay of priming observed in McKone (1995) with a stable long-term priming value reached by lag 4. Interestingly, priming was also shown to decay as a function of the time delay in the no-interference condition, though this decay was slower. Overall, the results of McKone's studies suggest that memory traces progressively decay with time in short-term memory, but that this decay affects a maximum of four items.

These findings shed light on a related study by Berman, Jonides, and Lewis (2009) that is often presented as evidence contradicting the hypothesis of temporal decay in short-term memory (for example, Lewandowsky et al. 2009). To test explicit short-term memory while avoiding any encouragement for rehearsal, Berman and colleagues used a recent-probes task in which participants are shown four target words to remember for a brief interval followed by a probe word. Their task is to judge whether this probe pertained or not to the stimulus set previously presented. The phenomenon of interest is that negative responses are delayed when the probe does not match a member of the current target set, but matches a word from the set presented in the previous trial. This delay in responding is due to the familiarity resulting from the recent study of the probe. The authors reasoned that if short-term memory decays with time, the recent probe effect should be affected by the duration of the inter-trial interval (ITI). Indeed, once a trial has ended, there is no reason to rehearse or keep in mind its target words. Thus, the memory traces of the previous trial should decline during ITI, with longer ITIs resulting in more decay and consequently in smaller recent probe effects. The results revealed that ITI manipulation had practically no effect, whereas increasing the number of intervening items by presenting an additional trial during the ITI resulted in a strong reduction of the recent-probe effect. This led the authors to conclude that short-term memories are subject to very small decay effects with the mere passage of time, but that interference plays a much larger role. Berman et al. considered their results as contradictory with those that found decay, such as McKone's studies, and suggested that these inconsistencies were due to differences in the processes involved in the tasks used.

However, and contrary to Berman et al. (2009) claims, their results are in line with McKone (1995, 1998) findings. As we have seen, McKone observed in the old-new recognition and in the lexical-decision task that decay-related effects disappear by lag 3 or 4. Critically, the recent-probes task used by Berman et al. systematically involved at least four intervening items (the four target words of the current trial) between the probe and its previous presentation. Thus, based on McKone's (1995) results, there was no reason to expect an effect of the ITI manipulation in Berman et al.'s study, because when the recent negative probe was presented, its matching target had already left working memory. Instead, and in line with McKone's studies, what Berman et al. have observed is that there is no temporal decay in long-term memory. What is more surprising is the fact that increasing the number of intervening items from four to eight abolished the recent probe effect as Figure 6 in Berman et al. indicates. The sudden disappearance of any effect of familiarity after eight intervening items remains difficult to understand knowing that McKone (1995, 1998) observed long-term priming effects at lag 23.

As we suggested above, the discontinuity in the phenomena observed by McKone (1995, 1998) does not fit very well with theories that conceive working memory as the activated part of long-term memory, with a focus of attention or a zone of direct access surrounded by items that have recently left this most activated area but remain relatively accessible due to their residual activation (Cowan 2005; Oberauer 2002). As surprising as it may seem, a word encountered four trials before is not better recognised and does not produce more repetition priming than a word encountered 23 trials before. This suggests that working memory is not that part of long-term memory activated above threshold that would gradually return to its resting level when leaving the focus of attention. The findings reviewed in this section are more in line with the idea that working memory consists of a limited number of items that are in a transient state that qualitatively differs from the resting state that characterises long-term memory. This does not mean that there is no long-term memory component in working memory performance. In Cowan *et al.* (2012), along with a fixed number of chunks and a process of decomposition of these chunks, the authors identified the need for a long-term memory component in verbal working memory performance. However, they noted that the extent to which long-term memory contributes to immediate memory depends on the measure. Chen and Cowan (2009) did not find a role for long-term memory in a recall task of lists of up to 12 items forming up to six chunks, and Cowan *et al.* (2012) found a moderate role for long-term memory in a recognition task (i.e., an increase of about 1.5 in the number of chunks accessed). Consequently, Cowan *et al.* assumed that the supplementation of working memory by long-term memory occurs only when there is sufficient contextual information for long-term memory retrieval, such as in recognition tasks. Thus, we assume that long-term memory constitutes the material for creating working memory representations, and that every working memory representation leaves a trace in long-term memory, but working memory is not that part of long-term memory temporarily enlightened by an attentional spotlight. Working memory is rather a system for constructing and manipulating transient mental representations whereas long-term memory contains inert and non-representational information.

Working memory as a primary memory retrieving memory traces from secondary memory

Unsworth and Engle (2007a, 2007b) have recently suggested that working memory comprises two functionally different components. A first component, referred to as primary memory, actively maintains information over the short term. According to Unsworth *et al.* (2010), this component is conceptually similar to the focus of attention in Cowan's theory. The second component, referred to as secondary memory, is needed to retrieve information that cannot be maintained in primary memory when its capacity is exhausted or its content is displaced by irrelevant distractors. In this case, retrieval from secondary memory would rely on a cue-dependent mechanism. For example, in a complex span task, memory items would be first stored in primary memory, but quickly displaced into secondary memory by the processing activity. At recall, the majority of the items would have to be retrieved from secondary memory through strategic search. By contrast, in simple span tasks, items could be held in primary memory, at least for short lists up to four items. With longer lists, items would be initially held in primary memory but some of them would be displaced into secondary memory.

This approach has the merit of reviving a venerable tradition initiated by James (1890) and introduces some simplicity by suggesting that working memory phenomena can be accounted for by the interplay between a short-term and a long-term memory. However, this approach does not fit very well with the results reported in the previous chapter concerning the effect of storage on processing. Because Unsworth and Engle (2007b) exclusively focused on verbal memory, it could be imagined that what they call primary memory corresponds to the phonological loop. Indeed, we have observed that this phonological loop can hold up to four items. When this capacity is exhausted, the executive loop works as a back-up system able to refresh working memory representations through a reconstruction mechanism akin to a retrieval process. This option was evoked by Jarrold et al. (2010) who suggested that primary memory capacity could be supported by rehearsal. Unfortunately, this account does not work because we have seen that the phonological loop can maintain verbal items without interfering with attention demanding activities, demonstrating that it is distinct from the focus of attention. As a consequence, the phonological loop cannot stand for the primary memory described by Unsworth and Engle (2007b) who consider primary memory and the focus of attention as equivalent constructs. Another possibility would be to consider that the primary memory consists in the assembly of the phonological and the executive loops, the secondary memory corresponding to long-term memory. However, we have seen that when participants were free to use verbal rehearsal for maintaining letters, that is when both the phonological and the executive loops could be used for maintenance purposes, they were able to maintain up to 6 letters while performing a distracting task, which is beyond the expected primary memory capacity.

Moreover, several findings are difficult to reconcile with the hypothesis that information is maintained in working memory through covert retrieval from long-term memory. First, the time course of the refreshing process, as estimated in the studies reported in the previous chapter (about 50ms per item), does not correspond to what is known about retrievals from long-term memory that take far longer (for example, about 180ms for retrieving a target word from the lexicon, Costa et al. 2009). Second, if memory items in complex spans were repeatedly retrieved from long-term memory, these repeated retrievals should lead to specific interference phenomena that do not occur. For example, as we have seen, Oberauer (2009a; Oberauer et al., 2004) observed that distractor words pertaining to the same semantic category as the words to be memorised did not produce a consistent effect of interference, whereas this semantic similarity should have created a high level of confusion if working memory was processed through the incessant search and retrieval of memory traces from long-term memory. This suggests that items in working memory are maintained in a distinctive state that prevents confusion with distractors. By contrast, when memory items are stored in long-term memory, interference resulting from semantic similarity occurs. For example, Beaman (2004) had participants memorise lists of 16 words presented on screen at a rate of two items per second followed by eight to-be-ignored words presented auditorily. These distractors were either semantically related or unrelated with the to-be-recalled words. Long lists of 16 words cannot be maintained in an active state in working memory and their recall probably involved retrieval from long-term memory. Accordingly, semantically related distractors involved poorer recall of the target words and a higher number of related-item intrusions. These findings suggest that working memory does not maintain information by recirculating within the focus of attention information that would be stored in long-term memory.

Working memory as the problem representation module in ACT-R architecture

Our model is also inspired by the ACT-R architecture (Anderson 1993, 2007; Anderson and Lebière 1998) and its procedural system. More recently, within this architecture, an 'imaginal module' was proposed, also called the 'representation module' or problem state resource, which could represent working memory (Borst et al. 2010). The imaginal module is used for storing intermediate information necessary for performing tasks and is comparable with the focus of attention in Cowan's (2005) theory or with Baddeley's episodic buffer. This module would be limited to only one coherent chunk of information with three or four slots and would create interference when it is requested by more than one task.

Though our proposals are akin to these conceptions, some differences remain. First, we have assumed that the executive loop can process up to four different representations or chunks at a time, or on a scale of tens of ms. Second, interference occurring in this central system seems more general than within the imaginal module. Borst et al. (2010) specify that not all tasks require the use of a problem state, such as, for example, when no intermediary results need to be stored or when all the necessary information is present in the world. Our conception differs because we assume that any process requiring an executive function involves the executive loop. Our results make clear that a simple response selection associated with the location of a stimulus on screen or the direct retrieval of parity information that does not require any intermediary result compete with concurrent maintenance of information within the episodic buffer. This suggests a more general and central representational role for the episodic buffer and the executive loop in our model than for the imaginal module postulated by ACT-R.

Conclusion

We have presented in this chapter an integrative view of working memory as a system for constructing, maintaining and transforming transient representations of internal and external states of the subject and the world. We have embedded this system in a cognitive architecture that relates working memory to other cognitive structures.

Thus, this model is not simply a description of working memory functioning, but makes proposals on how sensory systems, attention, executive functions and long-term memory interact to direct action. Nevertheless, we left many aspects unspecified, such as the precise functioning of sensory memories, the way attention selects information for further processing, the generation, selection and organisation of goals to direct behaviour, the monitoring of outcomes and the retroactive loops for corrections, as well as the precise functioning of long-term memory. The specific neural structures and mechanisms underlying these cognitive functions were only superficially evoked. We are also aware that key processes of our model need further empirical support and theoretical elaboration. For example, empirical evidence is still lacking for the construction of working memory representations from sensory input and retrieved information from long-term memory, for their unique nature contrasting with the non-representational status of long-term memory knowledge, but also for the interplay between the executive and phonological loops. In his excellent synthesis of his work, Baddeley (2012, p. 3) recalled Toulmin's (1953) stance that theories are 'like maps, way of organizing our existing knowledge of the world, providing tools both for interacting with the world and for further exploration'. This chapter is our modest attempt in this direction.

Notes

1 If Perruchet and Vinter (2002) as well as Dulany (1991, 1997) are correct, the focus of attention should not be conceived as a bright spot enlightening dormant representations that remain unchanged in nature whether they are activated or not. Thus, it could be inaccurate to present refreshing as a process that brings back representations under the attentional spotlight, but this is a convenient way to describe the mechanism of reconstruction.
2 It can be noted that the observed refreshing time is at odds with the parameter used by Oberauer and Lewandowsky (2011) in their attempt at a computational simulation of the TBRS model, named TBRS* (i.e., 80ms). This discrepancy could be at the origin of some outputs of the simulation that do not fit the predictions of the TBRS model such as the decline of recall performance with an increasing number of distractors processed at a constant pace.
3 The executive functions we refer to here are the discrete and atomistic processes described by cognitive psychologists such as switching, updating, inhibition, goal-directed retrieval from long-term memory, response selection, or refreshing, and not the metacognitive abilities known to involve PFC and thus considered by some neuroscientists as executive functions such as problem solving, abstracting, planning or strategy development and implementation (see, for example, Ardila 2008). The 'executive functions' in this latter tradition refer to highly complex activities requiring a myriad of cognitive steps and processes from the lowest to the highest levels of cognitive functioning. The clearest sign that the two traditions do not refer to the same theoretical construct when evoking 'executive functions' is probably that the second tradition often considers working memory itself as an executive function (for example, Ardila 2008; Diamond 2006).
4 The TBRS model assumes that there is a functional continuity between working memory and short-term memory, short-term memory corresponding to working memory when it is only used for storage and maintenance purposes (see Chapter 8 and Barrouillet et al. 2011a).
5 There were four operations, but because the last operation was immediately followed by recall, there was no refreshing opportunity after this operation.

6 Though these findings can be accounted for by assuming either the strengthening of a unique memory trace in long-term memory, like in Anderson's (1993) ACT-R approach, or the multiplication of instances as hypothesised by Logan (1988), this latter conception seems more compatible with our assumption of working memory representations that are distinct from long-term memory traces, each reconstruction in working memory through refreshing leaving a new trace in long-term memory.

7

WORKING MEMORY IN DEVELOPMENT AND INDIVIDUAL DIFFERENCES

Though the TBRS model was mainly developed and tested on adults, it was initially inspired by unanticipated developmental phenomena. As we have seen in Chapter 2, the question at the heart of our work was to understand the developmental increase in working memory capacity in childhood. The results we gathered in testing the task-switching model proposed by Towse and Hitch (1995) led us to develop the TBRS model as an alternative account. Along with the studies in adults, we continued to investigate working memory development. This chapter reviews some of these developmental studies. Beginning with studies that aimed at verifying the existence of a time-based resource sharing in children and adolescents as it is observed in adults, the chapter addresses in a second section the factors that can account for the development of working memory within the framework of the TBRS model. In a last section are presented the studies in which we tested the hypothesis that these factors might also be conceived of as sources of individual differences.

Time-based resource sharing in development

The TBRS model puts forward a new conception of the relationships between processing and storage in which the core mechanisms are time-constrained. Although we verified the main assumptions of our model in adults, it remained undetermined whether working memory functioning presents the same characteristics and constraints in childhood and adolescence. To address this question, we investigated the relationship between processing and storage in school-aged children and adolescents, as well as in younger children.

Time-based resource sharing in school-aged children and adolescents

The TBRS model predicts that the amount of information stored in working memory linearly decreases as the cognitive load of concurrent processing increases, a relationship that we frequently observed in adults. To assess this pivotal prediction in children, we followed the same research strategy as we used in adults. We first verified that any increase in the duration of the attentional capture involved in each step of the processing component of a working memory span task results in a correlative decrease in recall performance. This manipulation results in parameter a variations in the cognitive load equation. In a second series of experiments, we manipulated cognitive load by varying both the number of items to be processed between two successive memoranda and the time allowed to process them (N and T values in the cognitive load equation).

Portrat et al. (2009) replicated in 10-year-old children the experiment previously described in which adult participants had to maintain series of consonants while judging the location (up or down) of a square on screen (Barrouillet et al. 2007). As we did with adults, so the duration of the attentional capture induced by the location judgement task was varied by manipulating the discriminability of the two possible locations (close vs. distant), the close condition being expected to involve longer response selections and lower recall performance. The results were congruent with these predictions. The 'close' condition elicited slower responses than the 'distant' condition (488ms and 431ms respectively), a difference that had a direct impact on recall performance, children recalling less items in the 'close' (mean span = 2.86) than in the 'distant' (3.39) condition. A second experiment replicated this finding through a different manipulation of location discriminability. Another group of 10-year-old children were asked to perform a similar complex span task in which the squares appeared either in black (high contrast condition) or in dark gray (low contrast condition) on a light gray background. As for the previous experiment, we expected that the increasing difficulty to discriminate locations would make the judgement task more demanding, leading to reduced recall. The results confirmed this prediction. Response times were longer for the low than the high contrast condition (502ms vs. 431ms respectively), inducing lower working memory spans (3.30 vs. 3.58 respectively). As we observed in adults, even small increases in the duration of response selections had a disruptive effect on children's working memory and resulted in poorer recall performance.

Gavens and Barrouillet (2004) observed similar findings in a complex span task in which, contrary to the previous experiments, we took care to impede articulatory rehearsal. Eight- and 10-year-old children had to maintain series of consonants while reading aloud series of digits that appeared successively on screen either in a random order or in the numerical order (i.e., '1, 2, 3, 4 …'). In both conditions, the same digits had to be read, producing the same level of articulatory suppression. However, contrary to the numerical order condition, the random order condition not only did not permit children to anticipate the next digit to appear on screen, but required the inhibition of the conventional and highly automatised number sequence, making this condition more demanding. Accordingly, the random condition resulted in lower spans than the ordered condition in both 8- (1.50 vs. 1.97 respectively) and 10-year-old children (1.97 vs. 2.63). Because the two conditions did not differ in any dimension except the order of presentation of the digits to be read, such an effect can only result from the use of attentional refreshing to maintain verbal information. Thus, these three experiments provided clear evidence of the effect of cognitive load in children's working memory.

However, the TBRS model goes even further in predicting that if time-based resource sharing constrains children's working memory functioning, recall performance should decrease linearly with the cognitive load of the concurrent activity. We thus varied cognitive load by manipulating the number of distracting stimuli and the time allowed for their processing (Barrouillet et al. 2009). We presented 8-, 10-, 12- and 14-year-old children with the same reading digit span task we described above and that was used in Barrouillet et al. (2004a) to examine the relation between processing rates and spans in adults (Figure 3.3). Four different rates were selected (2, 1.2, 0.8 and 0.4 digits per second), resulting from the presentation of 12 digits within 6s, and of 12, 8 and 4 digits within 10s respectively. Besides a trivial age effect, the linear decrease in span with increasing paces appeared in each age group (Figure 7.1). This finding replicated in children and adolescents the observations we made in adults and confirmed one of the main assumptions of the TBRS model. Even children as young as 8 years are able to divert surreptitiously their attention from the series of digits to refresh memory traces, a refreshment that is more and more efficient as the concurrent task allows for longer free pauses.

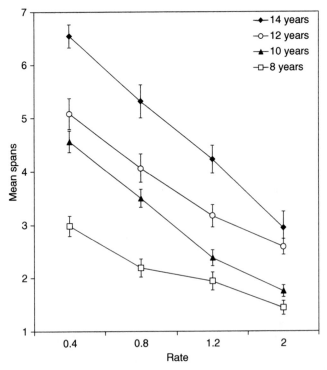

FIGURE 7.1 Mean spans as a function of the rate at which children aged 8, 10, 12 and 14 had to read digits after each memory item in Barrouillet et al. (2009)

However, the significant interaction between age and pace suggested that this refreshment differed in efficiency across age groups. While 8-year-old children exhibited an increase in span of 1.54 from the fastest to the slowest pace conditions (from 1.44 to 2.98), this increase was of 3.60 in 14-year-old children (from 2.94 to 6.54). This suggested that younger children are less able than their older peers to take advantage of the pauses freed by the slow pace conditions.

This phenomenon is consistent with Bayliss *et al.*'s (2005) idea that young children have a slower rate of reactivation than older children. In line with Cowan *et al.*'s (1994) observations, young children seem to be able to refresh only a limited number of digits per unit of time. Of course, other factors could account for this developmental difference, such as a lower capacity in young children to easily switch attention from processing to storage. Hitch (2006) has suggested that there might be a developmental shift from an early bias in favour of task switching and serial control to a greater degree of resource sharing and parallel processing. Younger children would devote all their attention to processing and then to storage when memory items appear, as the task-switching model describes, whereas older children would be able to rapidly switch their attention from processing to storage during the distracting activity, as in the TBRS model. Such a developmental shift would be underpinned by the development of executive processes and a greater capacity to control attention. Young children could exhibit a smaller pace effect owing to their lower capacity to disengage attention from processing as the current digit has been read. Before discussing in the following section the potential factors that could account for this phenomenon, and more generally for the development of working memory capacity, we have to consider if there is an age at which the time-based resource sharing does not operate.

Is there an age without time-based resource sharing?

Though several studies have addressed the development of working memory in school-aged children, little is known about this development in pre-school children. Although recall performance in school-aged children and adolescents reveal a time-based resource sharing, the question remains if such a mechanism is effective over the entire developmental period. If there is an age where children do not have such a mechanism at their disposal, what kind of recall performance pattern would result from such a working memory functioning? With no switch of attention during processing, attention would remain continuously occupied by the concurrent task except when a new memory item is presented. Such a functioning is exactly what Towse and Hitch (1995; Towse *et al.* 1998) described in their task-switching model. In this case, memory traces should suffer from a continuous decay during processing due to the absence of any attempt to refresh them. As a consequence, recall performance should remain unaffected by variations in cognitive load of the intervening task, and would only depend on the duration of this task. This does not imply that the intervening activity would have no effect on maintenance. The absence of any distracting task would allow attention to remain focused on the memory items to be maintained and should lead to better recall performance. Thus, if there is an age without any time-based resource sharing, recall performance should be impeded by the introduction of a concurrent task and decrease with its raw duration, but not with its cognitive load.

We have conducted two studies in pre-schoolers on this question showing a qualitative change in the use of refreshing. Testing children aged from 5 to 7 necessitated the adaptation of the material of our computer-paced span tasks to such a young population. In a new task, called the naming-colour span task, children were asked to memorise series of one to four animal nouns presented as drawings while they named the colour (blue, yellow or red) of smileys successively presented on screen after each animal. In a first experiment, 5- and 7-year-old children performed the naming-colour span task in which 8500-ms inter-animal intervals were either filled by the presentation of two or four smileys or remained empty (Barrouillet *et al.* 2009; Exp. 3). According to the TBRS model, the introducing of smileys to be named should reduce recall performance at any age. However, only children using a time-based resource sharing mechanism should have reduced span when the number of smileys increased in the constant inter-animal interval. Congruently with these predictions, both age groups exhibited a reduction in span when performing colour naming compared with an unfilled interval (mean spans of 1.12 and 2.11 respectively in 5-year olds, and 2.06 and 3.34, respectively in 7-year olds). However, while the increasing number of smileys led to a reduction of recall performance in the 7-year olds (2.45 *vs.* 1.67 for the 2- and 4-smiley conditions respectively), it left performance in 5-year olds unaffected (1.05 and 1.18 respectively). These findings support the idea of a qualitative change in the use of attentional refreshing, which does not seem to be used at 5. Nevertheless, it remains to be examined if such an absence of refreshing mechanism means that recall performance depends on the duration of the concurrent task.

In a further experiment using the same paradigm, we orthogonally varied the pace and the duration of the naming-colour task (Camos and Barrouillet 2011). Six- and 7-year-old children had to name the colour of either one smiley in a short 4000-ms interval, or two smileys presented in the same short interval of 4000ms or in a long 8000-ms interval. Whereas the two first conditions had the same duration (i.e., 4s) but differed in the number of distractors and consequently in their cognitive load, the first and third conditions induced the same cognitive load (one distractor every 4s) but differed in duration. The results were clear-cut. They replicated the pace effect in 7-year olds whose performance was sensitive to cognitive load, but not to raw duration. The one-colour-short-duration and two-colour-long-duration conditions induced the same and higher rate of correct recall (68 per cent) than the two-colour-short-duration (60 per cent). A totally different pattern of results emerged in 6-year-old children. Their performance was sensitive only to the raw duration of the naming-colour task but not to its cognitive load. Their percentage of correct recall did not differ between the two conditions that lasted the same duration (61 per cent in the one-colour-short-duration and 60 per cent in the two-colour-short-duration), although more distracting items were presented in the latter.

However, increasing the duration of the processing period in the two-colour-long-duration condition resulted in a decrease in recall performance (54 per cent). This result is also in favour with the hypothesis of a time-related decay of memory traces.

Overall, the findings from these two studies showed the qualitative change suggested by Hitch (2006) who proposed that the development of working memory in childhood might involve a shift from the macro-level switching described in the task-switching model, whereby attention is directed by the structure of the task, to the micro-level switching assumed by the TBRS model, whereby attention continuously switches between processing and storage, even during processing episodes. This shift would arise from the development of executive processes and a greater capacity to control attention (Zelazo and Frye 1998) that has been demonstrated in several behavioural (Bjorklund and Harnishfeger 1990) and neuroimaging studies (Posner 2004). Diamond (2006) proposed that such an improvement in cognitive flexibility would occur between 6 and 7 years of age, which is congruent with our findings that place the developmental shift between these ages. If the maturation of the frontal lobes can explain such a change, the TBRS model enlightens some factors that might underpin the observed developmental improvement in working memory performance.

Factors of working memory development in the TBRS model

Developmental psychology has from its inception tended to account for development by age-related changes in some core system underpinning cognition. While the Piagetian approach considered the structures of reasoning and rational thinking as this core system, the cognitive revolution in the 1950s launched more functionalist views and led to the conception that cognitive development results from the increase in capacity of some central general-purpose mechanism. The motor of development was to be found in the increase of M power (Pascual-Leone 1970), information processing resources (Andrews and Halford 2011) or mental capacity (Demetriou and Mouyi 2011) as revealed by the age-related increase in working memory spans (Case *et al.* 1982). The old question of the roots of cognitive development has consequently been refocused on the search for the determinants of working memory development.

Many studies have been dedicated to this question, leading to a variety of proposals (Barrouillet and Gaillard 2011; Cowan and Alloway 2009; Towse and Hitch 2007). Like several other approaches (Pascual-Leone 1970; Halford 1993), the TBRS model assumes that the main factor that could limit working memory functioning and performance in complex span tasks is the amount of attentional resources that can be shared between processing and storage. This factor could underpin developmental changes as well as individual differences, as we will see at the end of this chapter. However, accounting for working memory development by an increase in attentional resources has a poor explanatory value because it only replaces one concept with another. What is needed instead is to clarify the mechanisms by which this increase in attentional resources could operate to produce working memory development. A developmental increase in attentional resource may have several implications that impact working memory functioning through its time-based resource sharing. The first concerns the efficiency of processing. If older children have more attentional resources than their younger peers, they would perform cognitive activities more efficiently, resulting in higher processing speed. According to the TBRS model, this faster processing should, in turn, result in shorter periods of decay and longer periods during which attention is free to refresh memory traces. Second, an increasing amount of attentional resources could affect the efficiency of the maintenance mechanisms themselves. Finally, the third implication relates to the phenomenon of decay. To exemplify these phenomena, let us compare the performance in the location judgement task of 10-year-old children in Portrat et al. (2009; Exp. 1) with adults in Barrouillet et al. (2007; Exp. 2). In both studies, the same conditions of close and distant locations were compared. Whereas the difference in processing times between the two conditions was similar in both age groups, it induced a greater effect in recall performance for children than adults. The additional processing time of 57ms per square resulted in a reduction of 16 per cent ($d = 0.75$) in recall performance for children, compared with 5 per cent ($d = 0.29$) in adults for approximately the same extra processing time (63ms). This difference could result from two developmental changes. On the one hand, children could have a less efficient refreshing mechanism, adults taking a greater advantage from the short pauses left free between each processing step. On the other hand, higher attentional resources in adults could generate stronger and more elaborated memory traces, making them more resistant to decay.

Thus, our model assumes that age-related changes in processing efficiency, in the efficiency of refreshing, and in the rate of decay could contribute to working memory development. Before examining evidence on the developmental change in these three factors, we will evoke another important factor, the emergence of new strategies to maintain information.

The emergence of maintenance strategies

Among the various factors that are classically evoked in accounting for any developmental improvement, the discovery of new strategies and the change in strategy use have often been suggested (Flavell, 1979; Siegler 1996). Memory development is one of the main domains in which these changes in strategy use have been alleged and intensively researched as an essential determinant of development (Bjorklund et al. 2009; Schneider and Pressley 1997). However, in working memory literature, there is no consensus about the role of strategy in development. While the TBRS model evokes its leading role, other proposals such as the task-switching model of Towse and Hitch (1995) make no reference to any change in strategy, assuming that recall performance depends only on the duration of the concurrent task that determines the duration of decay without any attempt of reactivation. Thus, the emergence of such strategies during childhood would result in a determinant improvement in working memory functioning.

In the previous section, we reported two studies that brought evidence of a qualitative change with a shift from a passive to an active maintenance (Barrouillet *et al.* 2009; Camos and Barrouillet 2011). Neurophysiological studies suggest that the cognitive flexibility needed to switch attention back and forth from processing to maintenance activities develops critically between ages 7 and 9 in association with maturation of the frontal lobes (see Anderson 2002, for review). Besides the impact that such a change in the use of attentional refreshing may have in working memory development, we have already evoked the role of articulatory rehearsal in the maintenance of verbal information at short term. Several studies have been devoted to developmental changes in the use of verbal rehearsal by investigating the onset of the phenomena usually considered as clues for the use of this specific maintenance mechanism (for example, the correlation between articulation rate and span, or the effects of articulatory suppression and phonological similarity). As observed for the attentional refreshing, evidence speaks also in favour of a qualitative difference in the rehearsal status of children over and under 7 years of age (Henry 1991a, 1991b; but see Tam *et al.* 2010, for evidence of use of rehearsal at 6). Baddeley *et al.* (1975) suggested that a positive correlation between articulation rate and memory span is an index of the use of subvocal rehearsal (a faster rate allowing more items to be rehearsed), a correlation that was observed by Hulme *et al.* (1984) and Hitch *et al.* (1989) in children as young as 4. However, this correlation proved often non-significant under the age of 7 in subsequent studies (Cowan 1992; Gathercole and Adams 1993; Gathercole *et al.* 1994). Congruently, whereas concurrent articulation, which is assumed to impede subvocal rehearsal, reduces recall performance in older children and adults, it leaves 5-year-old children unaffected (Gathercole *et al.* 1992). Finally, the phonological similarity effect for visually presented items was often absent in children under the age of 7 who are instead sensitive to visual similarity (Hitch *et al.* 1989; Hitch *et al.* 1991; but see Henry *et al.* 2012 for an absence of visual similarity effect at 5, and Jarrold and Citroën 2013, for a critical discussion of the phonological similarity effect as a clue for verbal rehearsal).

Thus, in early childhood (i.e., before 7), children do not seem to spontaneously implement any of the two maintenance strategies described in the TBRS model, i.e., articulatory rehearsal and attentional refreshing. The emergence of these strategies would greatly improve maintenance efficacy and thus memory performance. However, after 7 and the appearance of these strategies, working memory spans continue to increase throughout childhood. Below, we will discuss some factors underlying this growth in working memory capacity.

Processing efficiency

Processing efficiency was among the first mechanisms evoked in the literature to account for working memory development. As we saw in Chapter 2, Case (1978) reduced developmental increase in memory spans to age-related changes in this unique factor. Diminishing the part of the Total Processing Space used by operations would free space available for short-term storage. To test this hypothesis, Case et al. (1982) equated the processing efficiency (i.e., counting speed) of young adults to that of kindergartners and did no longer observe any difference in recall performance. Above and beyond the importance of such a finding for Case's theory, the interest of this study relies also on its experimental design. To examine the impact of processing efficiency in the development of working memory, Case et al. (1982) aimed at equating processing efficiency to examine if the difference in working memory spans between two age groups vanished. In the same way, we equated across age groups the cognitive load of concurrent activities involved in computer-paced complex span tasks. This was done by manipulating each of the three determinant parameters of cognitive load (N, T and a in the cognitive load equation).

Gavens and Barrouillet (2004; Exp. 3) proposed to equate processing efficiency by tailoring the number of processing steps (N) to be performed between successive memory items. Nine- and 11-year-old children performed the continuous operation span task already described in Chapter 3 (see Figure 3.2). We have seen that when both age groups performed the same amount of processing steps in the span task (i.e., when performing two or four operations in the inter-letter interval), older children outperformed their younger peers (Gavens and Barrouillet 2004; Exp. 1; cf. Chapter 3). The rationale of this new experiment was to present older and younger children with concurrent tasks of the same level of difficulty. Thus, both age groups were asked to perform the same operation span task, except that younger children had to solve three operations in a 9-s inter-letter interval, whereas four operations were introduced in this interval for the older group. In line with the results issued from a pre-test, the rate of correct operation solving was similar across age groups, suggesting that the difficulty of the task was the same. However, though the developmental difference was reduced in comparison with a control condition, older children still outperformed younger children in recall performance (spans of 1.90 vs. 1.44, respectively). Thus, although the developmental difference in spans was reduced when the relative difficulty of the processing component of the task was kept constant, it did not vanish. The findings of this experiment do not support Case's hypothesis of an unchanged total processing space. Instead, they favour the idea that the age-related increase in working memory spans results in part from a greater efficiency of processing in older children, but that other factors intervene.

In a second attempt to equate the cognitive load of the concurrent activity, Barrouillet et al. (2009; Exp. 2) manipulated the time allowed to read series of digits (parameter T in the cognitive load equation). A pre-test revealed that 8-year-old children were slower than 14-year-old adolescents to read a single digit (622ms vs. 489ms respectively). Such a difference in processing times means that adolescents had probably more time available to refresh memory traces than younger children when performing the same reading digit span task as in Barrouillet et al. (2009; Exp. 1; described in the previous section). As a consequence, the age effect may have been heightened by the fact that memory traces would decay for longer durations in young children and could benefit from longer refreshment periods in adolescents. The interaction between age and pace observed in Barrouillet et al. could partially result from these variations in cognitive load between ages. Thus, to equate cognitive load across age, the time allowed to read each digit was fixed to either one, two or four mean reading times as assessed in the pre-test, resulting in three levels of cognitive load in each age group (for example, for the medium cognitive load, older children were given 2 × 489 = 978ms for reading a digit, while younger children had 2 × 622 = 1244ms). As in the previous experiment, adolescents still outperformed 8-year-old children (spans of 2.88 and 1.81 respectively), a difference that was nonetheless smaller than what Barrouillet *et al.* (2009, Exp. 1) observed when comparing groups of the same ages performing the same reading span task (4.76 *vs.* 2.14 respectively). Furthermore, the age × pace interaction observed when participants performed the same span task disappeared here when cognitive load was equated, suggesting that a substantial part of this interaction resulted from age-related differences in digit reading speed.

In a further experiment, we equated the cognitive load between two age groups by manipulating parameter *a* (Gaillard *et al.* 2011). To this end, participants performed slightly different tasks that induced similar processing times in 9- and 12-year-old children. Children had to maintain series of letters while performing additions on digits successively presented on screen. Two conditions were contrasted: one in which the two age groups performed the same additions (i.e., adding 1 to each digit), and another in which the difficulty of the additions was equated between groups by asking 9-year-old children to add 1 to each presented digit whereas 12-year olds added 2 (a pre-test revealed that response times were then equivalent in both age groups). We also varied the pace of this task in both conditions, with a digit presented every 1300ms, 2050ms or 2600ms. The control condition in which both groups performed the same task (i.e., adding 1 to each digit) revealed a strong age effect, older children outperforming younger children (3.05 *vs.* 1.79 respectively). Older children were also more affected by variations in cognitive load as the significant age × pace interaction testified, replicating Barrouillet *et al.* (2009; Figure 7.1). More interesting is the comparison with the other condition in which cognitive load was equated. The age effect was reduced but remained significant (2.31 and 1.72 respectively), whereas the pace effect, still significant, did no longer interact with age.

The findings of this third experiment echo the conclusions from the previous studies. As Case *et al.* (1982) discovered, processing efficiency is one factor that contributes to developmental differences in working memory. In three successive experiments that manipulated the number of processing steps to be performed, the time allowed to perform them, or their duration, equating processing efficiency between different age groups always resulted in reduced developmental differences. However, processing efficiency alone cannot account for all of the age-related differences in spans and, contrary to Case *et al.*'s observations, developmental differences were never abolished. This points towards a more complex processing-storage trade-off than hypothesised by Case (1978) who assumed that a common pool of resources would be shared between the two functions in a simple and continuous way. Other factors manifestly intervene to underpin the residual developmental difference.

As assumed by the TBRS model, the remaining source of this age-related difference may stand on changes in the efficiency of the attentional refreshing.

The efficiency of the attentional refreshing mechanism

We have seen in Chapter 2 that the phonological loop model assigns a pivotal role to the rate at which verbal information can be articulated and hence reactivated, and that children's memory span was strongly related with their articulation rate (Hitch et al. 1989; Hulme et al. 1984). Though these findings are of great interest and had a strong and justified impact in developmental psychology, they are limited to immediate serial recall of verbal items in simple span tasks and do not address the problem of working memory maintenance under the disruptive effect of concurrent activities. It is also possible that the observed relation between articulation rates and recall performance was not directly linked to reactivation mechanisms. Indeed, articulation rate could be the indicator of a more general processing rate that could be related to memory performance without having a causal role in the refreshment of decaying memory traces. In the following, we present a more direct test of the hypothesis of an involvement of the efficiency of refreshing mechanisms in working memory development.

Because the main hypothesis of the TBRS model is that attention can switch between processing and maintenance at a micro-level (i.e., during the processing episodes) to reactivate memory traces, the efficiency of this mechanism should have a direct and strong impact on working memory functioning. Any increase in the efficiency of this refreshing process during childhood means that older children should take a greater advantage from the short pauses left free between each processing step and available for refreshing activities. As a consequence, age-related changes in the efficiency of refreshing could play a central role in working memory development. We have seen above that Barrouillet et al. (2009) reduced developmental differences between 8- and 14-year-old children by equating processing efficiency in a reading digit span task through the manipulation of the time available to read the series of digits, a manipulation that also made the pace × age interaction disappear. However, when the spans were reanalysed, not as a function of the cognitive load, but according to the time available for refreshing (Figure 7.2), it turned out that adolescents benefitted more than children from this free time for refreshing memory traces. Linear regressions of the spans on these available times revealed a quasi-perfect linear function in each age group, with a steeper slope in older than in younger children. While 14-year-old children increased their recall performance by approximately one item for each additional second of time available after reading a digit (slope of 1.037), the same amount of time yielded only half of this increase in 8-year-old children (slope of 0.516). An important question is whether this developmental increase in reactivation rate goes beyond the general increase in processing speed.

When we examined the pace effect in different age groups, we showed that the slope relating pace to span was steeper in adolescents than in young children

Development and individual differences **157**

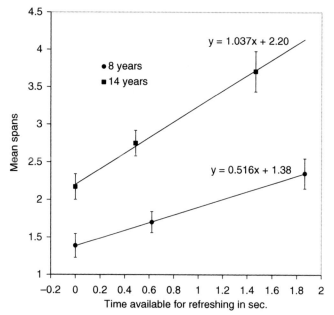

FIGURE 7.2 Mean spans as a function of age and free time available for refreshing in Barrouillet et al. (2009)

(see Figure 7.1). However, it should be noted that these variations in span were approximately in the same ratio. For example, increasing the pace led recall performance to drop from 3.60 to 1.53 in 8-year olds and from 4.57 to 2.14 in 14-year olds, a reduction of 58 per cent and 53 per cent respectively. If, at a first glance, the pace effect seems far stronger in adolescents than in children, it is in fact proportionate to recall performance. This was reflected by the fact that the age × pace interaction disappeared when recall performance were log-transformed (Barrouillet et al. 2009). Thus, developmental differences in the refreshing process seemed commensurate with differences in the most time-constrained conditions (i.e., at the highest pace) in which it can be assumed that this refreshing process has very little room and thus plays probably little role in working memory performance. This suggests that age-related differences in refreshing efficiency might be underpinned by a growth in a more general factor like processing speed.

To test the hypothesis that developmental differences in working memory spans are due to slower refreshing in younger children, reflecting a more general deficit in processing speed, we designed an experiment in which the time available for reactivation in younger children was tailored to their processing speed (Gaillard et al. 2011; Exp. 3). For this purpose, we first established in a pre-test the function relating the time taken by 9- and 12-year-old children to perform a variety of tasks such as articulating the numerical string, discriminating letters or solving simple arithmetic problems. A Brinley plot gave us the equation from which we were able to evaluate the free time needed by young children to achieve the same level of refreshing as older children if one assumes that the ratio of reactivation speed in the two groups is comparable to the ratio of processing speeds[1]. Then, we asked the two age groups to perform the same complex span task we previously used in which children performed additions on digits successively presented on screen while they maintained series of letters. As in this previous experiment, processing efficiency was equated, older children adding 2 to each digit, while 9-year-old children added 1. However, we also tailored to the processing speed of each group the time available for refreshing. In keeping with the design used by Gaillard et al. (2011), the refreshing times were determined by the presentation of blank screens that followed each digit to be processed, and fixed to either 0ms, 650ms or 1300ms in 12-year-old children. These durations were entered in the processing speed equation to compute the refreshing times given to the younger group, which were 0ms, 880ms and 1940ms respectively. We expected that, when processing times are equated, leading to comparable declines of memory traces in both age groups, providing younger children with the time they need to reactivate information as efficiently as older children should strongly reduce, if not abolish, developmental differences.

The results were twofold. First, the longer reactivation times from which the younger group benefited in this experiment resulted in an increase in recall performance. This was evidenced by comparing their recall performance with the mean span of the younger group in the previous experiment when processing times were equated but refreshing times kept constant between age groups. Tailoring refreshing times raised the mean span from 1.72 to 2.28. Second, this increase in spans practically abolished the residual developmental difference that remained in the previous experiment. Whereas the difference between the two age groups was still substantial when processing efficiency alone was equated (2.31 and 1.72 for 9- and 12-year olds respectively), this difference was no longer significant when processing efficiency was equated and refreshing times tailored (2.42 and 2.28 respectively). Giving young children the amount of time they actually need to reactivate memory traces, which is of course longer than the time that older children need, makes them perform at the same level as their older peers. Figure 7.3 illustrates the evolution of the developmental difference in span we observed in Gaillard et al. (2011) when successively equating processing efficiency and tailoring refreshing times in 9- and 12-year-old children. This suggests that working memory development, at least between these two ages, depends more strongly on quantitative changes, such as the speed and efficiency of reactivation of memory traces, than on qualitative changes, such as the propensity to use reactivation mechanisms (Tam et al. 2010).

Developmental changes in the rate of decay

At the beginning of this section, we evoked a third factor that could account for developmental differences within the TBRS model, which is a possible developmental change in the rate at which memory traces decay while the central bottleneck is occupied by concurrent activities. All other things being equal, the speed at which memory traces decline and fade away should affect their retrieval during recall.

Development and individual differences 159

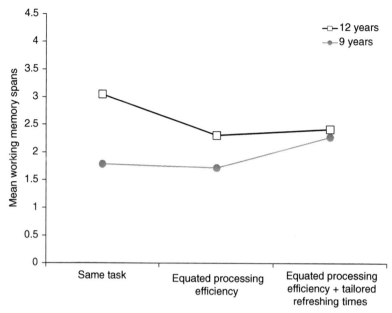

FIGURE 7.3 Evolution of the mean working memory spans in 9- and 12-year-old children when performing the same complex span task, when processing efficiency was equated, and when processing efficiency is equated and free time available for refreshing memory traces is tailored to processing speed in Gaillard et al. (2011)

Nelson Cowan and his collaborators conducted several studies to examine the rate of decay of information in the short term (Cowan et al. 2000; Keller and Cowan 1994; Saults and Cowan 1996). Because these studies were performed on children aged 6 and older, the authors assessed the effect of the delay of retention for digits, tone pitches or speech when they are ignored. In such a way, they prevented the use of mnemonic strategies susceptible to counteract the effect of decay at these ages. However, these studies provided quite divergent findings concerning a possible developmental change in the rate of forgetting through childhood. On the one hand, a developmental increase in the persistence of memory for pitch was reported between the ages of 6 to 7 years and adulthood (Keller and Cowan 1994) or for speech between the ages of 7 and 9 years and adulthood (Saults and Cowan 1996, Exp.2). On the other hand, contrary to these findings, Saults and Cowan (1996) observed in another experiment a similar rate of forgetting for speech between 7 and 10. More recently, Cowan et al. (2000) showed a similar loss of information across retention intervals for 8- and 11-year-old children as well as adults in an ability-adjusted paradigm (i.e., the length of the to-be-remembered series was adapted to the span of each participant). Nonetheless, in this latter study, a developmental increase in the persistence of memory was obtained only for the final item in an ignored list. The authors suggested that there might be an age difference in decay of an uninterrupted sensory memory (Cowan and Alloway 2009). Each item of the list may interrupt sensory memory for the previous items. Thus, only the last item benefits from that sort of memory. Overall, these studies do not provide a clear picture of the developmental change in the rate of forgetting through childhood.

Recently, Bertrand and Camos (submitted) re-examined the developmental change in rate of decay using a different research strategy. Instead of evaluating the rate of forgetting in late childhood with the necessity to impede maintenance mechanisms, we chose to assess it in a population that does not spontaneously use these mechanisms. As we have seen above, children in early childhood (i.e., between 4 and 6) do not seem to spontaneously implement any maintenance strategy. As a consequence, the maintenance of information in working memory between 4 and 6 should be affected by the mere passage of time, and recall performance in early childhood should depend on the delay between the presentation of memory items and recall. Thus, we developed a new span task, named 'the shopping span task'. Like the playing situation used by Istomina ([1948] 1977), our task is presented as a game that aims to do 'grocery shopping like mummy'. The experimenter took plastic fruits from a toy grocery shop and put them one after the other in a transparent bag, the child paying attention to the scene. After the experimenter's bag was hidden, the child had to reproduce the series of fruits by introducing the same fruits in her own bag. Four- to 6-year-old children were asked to reproduce these series either immediately or after a delay of 2, 4 or 6 seconds. We predicted that the absence of use of maintenance mechanisms would lead to poorer recall performance with longer delays. Accordingly, we observed that children's recall performance was affected by the delay of retention (Figure 7.4). Importantly, delay did not interact with age, suggesting a constant rate of decay over this age period. This effect was observed even when a single item had to be maintained.

It is worth noting that, though our participants did not seem to use any maintenance mechanism and that the rate of forgetting remained constant across age, our results nevertheless revealed a clear age-related increase in spans, with one additional object being recalled by the older compared with the younger children. Thus, among the main factors we mentioned to account for the developmental increase in working memory capacity, both changes in rate of forgetting and emergence of maintenance mechanisms could not explain the increase observed here between 4 and 6 years of age. It remains to understand what may drive the improvement of working memory in pre-schoolers.

Individual differences

Are individual differences of the same nature as developmental differences? This question is as old as psychology itself and can be traced back to Binet and Simon (1905). More than developmental differences, individual differences in working memory capacities have elicited an extensive literature. Along with studies aiming at establishing the predictive power of working memory capacity on a range of cognitive abilities, other studies have explored the factors underpinning individual differences in working memory capacity and suggested a variety of possible sources

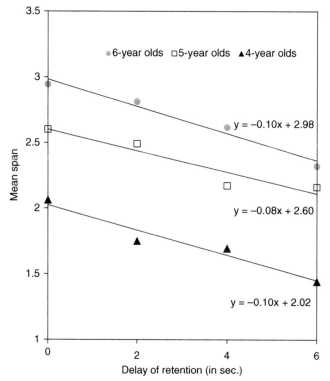

FIGURE 7.4 Mean span in children aged 4, 5 and 6 as a function of the delay of retention in the shopping span task in Bertrand and Camos (submitted)

(cf. for review Conway et al. 2007). Because, as we have seen, working memory functioning is characterised by a time-based resource sharing in children as well as in adults, we suggest that the factors that account in the TBRS model for developmental increase in working memory capacity are also at the root of individual differences. Before presenting some of our studies that have tried to identify the sources of these individual differences, we will examine a related topic, which concerns the predictivity of the complex span tasks we developed to test the TBRS model.

Predictivity of the computer-paced span tasks

As reported in several places in this book, our work on working memory led us to develop a new paradigm and design a new kind of working memory span task in which activities are time constrained. As we have seen in Chapter 3, Lépine et al. (2005b) showed that elementary processing steps can have the same detrimental effect as complex activities on the concurrent maintenance of information. Although the complexity of the processing component is not necessary to disrupt maintenance, it remains to be established whether our new complex span tasks assess the same capacity and have the same predictive power as traditional working memory span tasks. This is an important theoretical question because two alternative hypotheses were put forward in the literature to account for the relationships between working memory spans and performance in complex cognitive activities. According to the first hypothesis, traditional working memory tasks would evaluate some general cognitive capacity that is involved in any cognitive process requiring access and maintenance of items of knowledge (for example, Daneman and Carpenter 1980; Just and Carpenter 1992; Lovett et al. 1999). The measure of this general capacity does not require complexity, but only an activity that captures attention. However, this measure could be biased by the use of strategies to cope with dual tasking (Baddeley et al. 1985; Case et al. 1982; Daneman and Carpenter 1980; Turner and Engle 1989). Because our new tasks reduce the use of strategies due to their time-constrained nature, they should be more predictive of performance in high-level cognition than the traditional tasks. Alternatively, the second hypothesis assumes that traditional tasks evaluate some high-level executive capability that is essential both for the complex processes that they involve and for the use of strategies for dealing with the requirements of the dual task (Engle 2002). High-span individuals would be those who are better able to strategically plan and monitor their activity in complex situations, achieving better performance in working memory dual tasks and in higher-level cognition. According to this account, working memory spans are predictive because the traditional tasks mimic high-level cognitive activities. Such a hypothesis predicts that traditional spans will have a greater predictive value because our new tasks involve fewer strategic factors and only elementary processes.

To test these hypotheses, we examined the correlation between 12-year-old children's school achievement and their performance in traditional complex span tasks on the one hand, and new computer-paced TBRS span tasks on the other (Lépine et al. 2005a). The traditional span tasks were a reading span task inspired by Daneman and Carpenter (1980) and an operation span task inspired by Turner and Engle (1989). The new tasks were a computer-paced reading letter span task in which children read letters at a fixed pace while maintaining digits and a continuous operation span task (cf. Figure 3.2). To assess school achievement, we took advantage of the national academic achievement test that each French sixth grader takes at the beginning of the academic year. This test yields compound scores in literacy and mathematics, as well as a global score. The results showed that traditional and TBRS span tasks were highly correlated with each other, suggesting that both types of tasks aid in the evaluation of a common construct (r values ranging from .46 to .68). Compound scores for both types of tasks were calculated by averaging z values. TBRS tasks proved to be a better predictor than traditional tasks for the global scholastic score (.54 vs. .39 respectively), the literacy score (.50 vs. .34), and the mathematics score (.52 vs. .38). Moreover, traditional span tasks contributed no variance in addition to that already contributed by the TBRS tasks.

We ran a similar study in young adults (Lucidi et al. 2014). As in children, we contrasted traditional span tasks with our new computer-paced tasks and examined their correlation with measures of fluid intelligence. As in the children's study, we used as traditional tasks the reading span and the operation span tasks, and we added Case's counting span task. The TBRS span tasks were the reading letter span task and the upgrading span task used in the developmental studies by Gaillard et al. (2011) that requires maintaining consonants while adding 1 or 2 to digits successively displayed on screen. A third task, the enumeration span task, consisted in maintaining consonants while subitising small sets of dots. Gf was assessed through three tasks, namely Cattell's culture fair test, WAIS reasoning matrix and Raven's progressive matrices. We replicated the correlation between the TBRS and traditional tasks (r = .49, on average). To evaluate to what extent the working memory construct derived from the TBRS tasks was as predictive of Gf as the factor derived from traditional tasks, we tested a three-factor model distinguishing between the two types of tasks in relation to a Gf factor in which working memory constructs significantly correlated with Gf. Reinforcing the results observed in children, the correlation between the working memory factor derived from TBRS tasks and Gf was even significantly greater than the one between traditional tasks and Gf (.37 vs. .30, Figure 7.5, panel a). Nevertheless, a model in which the traditional and TBRS tasks loaded on a single working memory factor had a fit as good as the model with two distinct working memory factors (panel b). By extending to adults our findings in 12-year-old children, these results suggested that TBRS tasks are a valid measure of working memory capacity and as good predictor of Gf as the traditional span tasks.

In a further study in children, we contrasted the predictive validity of our TBRS tasks with measures of processing speed and articulation speed (Barrouillet et al. 2008a). We were also able to collect some information about the social-economic background of the pupils enrolled in the study, and to have access to the national evaluation of their school achievement at the ages of 9 and 12. Children were asked to perform the two same TBRS tasks used in our first study in 12-year-old children, i.e., the reading letter and the continuous operation span tasks. They also performed two processing speed tasks (a cancellation test and a Posner task in which they compared two digits), and we measured their articulation rate in several repetitions of the alphabet. Our results showed that working memory spans, processing speed and articulation rate were significantly correlated with each other. However, school achievement at 12 was only correlated with working memory spans and school achievement at 9. Congruently, regression analyses showed that only academic achievement at 9 and a compound working memory score accounted for the progression in school achievement between 9 and 12. Finally, we replicated the well-known effect of the impact of the socio-economic background on pupils' progression. Children coming from a lower socio-economic background experienced more difficulties in school learning. However, when working memory score was introduced in the regression analysis, the part of variance accounted for by the socio-economic background became non-significant.

Overall, these studies showed that our new computer-paced span tasks provide a more accurate evaluation of the capacity of the common mechanism reflected by

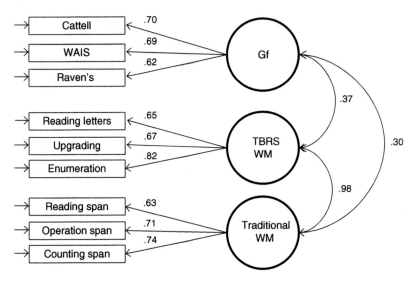

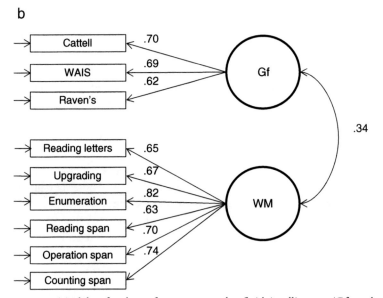

FIGURE 7.5 Models of task performance on the fluid intelligence (Gf) and working memory (WM) tests, variability of which is modelled as supported by three related constructs distinguishing the traditional and the TBRS tasks (panel a) or two related constructs including all the complex span tasks (panel b). Solid lines signify a significant loading or correlation at the $p < .05$ level

span measures than traditional tasks. This finding is all the more remarkable when considering that those tasks that involve the simplest activities and hamper the planning of sophisticated dual-task strategies turned out to be the most predictive of complex cognitive achievements. The predictive power of the new span tasks echoes previous observations by Fry and Hale (1996), who observed that performance on complex span tasks as simple as reporting the colours of items while maintaining their identities or locations in view of their subsequent recall was highly correlated with fluid intelligence. These findings are also congruent with Conlin et al. (2005) as well as Friedman and Miyake (2004), in which the correlation of span with higher cognition was better when the span task was conducted with a time limit rather than at the participant's own pace. Moreover, these results indicate that the predictive value of the traditional span tasks does not stem from their capacity to assess an ability to strategically cope with the demands of complex span tasks because, when the possibility of dealing strategically with the task is reduced by computer-paced presentation, this predictive value is increased. This does not mean that mnemonic strategies for encoding and maintaining memory items are unimportant in complex spans (McNamara and Scott 2001). However, our results show that complexity and strategies do not contribute to the predictive value of span tasks but rather introduce more noise than information into their relationship with high-level cognition.

As a consequence, increasing time constraints in our span tasks should reduce noise and increase the predictive power of the TBRS span tasks. In a further attempt to compare the traditional span tasks with ours, Camos et al. (2014) asked young adults to perform the traditional reading and operation span tasks, and one TBRS span task in which pace was varied. In this latter task, participants had to maintain letters while judging the parity of digits that were successively presented on screen at either a slow, medium or fast pace (one digit every 1600ms, 1200ms or 800ms respectively). We compared the correlation of these different span tasks with the score in the Raven's test. Replicating our previous results, a compound score of the TBRS span tasks was more strongly correlated with Raven score than the compound score derived from the traditional span tasks ($r = .28$ vs. $.20$ respectively). Moreover, in line with our suggestion that time constraints reduce noise in the measurement of working memory capacity, the correlation between the TBRS tasks and Raven increased with the pace of the parity judgement task from .20 to .23 and .29 for the slow, medium and fast paces respectively.

Sources of individual differences

The studies presented above showed that elementary activities, when performed under time constraints, are as disruptive as complex tasks for concurrent maintenance of information and as, if not more, predictive of higher level cognition. These results are in line with the TBRS model because cognitive cost is not a matter of complexity *per se*, very simple activities consuming cognitive resources to the extent that they require attention. However, two questions remain. First, if these elementary processes can involve a high cognitive load when performed under time constraints because they require attention, they should be sensitive to individual differences in working memory capacity conceived as the amount of available attention. Few studies have directly addressed this question and most often resulted in a negative answer. For example, Tuholski *et al.* (2001) observed that high-span were faster than low-span individuals in the complex activity of counting large arrays of dots, but they did not observe any difference in the speed of the more elementary process of subitising. By contrast, the TBRS model predicts that any activity involving attention should be sensitive to working memory capacity variations. Second, it is assumed that complex cognitive tasks require working memory because they involve the coordination of activities underpinned by multiple components of working memory (for example, Baddeley 1986). By contrast, within the TBRS model, complex activities are nothing more than the concatenation of elementary processes. Thus, the impact of working memory would result from the summation of small differences elicited by each attention demanding processing step. As a consequence, complex activities should not induce working memory differences beyond what could be expected from the differences elicited by their atomic constituents.

We tested these two hypotheses on a large sample of young adults contrasted on their working memory capacity (Barrouillet *et al.* 2008). Individual differences on elementary processes were assessed by presenting participants with numerical activities such as reading digits, solving very simple additions (the 16 possible additions with operands from 1 to 4), and subitising arrays of 1 to 4 dots. Following Anderson and Lebière (1998), the TBRS model assumes that these elementary activities, which require retrieval from long-term memory, necessitate the allocation of attention to activate the relevant declarative knowledge above threshold; the higher the amount of attention available, the faster the retrieval. Thus, we expected faster responses in individuals with higher working memory capacities. Finally, as Tuholski *et al.* (2001) reported, we expected high-span individuals to count large arrays of dots (from 5 to 12) faster than low-span individuals, but that these differences should be commensurate with, and should perfectly reflect, those elicited by the elementary activities. The results revealed the same pattern in the entire sample and in the extreme groups contrasted on their span. Besides replicating Tuholski *et al.*'s (2001) findings concerning counting of large arrays, higher working memory capacities were related with faster response times in all the elementary tasks (subitising, solving additions and reading digits). This result confirmed that any process occupying attention for a sizeable portion of time involves a cognitive cost and is thus sensitive to variations in working memory capacity. To test our second hypothesis about the fact that individual differences in complex activities should be perfectly commensurate with those observed in elementary activities, we first assessed the individual differences in elementary processes by plotting the mean response times in the low-span group against those in the high-span group for each item in each task involving elementary processes (32 different measures). The parameters of the regression analysis on these data were used to predict the differences that should be observed in the counting task if differences in complex activities do not go beyond those observed in elementary processes. When predicted times for the low-span group were calculated from the observed counting times in the high-span group using the linear function provided by the elementary processes analysis, the fit between the observed and predicted values for the low-span group was nearly perfect, with 99.7 per cent of the variance explained. Thus, a complex activity such as counting does not yield individual differences beyond what can be expected from the differences observed in the elementary components of this activity such as subitising small groups of dots and adding their results. The sequential functioning of working memory in the TBRS model accounts for this finding. The time needed to perform each processing step would depend on a basic general capacity, conceived as the amount of available attention needed to activate relevant items of knowledge and procedures. Individual differences in this basic capacity would result in small differences in the time needed to perform each attention-demanding processing step.

Finally, we will discuss the sources of the individual differences observed in complex span tasks. As we argued above in the developmental studies, two factors should limit working memory capacity and result in individual differences: processing efficiency that determines the time during which the memoranda suffer from temporal decay, and the efficiency of the processes in charge of refreshing these degraded memory traces during the free pauses. High-span individuals could be those who are more able than others to both avoid prolonged periods of decay by faster processing and to repair damaged memory traces through more efficient refreshing processes. In an unpublished study, Lucidi and Barrouillet (2012) tested these predictions with the same design as in the developmental study by Gaillard *et al.* (2011) presented above. A first experiment established a baseline by assessing the difference in spans between two extreme groups of adults performing the same upgrading span task in which participants added 2 to digits presented successively on screen while maintaining consonants. Three different levels of pace of the processing component were created by varying the time given to process each digit. In a second experiment, we tested the hypothesis that part of these individual differences depends on processing efficiency by equating processing times across groups. Low-span individuals had then to add 1 to each digit, an operation that took approximately the same time in this group as adding 2 in high-span individuals. In a third experiment, exactly as we did in children, the processing times were still equated across groups, but additionally the time available for refreshing was tailored to the processing speed of each group, resulting in more free time after each digit for low-span individuals. The two groups differed greatly when they performed the same span tasks (mean span of 4.93 and 3.03 for the high- and low-span participants respectively). In the same way as our developmental studies revealed a stronger pace effect in older children, the pace effect was more pronounced in the high-span group (3.71, 5.14 and 5.94 for the fast, medium and slow paces respectively) than in the low-span group (2.48, 3.07 and 3.50 respectively). Mimicking our findings in the developmental study, equating processing times reduced individual differences, but high-span individuals still outperformed low-span individuals (5.52 *vs.* 4.23 respectively) and pace did no longer interact with groups. Finally, when refreshing times were tailored to the differences in processing speed between the two groups (and processing times still equated), high-span individuals still outperformed low-span individuals (5.45 and 4.80 respectively), but this effect depended on pace. While the fast pace condition in which free time was the same in both groups (i.e., 100ms) revealed a large difference between groups (4.50 and 3.41 for the high- and low-span groups respectively), this difference was reduced in the medium pace (5.86 and 5.06 respectively) and disappeared in the slow pace condition (6.00 and 5.94 respectively). In this result, it is all the more noticeable that this latter condition elicited initially the larger difference between groups (5.94 and 3.50 respectively). Thus, equating between high- and low-span individuals the time devoted to perform the concurrent task and tailoring to their processing capacities the time available to reactivate memory traces resulted in a dramatic reduction of the difference in mean spans between the two groups. These experiments extend to individual differences what Gaillard *et al.* (2011) observed on developmental differences. Both kinds of differences result at least in part from differences in processing efficiency, more precisely in the time needed to perform the secondary task, and in the advantage that individuals can take from the pauses during which their attention is no longer occupied by processing and available for maintenance purposes.

An important question is to determine whether processing speed and efficiency of restoration processes constitute either one single or two independent sources of differences. We used in our studies the same measures of processing speed for equating processing times across groups and tailoring free times to the capacities of these groups. Consequently, this procedure could suggest that there is only one single factor. However, two facts prevent us from drawing such a conclusion. First, Bayliss *et al.* (2003, 2005) observed that processing efficiency on the one hand and storage capacity on the other contribute independent variance on span performance in children and adults. Under the plausible hypothesis that storage capacity has something in common with the efficiency of maintenance mechanisms, the findings from Bayliss and colleagues would speak in favour of the existence of two distinguishable factors. Second, individual differences remained even when free times were tailored to processing speed in low-span individuals, and it is probable that tailoring free time on another basis would have led to equivalent or even stronger reduction in individual differences. Thus, our results are not sufficient to support the conclusion that there is one general speed factor that would underpin WM span differences. In fact, studies that specifically addressed this question rejected the hypothesis of a general global rate of processing information that would determine working memory performance. For example, Cowan *et al.* (1998) reported that the rates of articulation and of retrieval of words from short-term memory are both related to children's memory spans but not with each other. In line with the idea that individual differences in WM are multi-determined, it should be noted that our results are entirely compatible with Unsworth and Engle's dual-component model. It could be assumed that differences in processing speed result from differences in attention control which is needed to sustain attention on the relevant items to be processed and avoid attention lapses, while differences in the efficiency of the restoration processes could reflect differences in the efficiency of the mechanism of retrieval from secondary memory.

Conclusion

As noted by Cowan and Alloway (2009), we certainly know that working memory increases with age, but there is still a lot of work left to do to understand how basic capacity contributes to that improvement. In this chapter, we evoked some of the factors that can account for this developmental improvement. However, it remains for other factors to be considered, like knowledge, strategies or automation through practice. For example, greater lexical knowledge in older children accounts at least in part for the greater lexicality effect (i.e., the advantage of words against non-words in immediate serial recall) observed in these age groups (Roodenrys et al. 1993). Greater knowledge could also result in stronger and more elaborated memory traces able to resist decay more efficiently and easier to reconstruct at recall through redintegration process. For strategies, we have already discussed the qualitative change in the use of subvocal rehearsal and attentional refreshing, but other strategies can be applied to working memory span tasks. For example, sorting items by category such as meaning or appearance, or elaborating semantic relations between the to-be-remembered items improve recall (Schneider et al. 2004). Strategies could also impact processing efficiency, having a direct role in the duration of the decaying periods. Automation through practice and exercise could be an additional factor impacting processing efficiency, as Case (1985) suggested. Klapp et al. (1991) demonstrated that automated processes become less and less disruptive of concurrent retrieval processes.

Moreover, we are aware that the three factors of development and individual differences we drew from the TBRS theoretical framework remain an oversimplification of working memory functioning. For example, processing efficiency and possibly refreshing efficiency cannot be clearly distinguished from a general processing speed factor which developmental role has been extensively explored both in childhood and aging (Kail 1991, 1996; Kail and Salthouse 1994; Salthouse 1996). In the same way, although we considered refreshing efficiency as a single and unique factor, a more fine-grained analysis could distinguish the efficiency of the maintenance process *per se* from the ease to switch attention back and forth between processing and storage activities. It is probable that there is a development of this switching process as with many other executive functions (Chevalier and Blaye 2008; Diamond 2006; Zelazo and Frye 1998). Concerning the rate of decay, and as we just mentioned, strength of encoding and quality of memory traces probably evolve with age, making them more and more resistant to decay and interference. Thus, a lot of work remains to be done to clarify the mechanisms underlying the developmental improvement and sources of individual differences in working memory.

Note

1 The equation was RT younger = RT older × 1.627 − 175. Due to its negative intercept, the equation returns a negative value when RT older = 0ms. Thus, we fixed to 0ms the corresponding refreshing time in the younger group.

8
CONTROVERSIES AND PROSPECTS IN WORKING MEMORY

In keeping with the seminal approach of Baddeley and Hitch (1974) who aimed at identifying, within the theoretical toolbox of psychology in the 1970s, the structure capable of providing the functions of a working memory, we have mainly focused in our work and in this book on the relationships between processing and storage. We have in the previous chapters proposed that these relationships result in an interplay between loss and reconstruction of the transient working memory representations on which cognition is based. This theoretical view did not only remain undisputed, but has heretofore led us to neglect important debated questions regarding working memory. This chapter aims at fixing some of these issues. We begin by discussing alternatives that have been proposed by distinguished researchers to our hypothesis of a time-based resource sharing in accounting for the pace effect. We then move to the hotly debated and complex problem of working memory capacity. Though our studies did not aim at addressing it, some of our results could be relevant to this question. The theoretical foundations of the problem of working memory capacity are linked with the larger question of working memory structure. Thus, the chapter ends with some thoughts about what is probably the main question regarding working memory, which is its genuine existence as a separate memory system.

Alternatives to a time-based resource-sharing mechanism in working memory

Our theory is based on the idea that working memory functioning is characterised by the alternation of processing and storage activities that compete on a temporal basis for the occupation of a common supply that we have described as an executive loop. When considering the effects that this functioning has on storage, ample empirical evidence has established that the amount of information that can be maintained in working memory is a function of the cognitive load of concurrent processing. We have explained this function by the interplay between two opposing processes, the loss of memory traces through temporal decay and interference, and their reconstruction by attentional refreshing and verbal rehearsal. The ubiquitous role of temporal factors in working memory performance led us to suppose that time had a causal effect on working memory loss, and we gathered evidence supporting this conjecture by demonstrating that the detrimental effect of concurrent activities on storage depended more on their duration than on their nature (Barrouillet *et al.* 2007, 2011a). Researchers who deny any time-based decay in short-term or working memory were faced with the challenge of accounting for the cognitive load function without assuming decay. This is the aim of the SOB-CS model (for Serial Order in a Box – Complex Span) designed by Oberauer *et al.* (2012). We have already evoked this model in Chapter 4 when discussing evidence for and against temporal decay. Here, we will present this model in greater detail and assess its capacity to account for the findings reported in this book.

The SOB-CS model

SOB-CS is a distributed neural-network model for complex span task. It is an extension of the SOB model, which aimed at accounting for verbal serial recall (Farrell and Lewandowsky 2002), and C-SOB (C standing for context) in which was introduced a two-structure layer with one layer representing serial position (i.e., the context) and the other representing items (Farrell 2006; Lewandowsky and Farrell 2008). As we explained in Chapter 4, these models already assumed that all the item-position associations are superimposed onto a common weight matrix resulting in their degradation through interference. At the heart of these models is the idea of novelty-gated encoding, which means that the encoding strength of an item is determined by its novelty, with more novel items receiving greater encoding weight and producing more interference. Accounting within this framework for working memory tasks that involve concurrent processing such as complex span tasks led to two further theoretical assumptions. The first is that processing a distractor inevitably results in encoding its representation into working memory in the same way as memory items are encoded, by associating the distractor with the same position marker as the memory item that this distractor immediately follows. Importantly, distractors incur the same novelty-gated encoding process as memory items. Consequently, distractors create interference with already encoded memoranda, the amount of which depends on their novelty. As we previously saw, this implies that the amount of interference increases with the number of novel distractors processed, whereas repeatedly processing the same distractor induces less or no additional interference.

The second assumption is more relevant for the issue discussed in the present chapter and concerns the mechanism of clearing working memory of no-longer-relevant contents. The small amount of information that working memory can hold in a readily accessible state is universally considered as a limitation of our cognitive system but, conversely, a working memory cluttered by no-longer-relevant information and the outcomes of past operations would rapidly become inefficient. As Oberauer et al. (2012) note, models assuming a time-related decay of working memory traces easily solve this problem: the cleaning up occurs by default, representations that are not actively maintained simply fade away. Things are different in models in which there is no temporal decay. All contents are now maintained by default, forgetting exclusively occurring through interference. Thus, the active restoration revealed by the cognitive load effect must reduce the impact of interference instead of counteracting the effects of decay. In SOB-CS, this is achieved by removing irrelevant representations through a Hebbian anti-learning process. Technically, this anti-learning takes the form of an unbinding process by which the association created at encoding between the distractor and its position marker is undone, the distractor representation being 'gradually removed from memory' (Oberauer et al. 2012, p. 782).

Four points are of particular importance here. First, this anti-learning process requires attentional focusing and can only take place when there is free time in-between distractor operations or during a pause between a processing episode and the presentation of the next memory item. Second, both encoding and anti-learning take time, the degree of encoding and the extent of removal increasing up to a point. Because encoding is rather fast, encoding strength approaching asymptote within 500ms, processing times have almost no impact on the amount of interference created by the distractor and hence no impact on forgetting. By contrast, the duration of free time matters because it determines the efficiency of the removal process and the strength of anti-learning. Removing an item would take between 1 and 2s according to Oberauer (2001, 2002). Third, and more importantly, SOB-CS does not include a maintenance process for the strengthening of memory items like rehearsal or refreshing. Restoration is assumed to be exclusively achieved by 'the removal of interfering material from memory, which by implication restores the quality of earlier memories' (Oberauer et al. 2012, p. 781).

The computational model proposed by Oberauer et al. (2012) was successful in simulating several benchmark findings including the effect of processing pace as well as the effects attributed by Lewandowsky et al. (2010) to the changing or repeated nature of distractors (see Chapter 4 for a reappraisal of these findings). However, beyond the originality of SOB-CS and the mathematical feat, does the interplay between interference and distractor removal constitute a plausible model of working memory, able to account not only for complex span task results but also for other working memory findings? As we will see, this does not seem to be the case. New empirical findings contradict the main tenets of the theory, *viz.* that there is no maintenance process for the strengthening of memory items and that the pace effect could be accounted for by a mechanism of removing interfering distractors. In the following, we elaborate on these two points.

Evidence contradicting the SOB-CS hypothesis of no active maintenance of memory items

Pertaining to a family of models, it does not come as a surprise that the SOB-CS model has inherited the strengths but also the limitations of its predecessors. In the same way as SOB and C-SOB were devoted to accounting for the sole task of serial recall, SOB-CS is limited to the complex span task and consequently focuses on the storage side of working memory. Of course, the need for simulating the disruptive effect of distractors on memory items led Oberauer *et al.* (2012) to modify the preceding models, but SOB-CS basically remains a model of short-term memory linking items to their position in a list, and not a model of working memory integrating the interactions between storage and processing. However, working memory is not limited to complex span tasks and, in the same way as processing affects storage, we have shown in Chapter 5 that storage affects processing. As Vergauwe *et al.* (2014) demonstrate, and in line with the predictions of the TBRS model, increasing memory load in a Brown-Peterson paradigm results in slower processing as long as the maintenance process relies on attention. When increasing the number of letters or spatial locations to be remembered, we observed a correlative increase in the time needed to perform parity or spatial fit judgements (see Figure 5.5). This increase in processing time proved to be proportionate to the number of memory items, whatever their verbal or visuospatial nature, and the nature of the processing task to be performed. These findings are totally incompatible with the SOB-CS model. Indeed, if there was no maintenance process operating on the memory items, and if cleaning up working memory was exclusively achieved by a mechanism of active removal of distractors as SOB-CS assumes, the number of memory items to be maintained would not have any effect on processing activities. In five successive experiments we proved that this is not the case. Our results revealed a linear function between memory load and processing times with a remarkable convergence in the successive estimates of its slope. Along with the function relating storage to cognitive load, a comprehensive theory of working memory must account for the function relating processing to memory load, a requirement that SOB-CS does not meet.

This illustrates, in our view, the dangers inherent in modelling tasks instead of cognitive processes or structures, which can lead to mistaking task-specific computational models for theories. However, the difficulties of SOB-CS are not limited to tasks for which it was not designed. The hypothesis of an interplay between interference and distractor removal is also contradicted by complex span tasks phenomena, and more precisely by the absence of effect of the number of distractors on recall when processed at a constant pace.

Evidence against the distractor-removal hypothesis

We have already evoked in Chapter 4 the study by Plancher and Barrouillet (2013) in which we tested SOB hypotheses in relation to the number of changing and repeated distractors. Let us have another look at some findings of this study that are particularly relevant for the problem here at hand, namely the nature of the opposing processes that underpin the cognitive load effect. This effect makes clear that some processes can partially counteract the disruptive effect of distractors, but are working memory traces restored by removing distractors or by refreshing and rehearsal? Recall that, in two experiments, Plancher and Barrouillet (2013) varied the number of changing distractors to be processed after each memorandum as well as the pace at which they had to be processed. Participants were asked to read series of five letters for further recall, each of these letters being followed by either two or four distractor words to be read either at a fast or a slow pace. For the sake of simplicity, we will collapse the data of the two experiments, which led to the same results, and consider first what happened when participants were presented with two changing distractors at a fast or a slow pace. As the TBRS model predicts, recall performance was higher for the slow than the fast pace condition (3.73 and 3.13 letters correctly recalled respectively), clearly indicating that the distractors processed at a fast pace induced more forgetting. According to the SOB-CS model, this stronger forgetting effect would be due to the fact that participants did not have sufficient time to remove the distractors to the same extent as they did in the slow pace condition. If this is the case, what would happen when adding two more distractors at the same fast pace after each letter? These two changing distractors would produce a further amount of interference with insufficient time to remove them, which would add to the interference already created by the first two distractors. The inescapable outcome should be a higher rate of forgetting. Contrary to this prediction, adding these two distractors had no effect at all, and processing four instead of two distractors resulted in an unchanged recall performance for both paces (3.74 and 3.15 letters correctly recalled for the slow and fast pace conditions respectively to be compared with the 3.73 and 3.13 observed with two distractors).

The same absence of effect of increasing the number of distractors processed at a constant pace was also observed by Barrouillet *et al.* (2011b). This study involved a task in which participants were presented with series of consonants to be remembered, each consonant being followed by either four or eight black squares displayed either in the upper or the lower part of the screen for a location judgement task. The pace at which the squares were presented was varied in such a way that, between two successive items, the total processing time during which memory traces are assumed to decay and the free time available for restoration were orthogonally manipulated. As the TBRS predicts, recall performance varied with the ratio between processing times and free times (i.e., with the cognitive load of the concurrent task). For example, as we predicted, doubling processing time while keeping free time constant resulted in poorer recall, whereas doubling free time while keeping pace constant had no effect. These findings contradict Lewandowsky and Oberauer's (2009) proposal that recall performance depends on the time available to restore the damage resulting from interference and that the time during which attention is occupied by processing would not have any effect *per se*.

These studies demonstrate that working memory performance does not depend on the relative efficiency of a process that would remove distractor representations. A simpler explanation is given by the TBRS model, which predicts that recall performance is a function of cognitive load conceived as the proportion of time during which processing prevents maintenance mechanisms to operate. Nonetheless, Oberauer *et al.* (2012) have argued that, contrary to our claims, the TBRS theory actually predicts, like SOB-CS, a decline in recall performance when the number of distractors processed at a constant pace increases. They reasoned that whenever the effect of decay is stronger than that of refreshing during a processing episode and the free time following it, the TBRS theory must predict that increasing the number of operations will lead to worse memory. This prediction was confirmed by TBRS★, a computational simulation of our theory proposed by Oberauer and Lewandowsky (2011). This is a common misunderstanding of the mechanisms by which the cognitive load affects memory, which suggests in turn that TBRS★ is an inadequate instantiation of the TBRS theory. Though some of our previous publications could have primed the idea that recall depends on the differential between decay and refreshing strengths (for example, Barrouillet et al. 2011a, Fig. 2; Gaillard et al. 2011, Fig. 1), what matters is the number of memory items that can be sufficiently refreshed during the free time to survive the next processing episode, something entirely dependent on cognitive load. The longer the free time, the higher this number. However, this number is also constrained by the degree of degradation undergone by memory traces during processing, with more degraded traces necessitating more time to be restored, and then less representations restored per unit of time. Through the processing of successive distractors, the two antagonistic mechanisms converge towards a point of equilibrium corresponding to the number of memory items that can be sufficiently restored during free time to be retrieved after the next processing episode. Once this equilibrium is reached, it can no longer be affected by the addition of distractors, provided that the durations of decay during processing and refreshing during free time remain unchanged. Thus, contrary to Oberauer et al.'s claim, the TBRS model does not predict variations in recall performance with the number of distractors when processed at a constant pace, because cognitive load remains unchanged.

In summary, the hypothesis put forward by Oberauer et al. (2012) and their SOB-CS model of a working memory, in which active restoration would be achieved by removing interfering distractors instead of operating on memory items to counteract the effects of decay and interference, lacks plausibility. Should we really believe that human beings try to maintain information in mind by directing their attention elsewhere (on the irrelevant items to remove them)? As we have seen, this idea is contradicted by facts.

Time pressure as an alternative to cognitive load

We already evoked the study by Oberauer and Lewandowsky (2013) that aimed at demonstrating that there is no decay in verbal working memory, in which participants maintained lists of consonants while performing visual search as a distracting task (Chapter 4). In a final series of experiments, they tried to disentangle cognitive load and the time pressure induced by the intervening task. Oberauer and Lewandowsky reasoned that in almost all our experiments, cognitive load is confounded with the degree of time pressure because, whichever way cognitive load is manipulated, the procedure always consists in reducing the time available to perform the task. To deconfound the two variables, they manipulated the time available for carrying out the visual search by introducing deadlines. For example, in their Experiment 8, a high and a low time pressure were created by fixing the deadline at 1.2s and 1.9s, which were the times taken by participants to complete about 50 per cent and 90 per cent respectively of the searches in a previous experiment. The search display disappeared from screen when the participant gave her response, or when the deadline was reached if the response did not intervene before. This procedure was used in three experiments in which were additionally varied either the free time (that followed the response or the deadline) or the duration of the attentional capture by varying the size of the visual display. In all these experiments, cognitive load defined as the ratio of attentional capture to the time allowed to perform the task was assumed to remain constant. In three experiments, higher time pressure resulted in lower recall performance. Oberauer and Lewandowsky concluded that the apparent cognitive load effect reported in many of our experiments did not arise from cognitive load as defined by the TBRS, but rather from time pressure. The challenge was to account for this time pressure effect when, contrary to the authors' expectations, the free time had no effect on recall unless the experiments included a manipulation of time pressure. Indeed, the visual search task proved not to interfere with the memoranda in several of their previous experiments. As a consequence, the time pressure effect could not be explained by an increased difficulty in removing the interference created by the distractors, as Oberauer et al. (2012) did to account for the pace effect. The solution imagined by the authors was to suppose that coping with time pressure involves increased cognitive control that uses representations susceptible to interfere with the memoranda, such as estimates of how much time is left for a response, the goal to work quickly, or to stop responses when the deadline is missed. The hypothesised verbal nature of these representations would have the potential to interfere with verbal memoranda.

There is no doubt that Oberauer and Lewandowsky made commendable efforts to account for the cognitive load effect without assuming temporal decay, and they developed complex experimental designs to disentangle cognitive load from a putative 'time pressure' that would have independent effects. It is worth noting that the idea of time pressure is not foreign to the TBRS theory, but in a way that totally differs from Oberauer and Lewandowsky's proposal. Let us recall that our theory assumes that increasing the pace of the secondary task has an effect on storage because this time pressure increases the proportion of time during which memory traces decay and reduces the time available for their refreshing. By contrast, for Oberauer and Lewandowsky, time does not play any causal role in the time pressure effect. Increased forgetting with higher cognitive load would result from the detrimental effect that the representations underpinning a higher cognitive control would have on memoranda. In other words, their explanation of the time pressure effect is just another way to reintroduce representation-based interference as the sole cause of forgetting. Although this 'time pressure' hypothesis sounds innovative and constitutes an appealing alternative to the TBRS theory, there are several reasons to remain sceptical about its explanatory value. In the following, we discuss in turn some aspects of Oberauer and Lewandowsky's experiments and explanation as well as some of our own results that could undermine their proposal.

Controversies and prospects **177**

First, it remains unclear how and why cognitive load was kept constant across conditions in Experiments 8–10, as claimed by Oberauer and Lewandowsky (2013). For example, in the four conditions of Experiment 8, participants were presented with the same search task with a deadline occurring after either 1.2s or 1.9s and followed by a free time of either 0.2s or 0.8s. As a consequence, the same work had to be done (i.e., the same search task) in four different delays (d = deadline + free time) ranging from 1.4s to 2.7s. In terms of cognitive load, which can be simply expressed as the amount of work to be done in a given period of time, the four conditions thus strongly vary. In Figure 8.1 we plot recall performance observed in Experiment 8 as a function of a grossly approximated cognitive load corresponding to $1/d$. The usual linear trend is observed, suggesting that recall performance, here as elsewhere, depends on cognitive load. Second, as Ricker *et al.* (2014) noted, the nature of the time pressure mechanism assumed to create interference with the memoranda remains vague. The representations generated by an increased cognitive control are assumed to be verbal in nature, producing the desired interference. The weakness of such an *ad hoc* explanation is that it remains unclear how this mechanism would produce the almost perfect linear trends relating memory performance to cognitive load (see, for example, Figures 3.3, 3.6 or 5.1). Moreover, assuming a verbal nature of the control-related representations is convenient when accounting for verbal recall, but how does it explain, within this framework, the cognitive load effects that affect visual and spatial maintenance, as we demonstrated

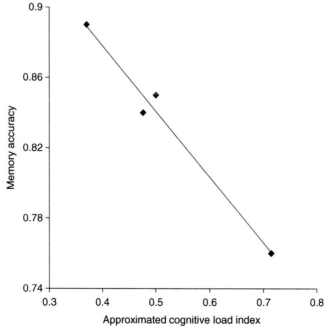

FIGURE 8.1 Memory accuracy as a function of an approximation of cognitive load given by the $1/d$ index (see text) in Oberauer and Lewandowsky (2013, Experiment 8)

on several occasions (see Chapters 3 and 5)? At the very least, the mechanism underlying the 'time pressure' account requires some further elaboration.

Moreover, several of our results related to cognitive load effects seem difficult to accommodate with Oberauer and Lewandowsky's hypothesis. To create time pressure effects, they designed extreme experimental conditions, like in their Experiment 8 in which people produced up to 50 per cent of time-outs. It is fairly possible that these conditions engendered parasitic thoughts interfering with the memory task, participants probably acquiring the conviction that they were facing an almost intractable task. However, this type of drastic constraint is not needed to observe cognitive load effects. For example, in Lépine et al.'s (2005b) study involving a continuous operation span task performed at either a slow or a fast pace, both conditions elicited 99 per cent of correct responses in the intervening task, clearly indicating that participants were perfectly able to perform the task, even at the faster pace. Nevertheless, pace had a dramatic effect on recall, which decreased by nearly 40 per cent (see Table 3.2). Moreover, we have already observed that increasing time pressure in performing the processing component of a working memory task does not necessarily disrupt concurrent maintenance. Recall the experiment by Barrouillet et al. (2007, Exp. 4, see Chapter 3, page 53) in which we used a simple reaction time task that does not involve attentional demand. Increasing from 5 to 11 the number of stimuli to process in a constant 6750ms interval, something that necessarily increased time pressure on participants, had nevertheless no effect on spans. This experiment demonstrated that increasing time pressure with no change in cognitive load does not affect storage in working memory. Overall, the time pressure hypothesis does not seem to be more convincing than the SOB-CS account of cognitive load. By now, the TBRS theory remains the sole theory able to account for both the cognitive load and the memory load effects.

The capacity of working memory

It is a fact of common observation that remembering in the short term is drastically limited. As Cowan (2008) recalls, if there is a difference between short-term and long-term memory, there are two ways in which the two stores may differ: duration and capacity. The limitation in capacity most probably reflects the fundamental structure and functioning of short-term or working memory. Accordingly, the constraints that restrict working memory in capacity as well as its 'real' size remain hot topics among working memory researchers. These questions are all the more important when considering that the available measures of this capacity prove highly predictive of Gf and high-level cognition. However, even defining working memory capacity is a task fraught with difficulties. In a very broad definition, one can consider working memory capacity as equivalent to short-term memory capacity, which is the ability to remember things in immediate memory tasks. However, eminent specialists have suggested that it differs from the capacity of short-term memory. Some assume that it can be better defined as executive attention (Engle 2002), a domain-free ability to control attention, whereas others suggest that we consider it as the amount of information an individual can hold in mind at one time (Cowan 2005). The next section will focus on this latter view.

Cowan's magical number four

In opening this book, we evoked one of the most famous papers in psychology where Miller (1956) estimated the span of immediate memory to seven plus or minus two items, which was, maybe coincidentally, equivalent to the mean capacity of the human information processing system. However, contrary to this appealing coincidence, subsequent studies suggested that Miller overestimated this capacity, which was re-evaluated to four in both the verbal (Sperling 1960) and the visuospatial domain (Luck and Vogel 1997). One reason that could explain this difference in estimation, as pointed out by Miller himself, is the ability to chunk information leading to the maintenance of more information, but in larger units, chunking being then an efficient strategy to maintain an increasing amount of information. This reassessment of the capacity of immediate memory to four chunks has mainly been empirically supported and theoretically motivated by Nelson Cowan (2001, 2005).

In a noteworthy *Behavioral and Brain Sciences* article, Cowan (2001) reviewed an impressive list of evidence for a capacity limit of about four items, ranging from immediate memory of spatial arrays, serial verbal retention under articulatory suppression, running span task, object tracking and enumeration, to sequential effects in implicit learning. In Cowan's embedded-processes model, this capacity limit would correspond to the size of the focus of attention, which determines the maximum number of chunks that people can attend at one time (Cowan 1988, 1995, 1999). Measuring the capacity of the focus of attention requires the avoidance of any corruption by various mnemonic strategies such as verbal rehearsal. Cowan used a variety of paradigms allowing for this control, such as the brief presentation of spatial arrays (Cowan et al. 2010), the simultaneous retention of visual and auditory arrays (Saults and Cowan 2007), or the recall from an unattended auditory channel (Cowan et al. 2000; Saults and Cowan 1996). In a notable series of experiments concerning immediate memory for verbal material under concurrent articulation, Chen and Cowan (2009) demonstrated that the size of four refers to a number of chunks and not of isolated items, their participants being able to recall as many word pairs as singletons. This conclusion was nonetheless tempered by recent results suggesting that working memory capacity is better described by a multi-factorial model which involves, in addition to a fixed chunk capacity limit, a long-term memory storage component and a process of chunk decomposition by which the probability of losing complex multiword chunks increases with their size (Cowan et al. 2012).

Alternative conceptions

Cowan's hypothesis of a working memory capacity limit of four chunks is closely related to his embedded-process model. Not surprisingly, other views of working memory lead to different estimates, or even conceptions, of its capacity. Some approaches, though retaining the idea of a focus of attention, disagree on its actual size, while others, distinguishing between different working-memory stores, envision several distinct capacity limits. Getting away from a simple storage-view of working memory, other scholars suggest the reintroduction of the limits that affect processing in the estimation of working memory capacity. Finally, defenders of the unitary view of memory, who deny the existence of separate short-term and long-term memories, envision working memory capacity as resulting from long-term memory mechanisms and limitations. We shall evoke in turn these different alternative conceptions.

Contrary to Cowan's estimate of the size of the focus of attention, several authors have suggested that this focus can only hold one item at a time. Reasoning that items should be retrieved more quickly when they are within than outside the focus of attention, they observed that this fast retrieval concerns only the last item in a list (Garavan 1998; McElree 1998, 2001). Oberauer's (2002) hierarchical model is based on this idea. Four would be the number of highly activated items easily retrievable in a region of direct access, only one of them being readily available for ongoing treatment in a one-chunk focus of attention. Cowan's and Oberauer's views could be reconciled if one considers, as Cowan et al. (2005) did, that the focus of attention could zoom in and zoom out according to the goal of the task at hand and individual abilities. Note that these various models all envision capacity as a structural limit determined by the fixed number of slots that some store contains. By contrast, the most popular phonological loop model adopts a functional view and conceives this limit as reflecting the number of items that a maintenance mechanism can preserve from forgetting (Baddeley et al. 1975). This idea can be extended to a variety of domains, leading to a multiple-capacities view of working memory (Baddeley 1986; Baddeley and Logie 1999; Wickens 1984).

Despite their divergences, the conceptions reviewed so far converge on the idea that working memory capacity, in the same way as short-term memory capacity, refers to the amount of information that some store or structure is able to hold. However, in conformity with the definition of working memory as a system devoted to the storage and processing of information, other theoretical approaches have defined working memory capacity as the complexity of the relations that can be processed in parallel (Halford et al. 1998). Interestingly, the maximum number of dimensions that can be integrated in these relations is also four. A further step in distinguishing between processing and storage capacities is to assume that working memory capacity consists of domain-specific storage capacities along with a domain-general processing efficiency, plus some capacity to coordinate the two functions (Bayliss et al. 2003). More generally, defining working memory capacity as the conjunction between storage capacity and processing efficiency is an idea shared by those theorists subscribing to the trade-off hypothesis described in Chapter 1 (Case 1985; Daneman and Carpenter 1980). As we already mentioned, this tradition is of importance for having designed the complex span tasks that are the most frequently used tools to measure working memory capacity. It is worth noting that processing efficiency is often equated with processing speed, as in Case's theory for example. Faster processes would in turn prevent memory traces for prolonged periods of decay and contribute to working memory capacity and cognitive performance, as in Salthouse's (1996) simultaneity mechanism hypothesis. Processing speed has consequently been considered as mental capacity (Kail and Salthouse 1994).

Finally, it has been suggested that working memory capacity could be viewed as the accessibility, through retrieval cues, of the content of long-term memory. These approaches, that deny the existence of a separate working memory, assume that the amount of information readily accessible for treatment is not limited by a fixed capacity, but depends on the efficiency of encoding and retrieval skills. Such a conception, famously illustrated by the long-term working memory model (Ericsson and Kintsch 1995), is largely adopted by the proponents of a unitary view of memory (McGeoch 1932; Nairne 2002). More will be said about this approach below.

A fixed capacity limit of the central system in the TBRS model?

Though the studies conducted within the TBRS framework and reported in this book did not explicitly aim at investigating the question of working memory capacity, many of them are relevant for this issue. Beginning by a presentation of findings that could shed some light on the problem of the size of the central working memory system (i.e., the focus of attention in Cowan's theory), we will discuss in the following section the implications of our results for a multi-capacities view of working memory and the possible role of processing efficiency on working memory capacity.

The TBRS model assumes a one-chunk focus of attention selecting a single working memory representation for the next cognitive operation among a limited number of representations held in an episodic buffer. This assumption of a one-item focus is a plausible theoretical stance compatible with the linearity of the functions relating processing to storage and storage to processing, even if we are aware that none of our studies brought definite evidence for this hypothesis (but see Garavan 1998 and McElree 1998). By contrast, the study by Vergauwe et al. (2014), in which participants were asked to maintain letters or spatial locations during a 12-sec. retention interval while performing intervening tasks, is certainly relevant to the question of the size of the episodic buffer as it investigated the effects of storage on processing (Chapter 5). Not reported previously are the estimates we made of working memory spans for each of the conditions studied. While doing a parity task, participants proved able to reliably maintain up to 3.95 letters under articulatory suppression but only 3.21 spatial locations, and 3.12 of these spatial locations when confronted with the spatial fit task. When discussing these results, we noted that these values were very close to the fixed capacity of the focus of attention suggested by Cowan (i.e., four), with some variations between domains. Though we attributed the advantage for the verbal material to supplementary involvement of long-term memory, as Cowan et al. (2012) proposed in their multi-factorial model, these results could also be considered as weakening the idea of a domain-general fixed capacity. Accordingly, these discrepancies and departures from the expected size value of four do not seem to be isolated or depending on our paradigm. For example, Cowan et al. (1999) reported a capacity limit for ignored lists between 3 and 3.5 in adults. Surprisingly, the mean number of verbal chunks recalled by adults, regardless of the position of recall, was not higher than 2.9 in Chen and Cowan (2009), and the capacity estimate (expressed in k value) dropped between 2 and 2.5 for colours in an array memory task (Cowan et al. 2010). At the same time, the mean span in Barrouillet et al. (2004a) under severe articulatory suppression was of 4.08 while taking order into account (see the rightmost value of the concurrent articulation condition in Figure 3.3).

It is important to remember that the capacity we are discussing here refers to a domain-general central system that is not exclusively dedicated to visual or verbal information (Baddeley 2000; Saults and Cowan 2007). Relevant for the question of the maintenance of chunks in a domain-general system is also the study by Langerock et al. (2014) in which we compared the maintenance of letters in spatial locations with the maintenance of the same letters or spatial locations in isolation. Not surprisingly, when considering that the tasks used did not involve any concurrent articulation, mean spans were higher for isolated letters than spatial locations (5.76 and 3.92 respectively). Note that the span for spatial information was very close to four. More interestingly, mean span for cross-domain information (i.e. letters in location) was lower than for locations alone (i.e., 2.79). This value dropped to 2.3 in a subsequent experiment.

At a first sight, variations in estimates of the central capacity could be taken as evidence against the idea of a fixed capacity limit. After all, reported values differ across tasks, domains and types of stimuli within a same domain, broadly varying from 2 to 4 in young adults. These variations seem more compatible with a model in which a common resource would be flexibly shared between memory items than with the view of a fixed number of slots, as has been advocated in visual working memory (for example, Bays et al. 2009; Bays and Husain 2008; Van den Berg et al. 2012). Within such a view, there would be no need for an upper limit in the number of objects that the central system can hold. However, the hypothesis of a central system containing a fixed limited amount of slots does not necessarily predict a constant level of recall at the maximum capacity. Indeed, suboptimal performance could result from decay and interference between stored representations. Although it is usually assumed that memory traces within the focus of attention are immune from degradation, decay and interference can occur within the rotating executive loop postulated by the TBRS model. Moreover, a process of chunk decomposition as suggested by Cowan et al. (2012) could operate, reducing the number of chunks recalled. This could account for the systematic drop in performance observed by Langerock et al. (2014) when presenting participants with cross-domain information. It is possible that the links binding letters to their location are especially fragile and easily corrupted and lost, reducing the amount of retrieved information. As a matter of fact, it remains that none of the estimates of central capacity exceeded four, in ours as in previous studies, lending support to Cowan's hypothesis.

Nonetheless, the difficult question of the origin of this magical number four remains. On the one hand, it might reflect a structural limit in the number of slots available in the central system of working memory. This hypothesis echoes the object-file model advocated in numerical cognition to account for the limitations in the exact representation of small quantities in adults, infants and even non-human primates (Simon 1997). This concept of object file has also been used to account for the binding of features of the same object into episodic traces (Kahneman, Triesman, and Gibbs 1992). On the other hand, the limit could emerge from the functional constraints imposed by the necessarily limited speed of the refreshing mechanism devoted to preventing working memory representations from their irremediable loss through decay and interference. Such an account is akin to the neurophysiological explanation of short-term memory limitation by Lisman and Idiart (1995) in which each item would be stored in gamma oscillation subcycles (about 40 Hz) within a theta neuron network oscillation (see Luck and Vogel 1998 for a similar account). It is clear that our results do not allow for disentangling the two options.

Beyond the central capacity: the limitations in working memory performance

Although the central storage system, conceived of as a focus of attention, a region of direct access or an episodic buffer, is a key determinant of working memory capacity, other systems and functions contribute to limit working memory performance. We have documented in Chapter 5 the independent contribution of an articulatory loop for the maintenance of verbal material, a system that appeared to be strongly limited in size, as we established in Vergauwe et al. (2014)[1]. When releasing the constraint of a concurrent articulation while maintaining letters during the completion of a parity judgement task, we observed that people were able to maintain and recall up to 4 letters without any impact on concurrent processing (see Figure 5.5). The fact that increasing the articulatory demand imposed by the memoranda (mono- and bi-syllabic words) progressively reduced this ability strongly suggests that the capacity of this peripheral verbal system does not depend on a number of slots but on the efficiency of the articulatory rehearsal system of maintenance, as proposed by the phonological loop model. Though we do not have any idea of the precise mechanism by which central and peripheral systems cooperate in their maintenance activities, Miller's magical number, based on immediate memory for letters and digits, is probably the product of their conjunct action. It is worth noting that, based on our own estimates, this conjunction operates with minimal waste. Indeed, the four letters that the articulatory loop can independently hold, added to the four chunks of the central system, fall within the interval set by Miller.

It could be argued that Miller's number seven corresponds to the capacity of short-term memory, whereas a measurement of the real capacity of working memory requires preventing the intervention of strategies like verbal rehearsal. However, when discussing the observed parameters of the processing-storage function and its intercept at 8.13 for a cognitive load of 0 (see Figure 3.6), Barrouillet et al. (2011a) suggested that short-term memory with its span of seven plus or minus two is nothing more than the working memory when it does not 'work', or when it works for maintenance purposes only. This was another way to say that considering working memory capacity as the size of the sole central mechanism of storage might constitute a restrictive approach to the question. After all, if working memory is that 'broad framework of interacting processes that involve the temporary storage and manipulation of information in the service of performing complex cognitive activities' (Baddeley et al. 2011, p. 1393), it could be pointless to focus on a single storage component in estimating its capacity. Accordingly, we have established that working memory spans vary with the cognitive load of the ongoing processes in such a way that it becomes difficult to consider that the spans obtained from some complex span task like the reading span or the operation span task correspond to 'the' working memory capacity of a given individual, whatever her age. Provided with some adequate fine tuning, young children appeared in Gaillard et al. (2011) to exhibit the same working memory capacity as older children. Thus, given the well-established trade-off between processing and storage, it could be argued that a more accurate measure of working memory capacity would require estimating both storage and processing capacities.

This is the criticism raised by Pascual-Leone (2001) when discussing Cowan's (2001) proposal for a magical number four. Pascual-Leone, in agreement with the constructivist neo-Piagetian approaches (Case and Okamoto 1996; Pascual-Leone 1970), noted that it is not sufficient when estimating working memory capacity to take into account the sole number of memory items. Indeed, some operative schemes are needed to account for their combination and integration in cognitive performance. Reintroducing operative aspects, Pascual-Leone reanalysed the paradigms mentioned by Cowan and found results consistent with Miller's number seven as an estimate of demand on working memory. In line with Pascual-Leone's theory, it should be noted that our own estimate of the central capacity (3.95 in Vergauwe et al. 2014) was obtained while participants were performing a concurrent parity judgement task. Applying Pascual-Leone's operative analysis would lead to adding to the four symbolic schemes corresponding to the maintained letters another symbolic scheme for representing the currently processed digit, and two operative schemes, one for retrieving its parity from long-term memory and another for selecting response, amounting to a total of seven schemes. Thus, when going back to the initial definition of working memory and focusing on the limitations of the information processing system rather than on some short-term buffer, as central as it may be, Miller's venerable estimate could keep all its interest and its significance.

Is there a short-term or a working memory?

At the beginning of this book, we emphasised the need in the information-processing approach for a working, or at least a short-term, memory able to maintain for some seconds relevant information in a state appropriate to its treatment. The optimism that could have arisen from the promising results that pioneers gathered in looking for such a memory (Broadbent 1958; Brown 1958; Miller 1956) was soon tempered by divergent results and reinterpretations and, about 60 years later, the question of the existence of a short-term or a working memory as a separate system from long-term memory has not yet been settled. The case for a single system, initially presented by Melton (1963), has never been abandoned, regularly attracting distinguished researchers (Brown *et al.* 2007; Brown and Lewandowsky 2010; Crowder 1982, 1993; Lewandowsky *et al.* 2004; Nairne 2002; Neath and Surprenant 2003). What is remarkable is the constancy of the arguments. Melton (1963) already argued against a separate short-term memory by discarding decay as a necessary ingredient of forgetting in the short term when interference offers a better account, and pointed out the influence of long-term memory phenomena on short-term performance such as the Hebb effect (Hebb 1961). Forty years later, Nairne (2002), in his case against what he called the 'standard model', evoked the problems encountered by the notions of rehearsal but also decay, and recalled that immediate recall is affected by long-term memory contributions producing effects related to the lexicality, concreteness or frequency of the words to be remembered.

What is the standard model that Nairne (2002) targeted? Simply the common idea that short-term storage arises from the activation of permanent knowledge that would come to reside 'in' short-term or working memory, becoming readily and immediately accessible for treatment. However, activation is assumed to be transient and rapidly lost through the process of decay. This process, which has adaptive value by removing the information that is no longer relevant, could be counteracted when needed by a process of rehearsal able to reactivate decayed memory traces. After having listed the difficulties encountered by the notions of rehearsal and decay, difficulties with which the reader is now familiar, Nairne addressed a probably more interesting point concerning the recovery of information from working memory. Rejecting Cowan's (1999) proposal that retrieval from activated memory and from long-term memory differ in important ways, as well as the idea that information in working memory is directly and effortlessly retrievable, he suggested the reconceptualisation of immediate retention as being essentially cue-driven, in the same way as long-term memory. The resulting unitary view of memory no longer considers that what sits in short-term memory are activated items immediately accessible and retrieved, but constellations of activated cues used to reconstruct what happened moments before. And Nairne (2002, p. 73) adds: 'These cues consist of remnants of prior processing records, for example records of just-presented list items that have become degraded through interference'. Short-term forgetting would occur because processing records are overwritten by subsequent material, the available cues becoming poor predictors of the target items. These ideas, or at least part of them, have shaped a number of models (for example, Brown *et al.* 2000; Nairne 1990; Oberauer and Kliegl 2006).

Of course, Baddeley (2007) was right in claiming that the standard model described by Nairne is an oversimplification that is not held by any theorist he has ever encountered but, when setting aside the details of the criticisms addressed to decay and rehearsal and taking a global view, Nairne's outline is not so caricatured. Several models of working memory indeed assume that its content is made of long-term memory items activated above threshold (Anderson 1993; Cowan 1988, 1999,

2005; Engle et al. 1999; Just and Carpenter 1992; Oberauer 2002, 2009b) or that rehearsal or refreshing mechanisms counteract decay, maintaining information in a highly accessible state (Baddeley 1986, 2007, 2012; Barrouillet et al. 2004a, 2011a; Cowan 1999). What makes, in our view, Nairne's case against the standard model disputable is less the fact that he reduces it to the phonological loop model, as Baddeley (2012) rightly notes, but rather that the proposed unitary view can hardly be taken as a genuine alternative to the standard model of working memory. We develop in the following section what looks, at a first glance, as a provocative statement.

We stressed above the striking continuity in arguments between Melton's (1963) defence of a unitary view of memory and modern expositions of this theoretical stance. However, Melton was explicit in admitting, and he insisted on this point, that his analyses only concerned storage and retrieval of verbal material in adults. The aim of this warning was probably to emphasise the limited scope concerning memory material and population, but it can also be extended to the processes under discussion. In keeping with Melton and his analyses and arguments, Nairne (2002) seems to be only concerned by storage and retrieval. However, from its very first inception (Miller et al. 1960) to its most recent descriptions (Baddeley 2012), working memory has been and is still considered as a system providing an interface between cognition and action rather than a mere store from which information can be retrieved. The unitary view put forward by Nairne assumes that what sits in short-term memory, and probably in working memory, are constellations of activated cues. However, these cues seem to be conceived of as pointers to long-term memory addresses rather than as mental states that could play a causal role in triggering action, which is what a working memory is for. A solution could be to suppose that this causal role is fulfilled not by the cues themselves, but by the information that is linked to these cues (recall that they would be 'used to reconstruct what happened moments before', Nairne 2002, p. 73). However, in this case, the content of short-term or working memory is not simply a collection of cues but the representations of the events that occurred moments before and that are retrieved (activated?) from long-term memory. As a consequence, the unitary view would not differ from the standard model.

Even more troublesome is Nairne's idea that these cues consist of remnants of prior processing records that have become degraded through interference. If the cues sit in short-term memory, and if they are remnants of processing records that have been degraded, this logically implies that these processing records were themselves in short-term memory before being degraded. In other words, we are back to the idea that short-term or working memory contains representations of the current internal and external state of affairs, representations that are degraded by some process the effects of which are more pronounced as time goes by. At this point, and considering the still uncertain outcome of the debate surrounding the existence of decay, the claim of a degradation through interference looks like a statement of belief that is no longer sufficient to demarcate the unitary view, as presented by Nairne, from the so-called standard model. Indeed, we are told that these cues are used to reconstruct the degraded processing records. In other words, what is described by Nairne is an interplay between processes of degradation and reconstruction of representations held in short-term memory, which is exactly what the unitary view was intended to avoid.

To be fair, apart from the rejection of any temporal decay, a difference can be drawn between Nairne's proposal and the standard model. It could be assumed that the records of processing stored and reconstructed in short-term memory are not simply long-term memory items activated above threshold, but transient mental models, as in the TBRS model, or multimodal representations as Baddeley's episodic buffer hypothesises. The TBRS model could even be seen as a synthesis between the standard model with its interplay between decay of activation and reactivation through rehearsal, and the cue-driven view of short-term memory in which remnants of previous processing records are used to reconstruct representations through a redintegration process. As Figure 8.2 illustrates, representations made of the assembly of contextual, sensory and semantic features may be degraded through decay and interference to the point where only some features are still available. If these remnants are recirculated into the executive loop before their complete loss, they can be used as retrieval cues to recruit elements from long-term memory that

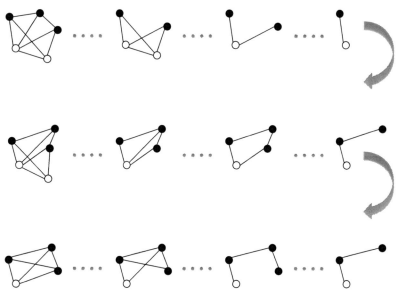

FIGURE 8.2 Cue-driven reconstruction within the TBRS model. Schematic illustration of a working memory representation as an assembly of contextual (empty circles) and object-inherent features (filled circles), and its progressive degradation up to the point at which only some features are remaining. These remnants are used as retrieval cues for reconstruction of the representation by the executive loop. This figure illustrates the fact that this reconstruction can recruit features that were not part of the initial representation, resulting in its possible modification (either degradation or enrichment). The figure shows two cycles of loss and reconstruction

constitute building blocks for a reconstruction. These cues, which are intrinsic to the items that were part of the representations but also contextual (i.e., positional, temporal, spatial), point to semantic but also episodic long-term memory. This process is at risk because the available cues, sometimes degraded or accidentally borrowed to another representation, may lead to both proactive and retroactive interference as well as distortion, or more simply be insufficient for a successful reconstruction, leading to forgetting in the short term.

This short discussion did not pretend to solve the intricate problem of the existence of a separate system of short-term memory and its potential interactions with long-term memory, but only to draw attention to the fact that it is not so easy to think about short-term retention without assuming any specifically dedicated system. The idea of a short-term memory containing simple cues for retrieving recently past events is appealing in its simplicity and parsimony as long as one remains within the boundaries of the serial recall exercise. However, further inquiry reveals the weaknesses inherent in this idea. If one wants to have mental states in which items of knowledge produce action, our intuition requires us to suppose that this knowledge is in some state that differs from its usual resting condition. In the standard model, that is what the concept of activation is for. Nairne's proposal is no exception to this rule, constellations of cues being 'activated' instead of items. The problem is that this idea could be a Trojan horse for the unitary view, because activation cannot be something else than a transient state. Of course, as McGeoch (1932) famously argued with his analogy with rust, time could not be ultimately responsible for the process by which the activated cues resume their resting state or disappear from short-term memory, but some process cleaning up short-term memory of no-longer-needed cues would be helpful, and decay of activation does not seem to be a bad solution. And what about the maintenance of these cues when needed for a prolonged period? Is not some mechanism necessary for avoiding their complete loss? It seems definitely difficult to envision ongoing cognition without some working memory distinct in its structure and functioning from long-term memory.

Note

1 It seems that the study by Vergauwe *et al.* (2014) provided the first estimate of the 'true' capacity of the phonological loop as the amount of verbal information that can be maintained without any detectable involvement of attention.

EPILOGUE

Searching for working memory

Forty years ago, Baddeley and Hitch (1974) asked whether the short-term storage buffer of the modal model was a good candidate for the role of the working memory needed by the information processing approach. We have seen that they concluded from their inquiry that this was not the case. Short-term memory did not seem to be a memory at work, at least if it was conceived of as a mental space shared between processing and storage. Paradoxically, this negative answer did not lead to a further quest for a more appropriate structure or mechanism. The processing component of working memory was relegated to some unfathomable and largely unexplored separate structure, the central executive, and the bulk of research was devoted to understanding the nature and functioning of the slave systems. In these investigations, researchers showed some predilection for the phonological buffer compared with its visuospatial counterpart, and the immediate serial recall paradigm. There is no doubt that considerable progress has been made on this domain, with the discovery of enlightening effects (of irrelevant speech, word length, phonological similarity or concurrent articulation), and the elaboration of heuristic hypotheses and models to account for them. The development of experimental methods such as the selective interference paradigm established the separability of these buffers and the new techniques of brain imagery allowed the identification of their neural correlates. Computational models helped in refining the predictions of concurrent models and detailing the mechanisms involved.

However, despite these advances, working memory is still like a receding and never-reached horizon. Having established that the system underpinning short-term memory span is not the working memory that cognitivism needed seems to have paradoxically resulted in a redoubling of efforts in the direction that should have been logically set aside, and working memory research has concentrated its efforts in understanding short-term memory as if the initial goal of describing the system in charge of the maintenance and on-line processing of information had been lost on the way. Interestingly, it seems that cognitive psychologists remain aware of having neglected a crucial aspect of the question. We have already quoted Conway and colleagues (2005) who noted that working memory would be unlikely to have evolved for the sole purpose of allowing an organism to store information for some seconds. As a matter of fact, it seems rather difficult to find an example of a significant human activity that would rely on the capacity to store items for the sole purpose of short-term storage without any planned treatment. Any professor of psychology has probably experienced this difficulty when trying to illustrate short-term memory. Of course, every psychology student knows the answer to the question 'what is short-term memory for?' Short-term memory is for remembering phone numbers for the short while between reading and dialing them. The fact that this example often stands alone in our lectures and that it seems difficult to find another one should challenge us, as some ironic and malicious dunce could retort 'and what was short-term memory for before Bell's invention?' Are we not investing time and efforts to understand the underpinnings of a task (i.e., immediate serial recall) that could turn out to have little to say about human cognition? It would not be the first time in cognitive psychology that a task becomes so popular and produces such intriguing phenomena that its study turns into an autonomous domain of research with few connections with relevant cognitive functions. In psychology of reasoning, Wason's selection task seems to be a good example of this evolution. The well-known enigma of the four cards (Wason 1966), initially intended to investigate people's capacity to understand and test conditional rules, rapidly became a domain of the psychology of reasoning on its own. It attracted so many empirical investigations and theoretical proposals during decades that, among the nine chapters of Evans *et al.*'s (1993) review on human reasoning, one chapter was exclusively devoted to this task. It turned out at the end, after fierce debates and controversies, that Wason's selection task does not greatly advance our understanding of conditional reasoning. It was even argued that it does not reveal anything profound about reasoning and does not provide evidence for or against different theories of human reasoning, the puzzling results it has brought to light being largely artefactual (Sperber *et al.* 1995). The astonishing enthusiasm in the last decade for the change detection task in the study of visual working memory might foretell a similar fate. There is no doubt that this paradigm has allowed a precise measure of the number of colour and shape features that can be simultaneously grasped in visual short-term memory, and revealed striking phenomena such as the sudden death of visual memory traces (for example, Zhang and Luck 2009). However, its relevance for understanding human high-level cognition could also be questioned, because it can be wondered if a working memory, the 'hub of human cognition' according to Haberlandt (1997), has evolved to detect colour changes occurring less than one second after a visual display has been flashed for 100ms.

This does not mean that the study of short-term maintenance in isolation to any processing activity has nothing to say about human memory, but it remains possible that it is not the best way to understand the mechanisms by which humans are able to preserve, from a continuous flow of information, some items in a state appropriate to their on-line treatment and, more importantly, how this temporary storage affects ongoing processing, and how this processing, in turn, impacts on the maintenance and accessibility of this information. Thus, we think that studying working memory, its structure, functioning and limitations, requires experimental paradigms that mimic the interplay between processing and storage, which distinguishes it from any other memory system. However, what the studies reviewed in this book revealed is that time is one of the main constraints weighting on this interplay. One cannot think of two things at the same time. Such a limitation, that Pascal considered as lucky for us, probably results from the fact that to think of something is nothing more than to build a representation of what we are thinking about, and our cognitive system does not seem to have the capacity to build more than one representation at a time. It is surprising that human beings, who are characterised within the animal kingdom as having selected intelligence as their main mode of adaptation to their environment, are not endowed with a more powerful system for high-level cognition than a strongly limited working memory. As Turing wrote, 'If we are trying to produce an intelligent machine, and are following the human model as closely as we can, we should begin with a machine with very little capacity to carry out elaborate operations or to react in a disciplined manner to orders' (Turing 1948 [1992], p. 118). This very little capacity is well illustrated by the small amount of information that can be kept in a state appropriate for its treatment, as Miller (1956) and Cowan (2001) demonstrated. However, we saw in this book that an at least as hurtful limitation concerns our incapacity to maintain even a few items in mind while performing the simplest activities, provided that they are performed under time constraints. Complex and sophisticated cogitations are not needed to fully occupy our mind. Repeating at a sufficiently fast pace the retrieval from long-term memory of the more deeply rooted knowledge is sufficient. It does not come as a surprise that catching a hare or following a ball constitute infallible remedies against intrusive thoughts. Stop paying attention to the ball, if only one moment, and you will miss it. Reading series of digits would have the same curative power if one could be as passionate about reading lists of digits as we are by playing with a ball.

The paradox of cognition is that this limited working memory led human beings to incredible achievements such as landing a man on the moon. However, this seems to be a paradox only if we conceive cognitive resources as a finite pool of energy shared in parallel among the several processes that human mental activities require. Things are different if time is taken into account. Complex processes can be seen as the rapid concatenation of elementary cognitive steps, the level of complexity of which is commensurate with the small amount of information that can be held simultaneously in mind. Reintroducing the temporal dynamic makes it possible to understand how a very simple device is able to produce complex results. It is even possible that restricting the amount of information simultaneously processed is the most efficient way to reach a maximum of cognitive complexity at the minimal cost for the biological system. The fact that performing at a fast pace very simple tasks such as reading digits has such dramatic effects on concurrent cognition suggests that these temporal constraints affect the keystone on which the equilibrium of the central cognitive system is based. What we have tried to do in this book is to provide evidence that this equilibrium results from the balance between loss and reconstruction of representations within working memory.

REFERENCES

Ackerman, P. L., Beier, M. E. and Boyle, M. O. (2002) 'Individual differences in working memory within a nomological network of cognitive and perceptual speed abilities'. *Journal of Experimental Psychology: General*, 131, pp. 567–589

Allen, R. J., Baddeley, A. D. and Hitch, G. J. (2006) 'Is the binding of visual features in working memory resource-demanding?' *Journal of Experimental Psychology: General*, 135, pp. 298–313

Allen, R. J., Hitch, G. J. and Baddeley, A. D. (2009) 'Cross-modal binding and working memory'. *Visual Cognition*, 17, pp. 83–102

Allport, A., Styles, E. A. and Hsieh S. (1994) 'Shifting intentional set: exploring the dynamic control of tasks' in C. Umiltà and M. Moscovitch (Eds) *Attention and Performance* (Vol. 15, pp. 421–452). Cambridge, MA: MIT Press

Altmann, E. M. and Schunn, C. D. (2012) 'Decay versus interference: a new look at an old interaction'. *Psychological Science*, 23, pp. 1435–1437

Anderson, J. R. (1983) *The Architecture of Cognition*. Cambridge, MA: Harvard University Press

Anderson, J. R. (1993) *Rules of the Mind*. Hillsdale, NJ: Lawrence Erlbaum Associates

Anderson, J. R. (2007) *How can the Human Mind Occur in the Physical Universe?* New York, NY: Oxford University Press

Anderson, J. R., Bothell, D., Byrne, M. D., Douglass, S., Lebiere, C. and Qin, Y. (2004) 'An integrated theory of mind'. *Psychological Review*, 111, pp. 1036–1060

Anderson, J. R., Bothell, D., Lebière, C. and Matessa, M. (1998) 'An integrated theory of list memory'. *Journal of Memory and Language*, 38, pp. 341–380

Anderson, J. R. and Lebière, C. (1998) *The Atomic Components of Thought*. Mawhaw, NJ: Lawrence Erlbaum Associates

Anderson, J. R., Reder, L. M. and Lebière, C. (1996) 'Working memory: activation limitations on retrieval'. *Cognitive Psychology*, 30, pp. 221–256

Anderson, P. (2002) 'Assessment and development of executive function (EF) during childhood'. *Child Neuropsychology*, 8, pp. 71–82

Andrade, J. and Donaldson, L. (2007) 'Evidence for an olfactory store in working memory?' *Psychologia*, 50, pp. 76–89

Andrews, G. and Halford, G. S. (2011) 'Recent advances in relational complexity theory and its application to cognitive development' in P. Barrouillet and V. Gaillard (Eds) *Cognitive Development and Working Memory* (pp. 47–68). Hove: Psychology Press

Ardila, A. (2008) 'On the evolutionary origins of executive functions'. *Brain and Cognition*, 68, pp. 92–99

Ashcraft, M. H. (2002) 'Math anxiety: personal, educational, and cognitive consequences'. *Current Directions in Psychological Sciences*, 11, pp. 181–185

Ashcraft, M. H. and Battaglia, J. (1978) 'Cognitive arithmetic: evidence for retrieval and decision processes in mental addition'. *Journal of Experimental Psychology: Human Learning and Memory*, 4, pp. 527–538

Atkinson, R. C. and Shiffrin, R. M. (1965) *Mathematical Models for Memory and Learning*. Technical report N° 79, Institute for Mathematical Studies in the Social Sciences, Stanford University

Atkinson, R. C. and Shiffrin, R. M. (1968) 'Human memory: a proposed system and its control processes' in K. W. Spence and J. T. Spence (Eds) *The Psychology of Learning and Motivation: Advances in Research and Theory* (Vol. 2, pp. 89–195). New York: Academic Press

Atkinson, R. C. and Shiffrin, R. M. (1971) 'The control of short-term memory'. *Scientific American*, 225, pp. 82–90

Baddeley, A. D. (1966) 'Short-term memory for word sequences as a function of acoustic, semantic, and formal similarity'. *Quarterly Journal of Experimental Psychology*, 18, pp. 362–366

Baddeley, A. D. (1986) *Working Memory*. Oxford: Clarendon Press

Baddeley, A. D. (1996) 'Exploring the central executive'. *Quarterly Journal of Experimental Psychology*, 49, pp. 5–28

Baddeley, A. D. (1997) *Human Memory: Theory and Practice*. Hove: Psychology Press

Baddeley, A. D. (2000) 'The episodic buffer: a new component of working memory?' *Trends in Cognitive Sciences*, 4, pp. 417–423

Baddeley, A. D. (2003) 'Working memory: looking back and looking forward'. *Nature Reviews Neuroscience*, 4, pp. 829–839

Baddeley, A. D. (2007) *Working Memory, Thought, and Action*. Oxford: Oxford University Press

Baddeley, A. D. (2012) 'Working memory: theories, models, and controversies'. *Annual Review of Psychology*, 63, pp. 1–29

Baddeley, A. D., Allen, R. J. and Hitch, G. J. (2010) 'Investigating the episodic buffer'. *Psychologica Belgica*, 50, pp. 223–243

Baddeley, A. D., Allen, R. J. and Hitch, G. J. (2011) 'Binding in visual working memory: the role of the episodic buffer'. *Neuropsychologia*, 49, pp. 1393–1400

Baddeley, A. D., Grant, S., Wight, E. and Thomson, N. (1973) 'Imagery and visual working memory' in P. M. Rabbit and S. Dornic (Eds) *Attention and Performance* (Vol. V, pp. 205–217). London: Academic Press

Baddeley, A. D. and Hitch, G. J. (1974) 'Working memory' in G. A. Bower (Ed.) *The Psychology of Learning and Motivation* (Vol. 8, pp. 647–667). New York: Academic Press

Baddeley, A. D. and Hitch, G. J. (1977) 'Recency re-examined' in S. Dornic (Ed.) *Attention and Performance VI* (pp. 647–671). Hillsdale, NJ: Erlbaum

Baddeley, A.D. and Larsen, J.D. (2007) 'The phonological loop unmasked? A comment on the evidence for a "perceptual-gestural" alternative'. *Quarterly Journal of Experimental Psychology*, 60, pp. 497–504

Baddeley, A. D., Lewis, V., Eldridge, M. and Thomson, N. (1984a) 'Attention and retrieval from long-term memory'. *Journal of Experimental Psychology: General*, 113, pp. 518–540

Baddeley, A. D., Lewis, V. and Vallar, G. (1984b) 'Exploring the articulatory loop'. *Quarterly Journal of Experimental Psychology*, 36, pp. 233–252

Baddeley, A. D. and Lieberman, K. (1980) 'Spatial working memory' in R. Nickerson (Ed.) *Attention and Performance VIII* (pp. (521–539). Hillsdale, NJ: Erlbaum

Baddeley, A. D. and Logie, R. H. (1999) 'Working memory: the multiple-component model' in A. Miyake and P. Shah (Eds) *Models of Working Memory: Mechanisms of Active Maintenance and Executive Control* (pp. 28–61). Cambridge: Cambridge University Press

Baddeley, A. D., Logie, R., Nimmo-Smith, I. and Brereton, N. (1985) 'Components of fluent reading'. *Journal of Memory and Language*, 24, pp. 119–131

Baddeley, A. D. and Scott, D. (1971) 'Short-term forgetting in the absence of proactive interference'. *Quarterly Journal of Experimental Psychology*, 23, pp. 275–283

Baddeley, A. D., Thomson, N. and Buchanan, M. (1975) 'Word length and the structure of short-term memory'. *Journal of Verbal Learning and Verbal Behavior*, 14, pp. 575–589

Baddeley, A. D. and Wilson, B. (1985) 'Phonological coding and short-term memory in patients without speech'. *Journal of Memory and Language*, 24, pp. 490–502

Badre, D. (2012) 'Opening the gate to working memory'. *Proceedings of the National Academy of Sciences*, USA, 109, pp. 19878–19879

Barrouillet, P. (1996) 'Transitive inferences from set-inclusion relations and working memory'. *Journal of Experimental Psychology: Learning, Memory, and Cognition*, 22, pp. 1408–1422

Barrouillet, P., Bernardin, S. and Camos, V. (2004a) 'Time constraints and resource-sharing in adults' working memory spans'. *Journal of Experimental Psychology: General*, 133, pp. 83–100

Barrouillet, P., Bernardin, S., Portrat, S., Vergauwe, E. and Camos, V. (2007) 'Time and cognitive load in working memory'. *Journal of Experimental Psychology: Learning, Memory and Cognition*, 33(3), pp. 570–585

Barrouillet, P. and Camos, V. (2001) 'Developmental increase in working memory span: resource sharing or temporal decay?' *Journal of Memory and Language*, 45, pp. 1–20

Barrouillet, P. and Camos, V. (2009) 'Interference: unique source of forgetting in working memory?' *Trends in Cognitive Sciences*, 13, pp. 145–146

Barrouillet, P. and Camos, V. (2010) 'Working memory and executive function: the TBRS approach'. *Psychological Belgica*, 50, pp. 353–382

Barrouillet, P. and Camos, V. (2012) 'As time goes by: temporal constraints in working memory'. *Current Directions in Psychological Science*, 21, pp. 413–419

Barrouillet, P., Camos, V., Morlaix, S. and Suchaut, B. (2008a) 'Compétences scolaires, capacités cognitives et origine sociale: quels liens à l'école élémentaire?' *Revue Française de Pédagogie*, 162, pp. 5–14

Barrouillet, P., Camos, V., Perruchet, P. and Seron, X. (2004b) 'A Developmental Asemantic Procedural Transcoding (ADAPT) model: from verbal to Arabic numerals'. *Psychological Review*, 111, pp. 368–394

Barrouillet, P., De Paepe, A. and Langerock, N. (2012) 'Time causes forgetting from working memory'. *Psychonomic Bulletin and Review*, 19, pp. 87–92

Barrouillet, P. and Gaillard, V. (2011) 'Introduction: from neo-Piagetian theories to working memory development studies' in P. Barrouillet and V. Gaillard (Eds) *Cognitive Development and Working Memory* (pp. 1–10). Hove: Psychology Press

Barrouillet, P., Gavens, N., Vergauwe, E., Gaillard, V. and Camos, V. (2009) 'Working memory span development: a Time-Based Resource-Sharing account'. *Developmental Psychology*, 45, pp. 477–490

Barrouillet, P., Lépine, R. and Camos, V. (2008) 'Is the influence of working memory capacity on high level cognition mediated by complexity or resource-dependent elementary processes?' *Psychonomic Bulletin and Review*, 15, pp. 528–534

Barrouillet, P., Plancher, G., Guida, A. and Camos, V. (2013) 'Forgetting at short term: when do event-based interference and temporal factors have an effect?' *Acta Psychologica*, 142, pp. 155–167

Barrouillet, P., Portrat, S. and Camos, V. (2011a) 'On the law relating processing and storage in working memory'. *Psychological Review*, 118, pp. 175–192

Barrouillet, P., Portrat, S., Vergauwe, E., Diependaele, K. and Camos, V. (2011b) Further evidence for temporal decay in working memory. *Journal of Experimental Psychology: Learning, Memory, and Cognition*, 37, pp. 1302–1317

Bayliss, D. M., Jarrold, C., Gunn, D. M. and Baddeley, A. D. (2003) 'The complexities of complex span: explaining individual differences in working memory in children and adults'. *Journal of Experimental Psychology: General*, 132, pp. 71–92

Bayliss, D. M., Jarrold, C., Baddeley, A. D., Gunn, D. M. and Leigh, E. (2005) 'Mapping the developmental constraints on working memory span performance'. *Developmental Psychology*, 41, pp. 579–597

Bays, P. M. and Husain, M. (2008) 'Dynamic shifts of limited working memory resources in human vision'. *Science*, 321, pp. 851–854

Bays, P. M., Catalao, R. F. G. and Husain, M. (2009) 'The precision of visual working memory is set by allocation of a shared resource'. *Journal of Vision*, 9(10):7, doi:10.1167/9.10.7

Beaman, C. P. (2004) 'The irrelevant sound phenomenon revisited: what role for working memory capacity?' *Journal of Experimental Psychology: Learning, Memory and Cognition*, 30, pp. 1106–1118

Berman, M., Jonides, J. and Lewis, R. L. (2009) 'In search of decay in verbal short-term memory'. *Journal of Experiment Psychology: Learning, Memory, and Cognition*, 35, pp. 317–333

Bertrand, R. and Camos, V. (submitted) 'Could developmental change in forgetting rate account for working memory in early childhood'. Unpublished manuscript

Berz, W. L. (1995) 'Working memory in music: a theoretical model'. *Music Perception*, 12, pp. 353–364

Binet, A. and Simon, T. (1905) Méthodes nouvelles pour le diagnostic du niveau intellectuel des anormaux. *L'Année Psychologique*, 11, pp. 191–244

Bjork, R. A. and Whitten, W. B. (1974) 'Recency-sensitive retrieval processes in long-term free recall'. *Cognitive Psychology*, 6, pp. 173–189

Bjorklund, D. F., Dukes, C. and Douglas Brown, R. (2009) 'The development of memory strategies' in M. L. Courage and N. Cowan (Eds) *The Development of Memory in Infancy and Childhood* (pp. 145–175). Hove: Psychology Press

Bjorklund, D. F. and Harnishfeger, K. K. (1990) 'The resources construct in cognitive development: diverse sources of evidence and a theory of inefficient inhibition'. *Developmental Review*, 10, pp. 48–71

Borst, J. P., Taatgen, N. A. and van Rijn, H. (2010) 'The problem state: a cognitive bottleneck in multitasking'. *Journal of Experimental Psychology: Learning, Memory, and Cognition*, 36, pp. 363–382

Brass, M., Derrfuss, J., Forstmann, B. and von Cramon, D. Y. (2005) 'The role of the inferior frontal junction area in cognitive control'. *Trends in Cognitive Sciences*, 9, pp. 314–316

Brass, M. and von Cramon, D. Y. (2004) 'Selection for cognitive control: an fMRI study on the selection of task relevant information'. *Journal of Neuroscience*, 24, pp. 8847–8852

Brass, M., Ullsperger, M., Knoesche, T. R., von Cramon, D. Y. and Phillips, N. A. (2005) 'Who comes first? The role of the prefrontal and parietal cortex in cognitive control'. *Journal of Cognitive Neuroscience*, 17, pp. 1367–1375

Braver, T. S. and Cohen, J. D. (2000) 'On the control of control: the role of dopamine in regulating prefrontal function and working memory' in S. Monsell and J. Driver (Eds) *Attention and Performance XVIII; Control of Cognitive Processes* (pp. 713–737). Cambridge, MA: MIT Press

Broadbent, D. E. (1958) *Perception and Communication*. London: Pergamon Press
Broadway, J. M. and Engle, R. W. (2010) 'Validating running memory span: measurement of working memory capacity and links with fluid intelligence'. *Behavior Research Methods*, 42, pp. 563–570
Brooks, L. R. (1968) 'Spatial and verbal components in the act of recall'. *Canadian Journal of Psychology*, 22, pp. 349–368
Brown, G. D. A. and Lewandowsky, S. (2010) 'Forgetting in memory models: arguments against trace decay and consolidation failure' in S. Della Sala (Ed.) *Forgetting* (pp. 49–75). Hove, UK: Psychology Press
Brown, G. D. A., Neath, I. and Chater, N. (2007) 'A temporal ratio model of memory'. *Psychological Review*, 114, pp. 539–576
Brown, G. D. A., Preece, T. and Hulme, C. (2000) 'Oscillator-based memory for serial order'. *Psychological Review*, 107, pp. 127–181
Brown, J. (1958) 'Some tests of the decay theory of immediate memory'. *Quarterly Journal of Experimental Psychology*, 10, pp. 12–21
Buchsbaum, B. R. and D'Esposito, M. (2008) 'The search for the phonological store: from loop to convolution'. *Journal of Cognitive Neuroscience*, 20, pp. 762–768
Buckner, R. L., Andrews-Hanna, J. R. and Schacter, D. L. (2008) 'The brain's default network: anatomy, function, and relevance to disease'. *Annals of the New York Academy of Science*, 1124, pp. 1–38
Bunting, M. F. (2006) 'Proactive interference and item similarity in working memory'. *Journal of Experimental Psychology: Learning, Memory, and Cognition*, 32, pp. 183–196
Burgess, G. C., Gray, J. R., Conway, A. R. A. and Braver, T. S. (2011) 'Neural mechanisms of interference control underlie the relationship between fluid intelligence and working memory span'. *Journal of Experimental Psychology: General*, 140, pp. 674–692
Burgess, N. and Hitch, G. J. (1999) 'Memory for serial order: a network model of the phonological loop and its timing'. *Psychological Review*, 106, pp. 551–581
Camos, V. and Barrouillet, P. (2011) 'Factors of working memory development: the time-based resource-sharing model approach' in P. Barrouillet and V. Gaillard (Eds) *Cognitive Development and Working Memory* (pp. 151–176). Hove: Psychology Press
Camos, V., Barrouillet, P. and Fayol, M. (2001) 'Does the coordination of verbal and motor information explain the development of counting in children?' *Journal of Experimental Child Psychology*, 78, pp. 240–262
Camos, V., Fayol, M. and Barrouillet, P. (1999) 'Counting in children: double task or procedure?' *L'Année Psychologique*, 99, pp. 623–645
Camos, V., Lagner, P. and Barrouillet, P. (2009) 'Two maintenance mechanisms of verbal information in working memory'. *Journal of Memory and Language*, 61, pp. 457–469
Camos, V., Lagner, P., Corbin, L. and Loaiza, V. (2014) 'Time pressure increases predictivity in working memory span task'. Unpublished manuscript
Camos, V., Mora, G. and Barrouillet, P. (2013) 'Phonological similarity effect in complex span task'. *Quarterly Journal of Experimental Psychology*, 66, pp. 1927–1950
Camos, V., Mora, G. and Oberauer, K. (2011) 'Adaptive choice between articulatory rehearsal and attentional refreshing in verbal working memory'. *Memory and Cognition*, 39, pp. 231–244
Camos, V. and Portrat, S. (submitted) 'The impact of cognitive load on delayed recall'.
Cantor, J. and Engle, R. W. (1993) 'Working-memory capacity as long-term memory activation: an individual-differences approach'. *Journal of Experimental Psychology: Learning, Memory and Cognition*, 5, pp. 1101–1114
Case, R. (1978) 'Intellectual development from birth to adulthood: a neo-Piagetian investigation' in R. S. Siegler (Ed.) *Children Thinking: What Develops?* (pp. 109–150). Hillsdale, NJ: Lawrence Erlbaum Associates

Case, R. (1985) *Intellectual Development: Birth to Adulthood*. New York: Academic Press
Case, R. (1992) *The Mind's Staircase: Exploring the Conceptual Underpinnings of Children's Thought and Knowledge*. Hillsdale, NJ: Lawrence Erlbaum Associates
Case, R., Kurland, M. and Goldberg, J. (1982) 'Operational efficiency and the growth of short-term memory'. *Journal of Experimental Child Psychology*, 33, pp. 386–404
Case, R. and Okamoto, Y. (1996) 'The role of central conceptual structures in the development of children's thought'. *Monographs of the Society for Research in Child Development*, Vol. 61, No. 245
Chein, J. M., Moore, A. B. and Conway, A. R. A. (2011) 'Domain-general mechanisms of complex working memory span'. *NeuroImage*, 54, pp. 550–559
Chen, Z. and Cowan, N. (2009) 'How verbal memory loads consume attention'. *Memory and Cognition*, 37, pp. 829–836
Chevalier, N. and Blaye, A. (2008) 'Cognitive flexibility in preschoolers: the role of representation activation and maintenance'. *Developmental Science*, 11, pp. 339–353
Chi, M. T. H. (1977) 'Age differences in memory span'. *Journal of Experimental Child Psychology*, 23, pp. 266–281
Chi, M. T. H. (1978) 'Knowledge structures and memory development' in R. S. Siegler (Ed.) *Children's Thinking: What Develops?* (pp. 73–96). Hillsdale, NJ: Lawrence Erlbaum Associates
Clément, S., Demany, L. and Semal, C. (1999) 'Memory for pitch versus memory for loudness'. *The Journal of the Acoustical Society of America*, 106, pp. 2805–2811
Cocchini, G., Logie, R. H., Della Sala, S., MacPherson, S. E. and Baddeley, A. D. (2002) 'Concurrent performance of two memory tasks: evidence for domain-specific working memory systems'. *Memory and Cognition*, 30, pp. 1086–1095
Colom, R., Rebollo, I., Abad, F.J. and Shih, P. C. (2006) 'Complex span tasks, simple span tasks, and cognitive abilities: a reanalysis of key studies'. *Memory and Cognition*, 34, pp. 158–171
Coltheart, V. (1972) 'The effects of acoustic and semantic similarity on concept identification'. *Quarterly Journal of Experimental Psychology*, 24, pp. 55–65
Coltheart, V. (1999) 'Comparing short-term memory and memory for rapidly presented visual stimuli'. *International Journal of Psychology*, 34(5), pp. 293–300
Conlin, J. A., Gathercole, S. E. and Adams, J. W. (2005) 'Stimulus similarity decrements in children's working memory span'. *Quarterly Journal of Experimental Psychology: Human Experimental Psychology*, 58, pp. 1434–1446
Conrad, R. (1964) 'Acoustic confusions in immediate memory'. *British Journal of Psychology*, 55(1), pp. 75–94
Conrad, R. and Hull, A. J. (1964) 'Information, acoustic confusion, and memory span'. *British Journal of Psychology*, 55, pp. 429–432
Conway, A. R. A., Jarrold, C. J., Kane, M. J., Miyake, A. and Towse, J. N. (2007) *Variation in Working Memory*. Oxford: Oxford University Press
Conway, A. R. A., Cowan, N., Bunting, M. F., Therriault, D. and Minkoff, S. (2002) 'A latent variable analysis of working memory capacity, short term memory capacity, processing speed, and general fluid intelligence'. *Intelligence*, 30, pp. 163–183
Conway, A. R. A., Kane, M. J., Bunting, M. F., Hambrick, D. Z., Wilhem, O. and Engle, R.W. (2005) 'Working memory span tasks: a methodological review and user's guide'. *Psychonomic Bulletin and Review*, 12, pp. 769–786
Costa A., Strijkers, K., Martin C. and Thierry G. (2009) 'The time-course of word retrieval revealed by event-related brain potentials during overt speech'. *Proceedings of the National Academy of Science*, 106, 21442–21446
Cowan, N. (1988) 'Evolving conceptions of memory storage, selective attention, and their natural constraints within the human information processing system'. *Psychological Bulletin*, 104, pp. 163–191

Cowan, N. (1992) 'Verbal memory span and the timing of spoken recall'. *Journal of Memory and Language*, 31, pp. 668–684

Cowan, N. (1995) *Attention and Memory: An Integrated Framework*. New York: Oxford University Press

Cowan, N. (1999) 'An embedded-process model of working memory' in A. Miyake and P. Shah (Eds) *Models of Working Memory: Mechanisms of Active Maintenance and Executive Control* (pp. 62–101). Cambridge: Cambridge University Press

Cowan, N. (2001) 'The magical number 4 in short-term memory: a reconsideration of mental storage capacity'. *Behavioral and Brain Sciences*, 24, pp. 87–185

Cowan, N. (2005) *Working Memory Capacity*. Hove, East Sussex, UK: Psychology Press

Cowan, N. (2008) 'What are the differences between long-term, short-term, and working memory?' in W.S. Sossin, J.-C. Lacaille, V.F. Castellucci and S. Belleville (Eds) *Progress in Brain Research: Vol. 169. Essence of Memory* (pp. 323–338). Amsterdam: Elsevier B.V.

Cowan, N. and Alloway, T. (2009) 'Development of working memory in childhood' in M. L. Courage and N. Cowan (Eds) *The Development of Memory in Infancy and Childhood* (pp. 303–342). Hove: Psychology Press

Cowan, N. and AuBuchon, A. M. (2008) 'Short-term memory loss over time without retroactive stimulus interference'. *Psychonomic Bulletin and Review*, 15, pp. 230–235

Cowan, N., Day, L., Saults, J. S., Keller, T. A., Johnson, T. and Flores, L. (1992) 'The role of verbal output time in the effects of word length on immediate memory'. *Journal of Memory and Language*, 31, pp. 1–17

Cowan, N., Elliott, E. M., Saults, J. S., Morey, C. C., Mattox, S., Hismjatullina, A. and Conway, A. R. A. (2005) 'On the capacity of attention: its estimation and its role in working memory and cognitive aptitudes'. *Cognitive Psychology*, 51, pp. 42–100

Cowan, N., Keller, T.A., Hulme, C., Roodenrys, S., McDougall, S. and Rack, J. (1994) 'Verbal memory span in children: speech timing clues to the mechanisms underlying age and word length effects'. *Journal of Memory and Language*, 33, pp. 234–250

Cowan, N., Morey, C. C., AuBuchon, A. M., Zwilling, C. E. and Gilchrist, A. L. (2010) 'Seven-year-olds allocate attention like adults unless working memory is overloaded'. *Developmental Science*, 13, pp. 120–133

Cowan, N., Nugent, L. D., Elliott, E. M., Ponomarev, I. and Saults, J. S. (1999) 'The role of attention in the development of short-term memory: age differences in the verbal span of apprehension'. *Child Development*, 70, pp. 1082–1097

Cowan, N., Nugent, L. D., Elliott, E. M. and Saults, J. S. (2000) 'Persistence of memory for ignored lists of digits: areas of developmental constancy and change'. *Journal of Experimental Child Psychology*, 76, pp. 151–172

Cowan, N., Rouder, J. N., Blume, C. L. and Saults, J. S. (2012) 'Models of verbal working memory capacity: what does it take to make them work?' *Psychological Review*, 119, pp. 480–499

Cowan, N., Saults, J. S. and Elliott, E. M. (2002) 'The search for what is fundamental in the development of working memory'. *Advances in Child Development and Behavior*, 29, pp. 1–49

Cowan, N., Saults, J. S. and Nugent, L. D. (1997) 'The role of absolute and relative amounts of time in forgetting within immediate memory: the case of tone-pitch comparisons'. *Psychonomic Bulletin and Review*, 4, pp. 393–397

Cowan, N., Wood, N. L., Wood, P.K., Keller, T. A. Nugent, L. D. and Keller, C. V. (1998) 'Two separate verbal processing rates contributing to short-term memory span'. *Journal of Experimental Psychology: General*, 127, pp. 141–160

Craik, F. I. M. and Lockhart, R. S. (1972) 'Levels of processing: a framework for memory research'. *Journal of Verbal Learning and Verbal Behavior*, 11(6), pp. 671–684

Craik, F. I. M. and Watkins, M. J. (1973) 'The role of rehearsal in short-term memory'. *Journal of Verbal Learning and Verbal Behavior*, 12(6), pp. 599–607

Crowder, R. G. (1982) 'The demise of short-term memory'. *Acta Psychologica*, 50, pp. 291–323

Crowder, R. G. (1993) 'Short-term memory: where do we stand?' *Memory and Cognition*, 21, pp. 142–145

D'Esposito, M., Detre, J. A., Alsop, D. C., Shin, R. K., Atlas, S. and Grossman, M. (1995) 'The neural basis of the central executive system of working memory'. *Nature*, 378, pp. 279–281

Daneman, M. and Carpenter, P. A. (1980) 'Individual differences in working memory and reading'. *Journal of Verbal Learning and Verbal Behavior*, 19, pp. 450–466

Daneman, M. and Tardif, T. (1987) 'Working memory and reading skill reexamined' in M. Coltheart (Ed.) *Attention and Performance* (pp. 491–508). Hillsdale, NJ: Erlbaum

Dang, C. P., Braeken, J., Ferrer, E. and Liu, C. (2012) 'Unitary or non-unitary nature of working memory? Evidence from its relation to general fluid and crystallized intelligence'. *Intelligence*, 40, pp. 499–508

Darling, S., Della Sala, S., Logie, R. H. and Cantagallo, A. (2006) 'Neuropsychological evidence for separating components of visuo-spatial working memory'. *Journal of Neurology*, 253, pp. 176–180

de Fockert, J. W., Rees, G., Frith, C. D. and Lavie, N. (2004) 'Neural correlates of attentional capture in visual search'. *Journal of Cognitive Neuroscience*, 16, pp. 751–759

Dehaene, S. (1992) 'Varieties of numerical abilities'. *Cognition*, 44, p. 1142

Dehaene, S., Bossini, S. and Giraux, P. (1993) 'The mental representation of parity and number magnitude'. *Journal of Experimental Psychology: General*, 122, pp. 391–396

Della Sala, S., Gray, C., Baddeley, A., Allamano, N. and Wilson, L. (1999) 'Pattern span: a tool for unwelding visuo-spatial memory'. *Neuropsychologia*, 37, pp. 1189–1199

Demany, L., Trost, W., Serman, M. and Semal, C. (2008) 'Auditory change detection: simple sounds are not memorized better than complex sounds'. *Psychological Science*, 19, pp. 85–91

Demetriou, A. and Mouyi, A. (2011) 'Processing efficiency, representational capacity, and reasoning: modeling their dynamic interactions' in P. Barrouillet and V. Gaillard (Eds) *Cognitive Development and Working Memory* (pp. 69–104). Hove: Psychology Press

Dempster, F. N. (1978) 'Memory span and short-term memory capacity: a developmental study'. *Journal of Experimental Child Psychology*, 26, pp. 419–431

Dempster, F. N. (1981) 'Memory span: sources of individual and developmental differences'. *Psychological Bulletin*, 89, pp. 63–100

Derrfuss, J., Brass, M. and von Cramon, D. Y. (2004) 'Cognitive control in the posterior frontolateral cortex: evidence from common activations in task coordination, interference control, and working memory'. *Neuroimage*, 23, pp. 604–612

Derrfuss, J., Brass, M., Neumann, J. and von Cramon, D. Y. (2005) 'Involvement of the inferior frontal junction in cognitive control: meta-analyses of switching and Stroop studies'. *Human Brain Mapping*, 25, pp. 22–34

Diamond, A. (2006) 'The early development of executive functions' in E. Bialystok and F. I. M. Craik (Eds) *Lifespan Cognition: Mechanisms of Change* (pp. 70–95). Oxford: Oxford University Press

Dillon, R. F. and Reid, L. S. (1969) 'Short-term memory as a function of information processing during the retention interval'. *Journal of Experimental Psychology*, 81, pp. 261–269.

Dirix, S. (2014) 'Time-related consolidation processes in working memory'. Unpublished internship dissertation, University of Geneva

Drew, T., Boettcher, S. and Wolfe, J. M. (2013) 'Hybrid visual and memory search remains efficient when visual working memory is full'. Paper presented at the 54th Annual Meeting of the Psychonomic Society, 14–17 November, Toronto

Duff, S. C. and Logie, R. H. (1999) 'Processing and storage in visuo-spatial working memory'. *Scandinavian Journal of Psychology*, 40, pp. 251–259

Duff, S. C. and Logie, R. H. (2001) 'Processing and storage in working memory span'. *Quarterly Journal of Experimental Psychology*, 54, pp. 31–48

Dulany, D. E. (1991) 'Conscious representation and thought systems' in R. S. Wyer, and T. K. Srull (Eds) *Advances in Social Cognition Vol. 4* (pp. 97–120). Hillsdale, NJ: Lawrence Erlbaum Associates

Dulany, D. E. (1997) 'Consciousness in the explicit (deliberative) and implicit (evocative)' in J. Cohen and J. Schooler (Eds) *Scientific Approaches to Consciousness* (pp. 179–211). Mahwah, NJ: Lawrence Erlbaum Associates

Dux, P. E., Ivanoff, J., Asplund, C. L. and Marois, R. (2006) 'Isolation of a central bottleneck of information processing with time-resolved fMRI'. *Neuron*, 52, pp. 1109–1120

Ebbinghaus, H. (1885) *Memory: A Contribution to Experimental Psychology*. New York: Teachers College

Ellis, N. C. and Hennelley, R. A. (1980) 'A bilingual word-length effect: implications for intelligence testing and the relative ease of mental calculation in Welsh and English'. *British Journal of Psychology*, 71, pp. 43–52

Elsley, J. V. and Parmentier, F. B. R. (2009) 'Is verbal-spatial binding in working memory impaired by a concurrent memory load? *Quarterly Journal of Experimental Psychology*, 62, pp. 1696–1705

Engle, R. W. (2002) 'Working memory capacity as executive attention'. *Current Directions in Psychological Science*, 11, pp. 19–23

Engle, R. W., Cantor, J. and Carullo, J. (1992) 'Individual differences in working memory and comprehension: a test of four hypotheses'. *Journal of Experimental Psychology: Learning, Memory and Cognition*, 18, pp. 972–992

Engle, R. W. and Kane, M. J. (2004) 'Executive attention, working memory capacity, and a two-factor theory of cognitive control' in B. Ross (Ed.) *The Psychology of Learning and Motivation* (Vol. 44, pp. 145–199). NY: Elsevier

Engle, R. W., Kane, M. J. and Tuholski, S. W. (1999) 'Individual differences in working memory capacity and what they tell us about controlled attention, general fluid intelligence and functions of the prefrontal cortex' in A. Miyake and P. Shah (Eds) *Models of Working Memory: Mechanisms of Active Maintenance and Executive Control* (pp. 102–134). Cambridge: Cambridge University Press

Engle, R. W. and Oransky, N. (1999) 'The evolution from short-term memory to working memory: multi-store to dynamic models of temporary storage' in R. J. Sternberg (Ed.) *The Nature of Cognition* (pp. 515–556). Cambridge, MA: MIT Press

Engle, R. W., Tuholski S. W., Laughlin J. E. and Conway, A. R. A. (1999) 'Working memory, short-term memory, and general fluid intelligence: a latent-variable approach'. *Journal of Experimental Psychology: General*, 128, pp. 309–331

Ericsson, K. A. and Kintsch, W. (1995) 'Long-term working memory'. *Psychological Review*, 102, pp. 211–245

Evans, J. St. B. T., Newstead, S. E. and Byrne, R. M. J. (1993) *Human Reasoning: The Psychology of Deduction*. Hillsdale, NJ: Lawrence Erlbaum

Fallon, A. B., Groves, K. and Tehan, G. (1999) 'Phonological similarity and trace degradation in the serial recall task: when CAT helps RAT, but not MAN'. *International Journal of Psychology*, 34, pp. 301–307

Farrell, S. (2006) 'Mixed-list phonological similarity effects in delayed serial recall'. *Journal of Memory and Language*, 55, pp. 587–600

Farrell, S. and Lewandowsky, S. (2002) 'An endogenous distributed model of ordering in serial recall'. *Psychonomic Bulletin and Review*, 9, pp. 59–79

Farmer, E.W., Berman, J.V.F. and Fletcher, Y.L. (1986) 'Evidence for a visuo-spatial scratch-pad in working memory'. *Quarterly Journal of Experimental Psychology*, 38A, pp. 675–688

Flavell, J. H. (1979) 'Metacognition and cognitive monitoring: a new area of cognitive-developmental inquiry'. *American Psychologist*, 34, pp. 906–911

Frank, M. J., Loughry, B. and O'Reilly, R. C. (2001) 'Interactions between the frontal cortex and basal ganglia in working memory: a computational model'. *Cognitive, Affective, and Behavioral Neuroscience*, 1, pp. 137–160

Friedman, N. P. and Miyake, A. (2004) 'The reading span test and its predictive power for reading comprehension ability'. *Journal of Memory and Language*, 51, pp. 136–158

Fry, A. F. and Hale, S. (1996) 'Processing speed, working memory, and fluid intelligence. *Psychological Science*, 7, pp. 237–241

Fuson, K.C. and Hall, J.W. (1983) 'The acquisition of early number word meanings' in H. Ginsburg (Ed.) *The Development of Children's Mathematical Thinking* (pp. 49–107). New York: Academic Press

Fuson, K.C., Richards, J. and Briars, D.J. (1982) 'The acquisition and elaboration of number word sequence' in C. Brainerd (Ed.) *Progress in Cognitive Development: Vol. 1 Children's Logical and Mathematical Cognition* (pp. 33–92). New York: Springer-Verlag

Gaillard, V., Barrouillet, P., Jarrold, C. and Camos V. (2011) 'Developmental differences in working memory: where do they come from?' *Journal of Experimental Child Psychology*, 110, pp. 469–479

Gardner, H. (1985) *The Mind's New Science: A History of the Cognitive Revolution*. New York: Basic Books

Garavan, H. (1998) 'Serial attention within working memory'. *Memory and Cognition*, 26, pp. 263–276

Gathercole, S. E. (1994) 'Neuropsychology and working memory: a review'. *Neuropsychology*, 8, pp. 499–505

Gathercole, S. E. and Adams, A.-M. (1993) 'Phonological working memory in very young children'. *Developmental Psychology*, 29, pp. 770–778

Gathercole, S. E., Adams, A.-M. and Hitch, G. J. (1994) 'Do young children rehearse? An individual differences analysis'. *Memory and Cognition*, 22, pp. 201–207

Gathercole, S. E. and Pickering, S. J. (2000) 'Working memory deficits in children with low achievements in the national curriculum at 7 years of age'. *British Journal of Educational Psychology*, 70, pp. 177–194

Gathercole, S. E., Pickering, S. J., Hall, M. and Peaker, S. M. (2001) 'Dissociable lexical and phonological influences on serial recognition and serial recall'. *Quarterly Journal of Experimental Psychology*, 54, pp. 1–30

Gathercole, S. E., Willis, C. and Baddeley, A. D. (1992) 'Phonological memory and vocabulary development during the early school years: evidence from a longitudinal study'. *Developmental Psychology*, 28, pp. 887–898

Gavens, N. and Barrouillet, P. (2004) 'Delays of retention, processing efficiency, and attentional resources in working memory span development'. *Journal of Memory and Language*, 51, pp. 644–657

Gilson, E. Q. and Baddeley, A. D. (1969) 'Tactile short-term memory'. *Quarterly Journal of Experimental Psychology*, 21, pp. 180–184

Glanzer, M. and Cunitz, A. R. (1966) 'Two storage mechanisms in free recall'. *Journal of Verbal Learning and Verbal Behavior*, 5, pp. 351–360

Glernberg, A., Smith, S.M. and Green, C. (1977) 'Type I rehearsal: maintenance and more'. *Journal of Verbal Learning and Verbal Behavior*, 16, pp. 339–352

Goldman-Rakic, P. S. (1992) 'Working memory and the mind'. *Scientific American*, 267, pp. 110–117

Gruber, O. and von Cramon, D.Y. (2003) 'The functional neuroanatomy of human working memory revisited: evidence from 3-T fMRI studies using classical domain-specific interference tasks'. *NeuroImage*, 19, pp. 797–809

Guttentag, R. E. (1984) 'The mental effort requirement of cumulative rehearsal: a developmental study'. *Journal of Experimental Child Psychology*, 37, pp. 92–106

Guttentag, R. E. (1989) 'Age differences in dual task performance: procedures, assumptions, and results'. *Developmental Review*, 9, pp. 146–170

Haberlandt, K. (1997) *Cognitive Psychology* (2nd Ed.). Boston: Allyn and Bacon

Halford, G. S. (1993) *Children's Understanding*. Hillsdale, NJ: Lawrence Erlbaum Associates

Halford, G. S. and Wilson, W. H. (1980) 'A category theory approach to cognitive development'. *Cognitive Psychology*, 12, pp. 356–411

Halford, G.S., Wilson, W.H. and Phillips, S. (1998) 'Processing capacity defined by relational complexity: implications for comparative, developmental, and cognitive psychology'. *Behavioral and Brain Sciences*, 21, pp. 803–864

Hamilton, A.C., Martin, R.C. and Burton, P.C. (2009) 'Converging functional magnetic resonance imaging evidence for a role of the left inferior frontal lobe in semantic retention during language comprehension'. *Cognitive Neuropsychology*, 26, pp. 685–704

Hammerton, M. (1969) 'Interference between low information verbal output and a cognitive task'. *Nature*, 222, 196–196

Hanten, G. and Martin, R.C. (2000) 'Contributions of phonological and semantic short-term memory to sentence processing: evidence from two cases of closed head injury in children'. *Journal of Memory and Language*, 43, pp. 335–361

Harris, J. D. (1952) 'The decline of pitch discrimination with time'. *Journal of Experimental Psychology*, 43, pp. 96–99

Hazy, T. E., Frank, M. J. and O'Reilly, R. C. (2006) 'Banishing the homunculus: making working memory work'. *Neuroscience*, 139, pp. 105–118

Hebb, D. O. (1961) 'Distinctive features of learning in the higher animal' in J. F. Delafresnaye (Ed.) *Brain Mechanisms and Learning* (pp. 37–46). Oxford, U.K.: Blackwell

Henry, L. A. (1991a) 'The effects of word length and phonemic similarity in young children's short-term memory'. *Quarterly Journal of Experimental Psychology*, 43, pp. 35–52

Henry, L. A. (1991b) 'Development of auditory memory span: the role of rehearsal'. *British Journal of Developmental Psychology*, 9, pp. 493–511

Henry, L. A., Messer, D., Luger-Klein, S. and Crane, L. (2012) 'Phonological, visual and semantic coding strategies and children's short-term picture memory span'. *Quarterly Journal of Experimental Psychology*, 65, pp. 2033–2053

Henson, R. N. (1998) 'Short-term memory for serial order: the Start-End Model'. *Cognitive Psychology*, 36, pp. 73–137

Hitch, G. J. (2006) 'Working memory in children: a cognitive approach' in E. Bialystock and F. I. M. Craik (Eds) *Lifespan Cognition: Mechanisms of Change* (pp. 112–127). Oxford: Oxford University Press

Hitch, G. J., Halliday, M. S. and Littler, J. E. (1989) 'Item identification time, rehearsal rate and memory span in children'. *Quarterly Journal of Experimental Psychology*, 41, pp. 321–337

Hitch, G. J., Halliday, M. S. and Littler, J. E. (1993) 'Development of memory span for spoken words: the role of rehearsal and item identification processes'. *British Journal of Developmental Psychology*, 11, pp. 159–169

Hitch, G. J., Halliday, M. S., Dodd, A. and Littler, J. E. (1989) 'Development of rehearsal in short-term memory: differences between pictorial and spoken stimuli'. *British Journal of Developmental Psychology*, 7, pp. 347–362

Hitch, G. J., Halliday, M. S., Schaafstal, A. M. and Heffernan, T. E. (1991) 'Speech, "inner speech" and the development of short-term memory: effects of picture-labelling on recall'. *Journal of Experimental Child Psychology*, 51, pp. 220–234

Hitch, G. J. and Towse, J. (1995) 'Working memory: what develops?' in W. Schneider and F. E. Weinert (Eds) *Memory Performance and Competencies: Issues in Growth and Development* (pp. 3–22). Hillsdale, NJ: Lawrence Erlbaum Associates

Hitch, G., Towse, J.N. and Hutton, U. (2001) 'What limits children's working memory span? Theoretical accounts and applications for scholastic development'. *Journal of Experimental Psychology: General*, 130, pp. 184–198

Hudjetz, A. and Oberauer, K. (2007) 'The effects of processing time and processing rate on forgetting in working memory: testing four models of the complex span paradigm'. *Memory and Cognition*, 35, pp. 1675–1684

Hulme, C., Maugham, S. and Brown, G. D. A. (1991) 'Memory for familiar and unfamiliar words: evidence for a long-term memory contribution to short-term memory span'. *Journal of Memory and Language*, 30, pp. 685–701

Hulme, C., Roodenrys, S., Schweickert, R., Brown, G. D. A., Martin, S. and Stuart, G. (1997) 'Word-frequency effects on short-term memory tasks: evidence for a redintegration process in immediate serial recall'. *Journal of Experimental Psychology: Learning, Memory, and Cognition*, 23, pp. 1217–1232

Hulme, C., Thomson, N., Muir, C. and Lawrence, A. (1984) 'Speech rate and the development of short-term memory span'. *Journal of Experimental Child Psychology*, 38, pp. 241–253

Hunt, E. B. (1971) 'What kind of computer is man?' *Cognitive Psychology*, 2, pp. 57–98

Hunter, I. M. L. (1964) *Memory*. Baltimore: Penguin Books

Istomina, Z. M. (1977) 'The development of voluntary memory in preschool-age children' in M. Cole (Ed.) *Soviet Developmental Psychology* (pp. 100–159). White Plains, NY: Sharpe [originally published in Russian in 1948]

James, W. (1890) *The Principles of Psychology*. New York: Henry Holt

Jarrold, C. and Citroën, R. (2013) 'Re-evaluating key evidence for the development of rehearsal: phonological similarity effects in children are subject to proportional scaling artifacts'. *Developmental Psychology*, 49, pp. 837–847

Jarrold, C., Tam, H., Baddeley, A. D. and Harvey, C. E. (2010) 'The nature and the position of processing determines why forgetting occurs in working memory tasks'. *Psychonomic Bulletin and Review*, 17, pp. 772–777

Jilk, D. J., Lebiere, C., O'Reilly, R. C. and Anderson, J. R. (2008) 'SAL: an explicitly pluralistic cognitive architecture'. *Journal of Experimental and Theoretical Artificial Intelligence*, 20, pp. 197–218

Johnson, M. K., Raye, C. L., Mitchell, K. J., Greene, E. J., Cunningham, W. A. and Sanislow, C. A. (2005) 'Using fMRI to investigate a component process of reflection: prefrontal correlates of refreshing a just-activated representation'. *Cognitive, Affective & Behavioral Neuroscience*, 5, pp. 339–361

Johnson-Laird, P. N. (1983) *Mental Models*. Cambridge: Cambridge University Press

Johnson-Laird, P. N. (2006) *How We Reason*. Oxford: Oxford University Press

Jolicoeur, P. and Dell'Acqua, R. (1998) 'The demonstration of short-term consolidation'. *Cognitive Psychology*, 36, pp. 138–202

Jurden, F. H. (1995) 'Individual differences in working memory and complex cognition'. *Journal of Educational Psychology*, 87, pp. 93–102

Just, M. A. and Carpenter, P. A. (1992) 'A capacity theory of comprehension: individual differences in working memory'. *Psychological Review*, 99, pp. 122–149

Kaernbach, C. (2004) 'Auditory sensory memory and short-term memory' in C. Kaernbach, E. Schröger and H. Müller (Eds) *Psychophysics Beyond Sensation: Laws and Invariants of Human Cognition* (pp. 331–348). Hillsdale, NJ: Erlbaum

Kaernbach, C. and Schlemmer, K. (2008) 'The decay of pitch memory during rehearsal'. *The Journal of the Acoustical Society of America*, 123, pp. 1846–1849

Kahneman, D. (1973) *Attention and Effort*. Englewood Cliffs, NJ: Prentice-Hall

Kahneman, D., Triesman, A. and Gibbs, B. J. (1992) 'The reviewing of object files: object-specific integration of information'. *Cognitive Psychology*, 24, pp. 175–219

Kail, R. (1991) 'Developmental change in speed of processing during childhood and adolescence'. *Psychological Bulletin*, 109, pp. 490–501

Kail, R. (1996) 'Nature and consequences of developmental change in speed of processing'. *Swiss Journal of Psychology*, 55, pp. 133–138

Kail, R. and Salthouse, T. A. (1994) 'Processing speed as a mental capacity'. *Acta Psychologica*, 86, pp. 199–225

Kane, M. J., Conway, A. R. A., Hambrick, D. Z. and Engle, R. W. (2007) 'Variation in working memory capacity as variation in executive attention and control' in A. R. A Conway, C. Jarrold, M. J. Kane, A. Miyake and J. N. Towse (Eds) *Variation in Working Memory* (pp. 21–48). NY: Oxford University Press

Kane, M. J. and Engle, R. W. (2002) 'The role of prefrontal cortex in working-memory capacity, executive attention, and general fluid intelligence: an individual differences perspective'. *Psychonomic Bulletin and Review*, 9, pp. 637–671

Kane, M. J. and Engle, R.W. (2003) 'Working-memory capacity and the control of attention: the contributions of goal neglect, response competition, and task set to Stroop interference'. *Journal of Experimental Psychology: General*, 132, pp. 47–70

Kane, M. J., Hambrick, D. Z., Tuholski, S. W., Wilhelm, O., Payne, T. W. and Engle, R. W. (2004) 'The generality of working memory capacity: a latent-variable approach to verbal and visuospatial memory span and reasoning'. *Journal of Experimental Psychology: General*, 133, pp. 189–217

Kane, M. J., Poole, B. J., Tuholski, S. W. and Engle, R. W. (2006) 'Working memory capacity and the top-down control of visual search: exploring the boundaries of "executive attention"'. *Journal of Experimental Psychology: Learning, Memory, and Cognition*, 32, pp. 749–777

Keller, T. A. and Cowan, N. (1994) 'Developmental increase in the duration of memory for tone pitch'. *Developmental Psychology*, 30, pp. 855–863

Keller, T. A., Cowan, N. and Saults, J. S. (1995) 'Can auditory memory for tone pitch be rehearsed?' *Journal of Experimental Psychology: Learning, Memory, and Cognition*, 21, pp. 635–645

Kemps, E., De Rammelaere, S. and Desmet, T. (2000) 'The development of working memory: exploring the complementarity of two models'. *Journal of Experimental Child Psychology*, 77, pp. 89–109

Keppel, G. and Underwood, B. J. (1962) 'Proactive inhibition in short-term retention of single items'. *Journal of Verbal Learning and Verbal Behavior*, 1, pp. 153–161

Kim, C., Cilles, S. E., Johnsin, N. F. and Gold, B. T. (2012) 'Domain general and domain preferential brain regions associated with different types of task switching: a meta-analysis'. *Human Brain Mapping*, 33, pp. 130–142

Kinchla, R. A. and Smyzer, F. (1967) 'A diffusion model of perceptual memory'. *Perception and Psychophysics*, 2, pp. 219–229

Kintsch, W., Healy, A., Hegarty, M., Pennington, B. and Salthouse, T. (1999) 'Models of working memory: eight questions and some general answers' in A. Miyake and P. Shah, (Eds) *Models of Working Memory* (pp. 412–441). New York, NY: Cambridge University Press

Klapp, S. T., Boches, C. A., Trabert, M. L. and Logan, G. D. (1991) 'Automatizing alphabet arithmetic: II. Are there practice effects after automaticity is attained?' *Journal of Experimental Psychology: Learning, Memory, and Cognition*, 17, pp. 196–209

Klauer, K. C. and Zhao, Z. (2004) 'Double dissociations in visual and spatial short-term memory'. *Journal of Experimental Psychology: General*, 133, pp. 355–381

Kroll, N. E. A., Parks, T., Parkinson, S. R., Bieber, S. L. and Johnson, A. L. (1970) 'Short-term memory while shadowing: recall of visually and aurally presented letters'. *Journal of Experimental Psychology*, 85, pp. 220–224

Kyllonen, P. C. and Christal, R. E. (1990) 'Reasoning ability is (little more than) working memory capacity?' *Intelligence*, 14, pp. 389–433

Kyllonen, P. C. (1993) 'Aptitude testing inspired by information processing: a test of the four-sources model'. *Journal of General Psychology*, 120, pp. 375–405

Kyndt, E., Cascallar, E. and Dochy, F. (2012) 'Individual differences in working memory capacity and attention, and their relationship with students' approaches to learning'. *Higher Education*, 64, pp. 285–297

Kyndt, E., Dochy, F., Struyven, K. and Cascallar, E. (2012) 'Looking at learning approaches from the angle of student profiles'. *Educational Psychology*, 32, pp. 493–513

Lange, E. B. and Oberauer, K. (2005) 'Overwriting of phonemic features in serial recall'. *Memory*, 13, pp. 333–339

Langerock, N., Vergauwe, E. and Barrouillet, P. (2014) 'The maintenance of cross-domain associations in the episodic buffer'. *Journal of Experimental Psychology: Learning, Memory, and Cognition* 40(4), pp. 1096-1109

La Pointe, L. B. and Engle, R. W. (1990) 'Simple and complex word spans as measures of working memory capacity'. *Journal of Experimental Psychology: Learning, Memory, and Cognition*, 16, pp. 1118–1133

Lépine, R., Barrouillet, P. and Camos, V. (2005a) 'What makes working memory spans so predictive of high-level cognition?' *Psychonomic Bulletin and Review*, 12, pp. 165–170

Lépine, R., Bernardin, S. and Barrouillet, P. (2005b) 'Attention switching and working memory spans'. *European Journal of Cognitive Psychology*, 17, pp. 329–346

Lewandowsky, S., Duncan, M. and Brown, G. D. A. (2004) 'Time does not cause forgetting in short-term serial recall'. *Psychonomic Bulletin and Review*, 11, pp. 771–790

Lewandowsky, S. and Farrell, S. (2008) 'Phonological similarity in serial recall: constraints on theories of memory'. *Journal of Memory and Language*, 58, pp. 429–4

Lewandowsky, S., Geiger, S. M., Morrell, D. B. and Oberauer, K. (2010) 'Turning simple span into complex span: time for decay or interference from distractors?' *Journal of Experimental Psychology: Learning, Memory, and Cognition*, 36, pp. 958–978

Lewandowsky, S., Geiger, S. M. and Oberauer, K. (2008) 'Interference-based forgetting in verbal short-term memory'. *Journal of Memory and Language*, 59, pp. 200–222

Lewandowsky, S. and Oberauer, K. (2008) 'The word-length effect provides no evidence for decay in short-term memory'. *Psychonomic Bulletin and Review*, 15, pp. 875–888

Lewandowsky, S. and Oberauer, K. (2009) 'No evidence for temporal decay in working memory'. *Journal of Experimental Psychology: Learning, Memory, and Cognition*, 35, pp. 1545–1551

Lewandowsky, S., Oberauer, K. and Brown, G. D. A. (2009) 'No temporal decay in verbal short-term memory'. *Trends in Cognitive Sciences*, 13, pp. 120–126

Liefooghe, B., Barrouillet, P., Vandierendonck, A. and Camos, V. (2008) 'Working memory costs of task switching'. *Journal of Experimental Psychology: Learning, Memory, and Cognition*, 34, pp. 478–494

Lisman, J. E. and Idiart, M. A. P. (1995) 'Storage of 7 ± 2 short-term memories in oscillatory subcycles'. *Science*, 267, pp. 1512–1515

Loaiza, V. M. and McCabe, D. P. (2012) 'Temporal-contextual processing in working memory: evidence from delayed cued recall and delayed free recall tests'. *Memory and Cognition*, 40, pp. 193–203

Loaiza, V. M. and McCabe, D. P. (2013) 'The influence of aging on attentional refreshing and articulatory rehearsal during working memory on later episodic memory performance'. *Aging, Neuropsychology, and Cognition*, 20, pp. 471–493

Lobley, K. J., Baddeley, A. D. and Gathercole, S. E. (2005) 'Phonological similarity effects in verbal complex span'. *Quarterly Journal of Experimental Psychology*, 58(8), pp. 1462–1478

Logan, G. D. (1976) 'Converging evidence for automatic perceptual processing in visual search'. *Canadian Journal of Psychology*, 30, pp. 193–200

Logan, G. D. (1988) 'Toward an instance theory of automatization'. *Psychological Review*, 95, pp. 492–527

Logan, G. D. (1995) 'The Weibull distribution, the power law, and the instance theory of automaticity'. *Psychological Review*, 102, pp. 751–756

Logan, G. D. (1998) 'What is learned during automatization? II: obligatory encoding of location information'. *Journal of Experimental Psychology: Human Perception and Performance*, 24, pp. 1720–1736

Logan, G. D. and Etherton, J. L. (1994) 'What is learned during automatization? The role of attention in constructing an instance'. *Journal of Experimental Psychology: Learning, Memory and Cognition*, 20, pp. 1022–1050

Logie, R. H. (1986) 'Visuo-spatial processing in working memory'. *Quarterly Journal of Experimental Psychology*, 38, pp. 229–247

Logie, R. H. (1995) *Visuo-spatial working memory*. Hove, UK: Erlbaum

Logie, R. H. and Duff, S. C. (1996) 'Processing and storage in working memory: multiple components?' Poster presented at the annual meeting of the Psychonomic Society, Chicago, IL

Logie, R. H. and Duff, S. C. (2007) 'Separating processing from storage in working memory operation span' in N. Osaka, R. Logie and M. D'Esposito (Eds) *Working Memory: Behavioral and Neural Correlates* (pp. 119–135). Oxford: Oxford University Press

Logie, R. H. and Marchetti, C. (1991) 'Visuo-spatial working memory: visual, spatial or central executive?' in C. Cornoldi and M. A. McDaniels (Eds) *Mental Images in Human Cognition* (pp. 72–102). New York: Springer

Logie, R. H., Zucco, G. M. and Baddeley, A. D. (1990) 'Interference with visual short-term memory'. *Acta Psychologica*, 75, pp. 55–74

Lovett, M. C., Reder, L. M. and Lebière, C. (1999) 'Modeling working memory in a unified architecture: an ACT-R perspective' in A. Miyake, and P. Shah (Eds) *Models of Working Memory: Mechanisms of Active Maintenance and Executive Control* (pp. 135–182). Cambridge: Cambridge University Press

Lucidi, A. and Barrouillet, P. (2012) 'Where do individual differences in working memory capacity come from? A Time-Based Resource-Sharing account'. Unpublished manuscript.

Lucidi, A., Loaiza, V., Camos, V. and Barrouillet, P. (2014) 'Assessing working memory capacity through time-constrained elementary activities'. *Journal of General Psychology*, 141(2), pp. 98–112

Luck, S. J. and Vogel, E. K. (1997) 'The capacity of visual working memory for features and conjunctions'. *Nature*, 390, pp. 279–281

Luck, S. J. and Vogel, E. K. (1998) 'Response to visual and auditory working memory capacity by N. Cowan'. *Trends in Cognitive Sciences*, 2, pp. 78–80

Lustig, C., May, C. P. and Hasher, L. (2001) 'Working memory span and the role of proactive interference'. *Journal of Experimental Psychology: General*, 130, pp. 199–207

Macken, W. J. and Jones, D. M. (1995) 'Functional characteristics of the inner voice and the inner ear: single or double agency?'. *Journal of Experimental Psychology: Learning, Memory, and Cognition*, 21, pp. 436–448

Macnamara, B. N., Moore, A. B. and Conway, A. R. A. (2011) 'Phonological similarity effects in simple and complex span tasks'. *Memory and Cognition*, 39, pp. 1174–1186

Martin, R. C. (1993) 'Short-term memory and sentence processing: evidence from neuropsychology'. *Memory and Cognition*, 21, pp. 176–183

Martin, R. C. (2003) 'Language processing: functional organization and neuroanatomical basis'. *Annual Review of Psychology*, 54, pp. 55–89

Martin, R. C. (2005) 'Components of short-term memory and their relation to language processing: evidence from neuropsychology and neuroimaging'. *Current Directions in Psychological Science*, 14, pp. 204–208

Martinez, K. and Colom, R. (2008) 'Working memory capacity and processing efficiency predict fluid but not crystallized and spatial intelligence: evidence supporting the neural noise hypothesis'. *Personality and Individual Differences*, 46, pp. 281–286

Massaro, D. W. (1970) 'Forgetting: interference or decay?'. *Journal of Experimental Psychology*, 83, pp. 238–243

May, C. P., Hasher, L. and Kane, M. J. (1999) 'The role of interference in memory span'. *Memory and Cognition*, 27, pp. 759–767

Mazuryk, G. F. and Lockhart, R. S. (1974) 'Negative recency and levels of processing in free recall'. *Canadian Journal of Psychology*, 23, pp. 114–123

McCabe, D. P. (2008) 'The role of covert retrieval in working memory span tasks: evidence from delayed recall tests'. *Journal of Memory and Language*, 58, pp. 480–494

McElree, B. (1998) 'Attended and non-attended states in working memory: accessing categorized structures'. *Journal of Memory and Language*, 38, pp. 225–252

McElree, B. (2001) 'Working memory and focal attention'. *Journal of Experimental Psychology: Learning, Memory and Cognition*, 27, pp. 817–835

McElree, B. and Dosher, B. A. (1989) 'Serial position and set size in short-term memory: the time course of recognition'. *Journal of Experimental Psychology: General*, 118, pp. 346–373

McGeoch, J. A. (1932) 'Forgetting and the law of disuse'. *Psychological Review*, 39, pp. 352–70

McGeoch, J. A. (1942) *The Psychology of Human Learning*. Longmans, Green: New York

McKeown, D. and Mercer, T. (2012) 'Short-term forgetting without interference'. *Journal of Experimental Psychology: Learning, Memory, and Cognition*, 38, pp. 1057–1068

McKeown, D., Holt, J., Delvenne, J. F., Smith, A. and Griffiths, B. (2014) 'Active versus passive maintenance of visual nonverbal memory'. *Psychonomic Bulletin and Review* (in press)

McKone, E. (1995) 'Short term implicit memory for words and non-words'. *Journal of Experimental Psychology: Learning, Memory, and Cognition*, 21, pp. 1108–1126

McKone, E. (1998) 'The decay of short-term implicit memory: unpacking lag'. *Memory and Cognition*, 26, pp. 1173–1186

McKone, E. (2001) 'Capacity limits in continuous old-new recognition, and in short-term implicit memory. (Commentary on Cowan 2001 "The magical number 4 in short-term memory: a reconsideration of mental storage capacity")'. *Behavioural and Brain Sciences*, 24, pp. 130–131

McNamara, D. S. and Scott, J. L. (2001) 'Working memory capacity and strategy use'. *Memory and Cognition*, 29, pp. 10–17

Meiser, T. and Klauer, K. C. (1999) 'Working memory and changing-state hypothesis'. *Journal of Experimental Psychology: Learning, Memory, and Cognition*, 25, pp. 1272–1299

Melton, A. W. (1963) 'Implications of short-term memory for a general theory of memory'. *Journal of Verbal Learning and Verbal Behavior*, 2, pp. 1–21

Miles, C. and Borthwick, H. (1996) 'Tactile short-term memory revisited'. *Memory*, 4, pp. 655–668

Miller, G. A. (1956) 'The magical number seven, plus or minus two: some limits on our capacity for processing information'. *Psychological Review*, 63, pp. 81–97

Miller, G. A., Galanter, E. and Pribam, K. H. (1960) *Plans and the Structure of Behavior*. New York: Holt, Rinehart and Winston

Miller, K. F. and Stigler, J. W. (1987) 'Counting in Chinese: cultural variation in a basic cognitive skill'. *Cognitive Development*, 2, pp. 279–305

Miyake, A., Friedman, N.P., Emerson, M.J., Witzki, A.H., Howerter, A. and Wager, T. (2000) 'The unity and diversity of executive functions and their contributions to complex "frontal lobe" tasks: a latent variable analysis'. *Cognitive Psychology*, 41, pp. 49–100

Miyake, A. and Shah, P. (1999) *Models of Working Memory: Mechanisms of Active Maintenance and Executive Control*. New York: Cambridge University Press

Monsell, S. (1984) 'Components of working memory underlying verbal skills – a Distributed Capacities view – a tutorial review'. *Attention and Performance*, 10, pp. 327–350

Mora, G. and Camos, V. (2013) 'Two systems of maintenance in verbal working memory: evidence from the word length effect'. *PLoS One*, 8(7), e70026

Morey, C. C. and Bieler, M. (2013) 'Visual short-term memory always requires general attention'. *Psychonomic Bulletin and Review*, 20, pp. 163–170

Morey, C. C. and Cowan, N. (2004) 'When visual and verbal memories compete: evidence of cross-domain limits in working memory'. *Psychonomic Bulletin and Review*, 11, pp. 296–301

Morey, C. C. and Cowan, N. (2005) 'When do visual and verbal memories conflict? The importance of working-memory load and retrieval'. *Journal of Experimental Psychology: Learning Memory and Cognition*, 31, pp. 703–713

Moss, S. M., Myers, J. L. and Filmore, T. (1970) 'Short-term recognition memory of tones'. *Perception and Psychophysics*, 7, pp. 369–373

Murdock, B. B. (1967) 'Recent developments in short-term memory'. *British Journal of Psychology*, 58, pp. 421–433

Murray, D. J. (1967) 'The role of speech responses in short-term memory'. *Canadian Journal of Psychology*, 21, pp. 263–276

Nairne, J. S. (1990) 'A feature model of immediate memory'. *Memory and Cognition*, 18, pp. 251–269

Nairne, J. S. (2002) 'Remembering over the short-term: the case against the standard model'. *Annual Review of Psychology*, 52, pp. 53–81

Nairne, J. S. (2003) 'Sensory and working memory' in A. F. Healy and R. W. Proctor (Eds) *Comprehensive Handbook of Psychology* (Vol. 4: *Experimental Psychology*, pp. 423–444). New York: Wiley

Nairne, J. S., Whiteman, H. L. and Kelley, M. R. (1999) 'Short-term forgetting of order under conditions of reduced interference'. *Quarterly Journal of Experimental Psychology*, 52, pp. 241–251

Naveh-Benjamin, M. and Ayres, T.J. (1986) 'Digit span, reading rate, and linguistic relativity'. *Quarterly Journal of Experimental Psychology*, 38, pp. 739–751

Naveh-Benjamin, M. and Jonides, J. (1984) 'Maintenance rehearsal: a two-component analysis'. *Journal of Experimental Psychology: Learning, Memory, and Cognition*, 10, pp. 369–385

Navon, D. (1984) 'Resources – a theoretical soup stone?' *Psychological Review*, 91, pp. 216–234

Neath, I. and Brown, G. D. A. (2012) 'Arguments against memory trace decay: a SIMPLE account of Baddeley and Scott'. *Frontiers in Psychology*, 3, doi: 10.3389/fpsyg.2012.00035

Neath, I. and Surprenant, A. M. (2003) *Human Memory: An Introduction to Research, Data and Theory*. Belmont, CA: Wadsworth

Newell, A. (1990) *Unified Theories of Cognition*. Harvard, MA: Harvard University Press

Newell, A. and Simon, H. A. (1956) 'The logic theory machine: a complex information processing system'. *IRE Transactions on Information Theory*, 2, pp. 61–79

Newell, A., Shaw, J. C. and Simon, H. A. (1958) 'Chess-playing programs and the problem of complexity'. *IBM Journal of Research and Development*, 2, pp. 320–335

Nicolson, R. (1981) 'The relationship between memory span and processing speed' in M. Friedman, J. P. Das and N. O'Connor (Eds) *Intelligence and Learning* (pp. 179–184). New York: Plenum Press

Noël, M. P., Fias, W. and Brysbaert, M. (1997) 'About the influence of the representation format on arithmetical-fact retrieval processes'. *Cognition*, 63, pp. 335–374

Norman, D. A. and Shallice, T. (1986) 'Attention to action: willed and automatic control of behavior' in R. J. Davidson, G. E. Schwartz and D. Shapiro (Eds.) *Consciousness and Self-regulation*. New York: Plenum Press

Oberauer, K. (2001) 'Removing irrelevant information from working memory: a cognitive aging study with the modified Sternberg task'. *Journal of Experimental Psychology: Learning, Memory, and Cognition*, 27, pp. 948–957

Oberauer, K. (2002) 'Access to information in working memory: exploring the focus of attention'. *Journal of Experimental Psychology: Learning, Memory, and Cognition*, 28, pp. 411–421

Oberauer, K. (2005) 'Control of the contents of working memory: a comparison of two paradigms and two age groups'. *Journal of Experimental Psychology: Learning, Memory, and Cognition*, 31, pp. 714–728

Oberauer, K. (2009a) 'Interference between storage and processing in working memory: feature overwriting, not similarity-based competition'. *Memory and Cognition*, 37, pp. 346–357

Oberauer, K. (2009b) 'Design for a working memory'. *Psychology of Learning and Motivation*, 51, pp. 45–100

Oberauer, K. and Kliegl, R. (2006) 'A formal model capacity limits in working memory'. *Journal of Memory and Language*, 55, pp. 601–626

Oberauer, K. and Lange, E. B. (2008) 'Interference in verbal working memory: distinguishing similarity-based confusion, feature overwriting, and feature migration'. *Journal of Memory and Language*, 58, pp. 730–745

Oberauer, K., Lange, E. and Engle, R. W. (2004) 'Working memory capacity and resistance to interference'. *Journal of Memory and Language*, 51, pp. 80–96

Oberauer, K. and Lewandowsky, S. (2008) 'Forgetting in immediate serial recall: decay, temporal distinctiveness, or interference?' *Psychological Review*, 115, pp. 544–576

Oberauer, K. and Lewandowsky, S. (2011) 'Modeling working memory: a computational implementation of the Time-Based Resource-Sharing theory'. *Psychonomic Bulletin and Review*, 18, pp. 10–45

Oberauer, K. and Lewandowsky, S. (2013) 'Evidence against decay in verbal working memory'. *Journal of Experimental Psychology: General*, 142, pp. 380–411

Oberauer, K., Lewandowsky, S., Farrell, S., Jarrold, C. and Greaves, M. (2012) 'Modeling working memory: an interference model of complex span'. *Psychonomic Bulletin and Review*, 19, pp. 779–819

Oberauer, K., Süß, H.-M., Wilhelm, O. and Wittmann, W. W. (2003) 'The multiple faces of working memory: storage, processing, supervision, and coordination'. *Intelligence*, 31, pp. 167–193

O'Reilly, R. C. (2006) 'Biologically based computational models of high-level cognition'. *Science*, 314, pp. 91–94

O'Reilly, R. C. and Frank, M. J. (2006) 'Making working memory work: a computational model of learning in the frontal cortex and basal ganglia. *Neural Computation*, 18, pp. 283–328

Packard, M. G. and Knowlton, B. J. (2002) 'Learning and memory functions of the basal ganglia'. *Annual Review of Neuroscience*, 25, pp. 563–593

Page, M. P. and Norris, D. (1998) 'The primacy model: a new model of immediate serial recall'. *Psychological Review*, 105, pp. 761–781

Pascual-Leone, J. A. (1970) 'A mathematical model for the transition rule in Piaget's developmental stage'. *Acta Psychologica*, 32, pp. 301–345

Pascual-Leone, J. A. (2001) 'If the magical number is 4, how does one account for operations within working memory?' *Behavioral and Brain Sciences*, 24, pp. 136–138

Pashler, H. E. (1998) *The Psychology of Attention*. Cambridge, MA: MIT Press

Patterson, K. A. (1971) 'Limitations on retrieval from long-term memory'. Unpublished doctoral dissertation, University of California, San Diego

Perruchet, P. and Vinter, A. (2002) 'The self-organizing consciousness'. *Behavioral and Brain Sciences*, 25, pp. 297–388

Pertzov, Y., Bays, P. M., Joseph, S. and Husain, M. (2013) 'Rapid forgetting prevented by retrospective attention cues. *Journal of Experimental Psychology: Human Perception and Performance*, 39, pp. 1224–1231

Peterson, L. R. (1966) 'Short-term verbal memory and learning'. *Psychological Review*, 73, pp. 193–207

Peterson, L. R. and Peterson, M. J. (1959) 'Short-term retention of individual verbal items'. *Journal of Experimental Psychology*, 58, pp. 193–198

Pillsbury, W. B. and Sylvester, A. (1940) 'Retroactive and proactive inhibition in immediate memory'. *Journal of Experimental Psychology*, 27, pp. 532–545

Plancher, G. and Barrouillet, P. (2013) 'Forgetting from working memory: does novelty encoding matter?' *Journal of Experimental Psychology: Learning, Memory, and Cognition*, 39, pp. 110–125

Portrat, S., Barrouillet, P. and Camos, V. (2008) 'Time-decay or interference-based interference forgetting in working memory?' *Journal of Experimental Psychology: Learning, Memory and Cognition*, 34(6), pp. 1561–1564

Portrat, S., Camos, V. and Barrouillet, P. (2009) 'Working memory in children: a time-related functioning similar to adults'. *Journal of Experimental Child Psychology*, 102, pp. 368–374

Posner, M. I. (1967) 'Short-term memory systems in human information processing'. *Acta Psychologica*, 27, pp. 267–284

Posner, M. I. (2004) *Cognitive Neuroscience of Attention*. New York: Guildford Press

Postle, B. R. and d'Esposito, M. (1999) 'Dissociation of human caudate nucleus activity in spatial and nonspatial working memory'. *Cognitive Brain Research*, 8, pp. 107–115

Postman, L. and Phillips, L. W. (1965) 'Short-term temporal changes in free recall'. *Quarterly Journal of Experimental Psychology*, 17, pp. 132–138

Potter, M. C. (1993) 'Very short-term conceptual memory'. *Memory and Cognition*, 21, pp. 156–161

Potter, M. C. and Levy, E. I. (1986) 'Spatial enumeration without counting'. *Child Development*, 39, pp. 265–272

Quinn, J. G. and McConnell, J. (1996) 'Irrelevant pictures in visual working memory'. *Quarterly Journal of Experimental Psychology*, 49, pp. 200–215

Raye, C. L., Johnson, M. K., Mitchell, K. J., Greene, E. J. and Johnson, M. R. (2007) 'Refreshing: a minimal executive function'. *Cortex*, 43, pp. 135–145

Raye, C. L., Johnson, M. K., Mitchell, K. J., Reeder, J. A. and Greene, E. J. (2002) 'Neuroimaging a single thought: dorsolateral PFC activity associated with refreshing just-activated information'. *NeuroImage*, 15, pp. 447–453

Redick, T. S., Unsworth, N., Kelly, A. J. and Engle, R.W. (2012) 'Faster, smarter? Working memory capacity and perceptual speed in relation to fluid intelligence'. *Journal of Cognitive Psychology*, 24, pp. 844–854

Reitman, J. S. (1974) 'Without surreptitious rehearsal, information in short-term memory decays'. *Journal of Verbal Learning and Verbal Behavior*, 13, pp. 365–377

Repovs, G. and Baddeley, A. D. (2006) 'The multi-component model of working memory: explorations in experimental cognitive psychology'. *Neuroscience*, 139, pp. 5–21

Ricker, T. J. and Cowan, N. (2010) 'Loss of visual working memory within seconds: the combined use of refreshable and non-refreshable features'. *Journal of Experimental Psychology: Learning, Memory, and Cognition*, 36, pp. 1355–1368

Ricker, T.J. and Cowan, N. (2014) 'Differences between presentation methods in working memory procedures: a matter of working memory consolidation'. *Journal of Experimental Psychology: Learning, Memory, and Cognition*, 40(2), pp. 417–428

Ricker, T. J., Vergauwe, E. and Cowan, N. (2014) 'Decay theory of immediate memory: from Brown (1958) to today (2014)'. *Quarterly Journal of Experimental Psychology*, 141(2), pp. 98–112

Roediger, H. L., Weinstein, Y. and Argawal, P. K. (2010) 'Forgetting: preliminary considerations' in S. Della Sala (Ed.) *Forgetting* (pp. 1–22). Hove, UK: Psychology Press

Rohrer, D., Pashler, H. and Etchegaray, J. (1998) 'When two memories can and cannot be retrieved concurrently'. *Memory and Cognition*, 26, pp. 731–739

Roodenrys, S., Hulme, C. and Brown, G. (1993) 'The development of short-term memory span: separable effects of speech rate and long-term memory'. *Journal of Experimental Child Psychology*, 56, pp. 431–442

Rose, N. S., Buchsbaum, B. R. and Craik, F. I. M. (2014) 'Short-term retention of a single word rely on retrieval from long-term memory when both rehearsal and refreshing are disrupted'. *Memory and Cognition*, doi: 10.3758/s13420-014-0398-x

Rose, N. S., Olsen, R. K., Craik, F. I. M. and Rosenbaum, R. S. (2012) 'Working memory and amnesia: the role of stimulus novelty'. *Neuropsychologia*, 50, pp. 11–18

Rose, N. S., Myerson, J., Roediger, H. L. and Hale, S. (2010) 'Similarities and differences between working memory and long-term memory: evidence from the levels-of-processing span task'. *Journal of Experimental Psychology: Learning, Memory and Cognition*, 36(2), pp. 471–483

Rosen, V. M. and Engle, R. W. (1998) 'Working memory capacity and suppression'. *Journal of Memory and Language*, 39, pp. 418–436

Ruchkin, D. S., Grafman, J., Cameron, K. and Berndt, R. S. (2003) 'Working memory retention systems: a state of activated long-term memory'. *Behavioral and Brain Sciences*, 26, pp. 709–777

Rumelhart, D. E., Lindsay, P. H. and Norman, D. A. (1972) 'A process model for long-term memory' in E. Tulving and W. Donaldson (Eds) *Organization of Memory*. New York: Academic Press

Rundus, D. (1977) 'Maintenance rehearsal and single-level processing'. *Journal of Verbal Learning and Verbal Behavior*, 16(6), pp. 665–681

Rybash, J. M. and Hoyer, W. J. (1992) 'Hemispheric specialization for categorical and coordinate spatial representations: a reappraisal'. *Memory and Cognition*, 20, pp. 271–276

Saito, S. (1997) 'When articulatory suppression does not suppress the activity of the phonological loop'. *British Journal of Psychology*, 88, pp. 565–578

Saito, S. and Miyake, A. (2004) 'On the nature of forgetting and the processing-storage relationship in reading span performance'. *Journal of Memory and Language*, 50, pp. 425–443

Salamé, P. and Baddeley, A. D. (1986) 'Phonological factors in STM: similarity and the unattended speech effect'. *Bulletin of the Psychonomic Society*, 24, pp. 263–265

Salthouse, T.A. (1996) 'The processing speed theory of adult age differences in cognition'. *Psychological Review*, 103, pp. 403–428

Salway, A. F. S. and Logie, R. H. (1995) 'Visuo-spatial working memory, movement control and executive demands'. *British Journal of Psychology*, 86, pp. 253–269

Saults, J. S. and Cowan, N. (1996) 'The development of memory for ignored speech'. *Journal of Experimental Child Psychology*, 63, pp. 239–261

Saults, J.S. and Cowan, N. (2007) 'A central capacity limit to the simultaneous storage of visual and auditory arrays in working memory'. *Journal of Experimental Psychology: General*, 136, pp. 663–684

Scarborough, D. L, Cortese, C. and Scarborough, H. S. (1977) 'Frequency and repetition effects in lexical memory'. *Journal of Experimental Psychology: Human Perception and Performance*, 3, pp. 1–17

Schneider, W. and Detweiler, M. (1987) 'A connectionist/control architecture for working memory' in G. H. Bower (Ed.) *The Psychology of Learning and Motivation* (Vol. 21, pp. 54–119). New York: Academic Press

Schneider, W., Kron, V., Hünnerkopf, M. and Krajewski, K. (2004) 'The development of young children's memory strategies: first findings from the Würzburg Longitudinal Memory Study'. *Journal of Experimental Child Psychology*, 88, pp. 193–209

Schneider, W. and Pressley, M. (1997) *Memory Development between Two and Twenty* (2nd Ed.). Mahwah, NJ: Erlbaum

Schubert, T. (1999) 'Processing differences between simple and choice reactions affect bottleneck localization in overlapping tasks'. *Journal of Experimental Psychology: Human Perception and Performance*, 25, pp. 408–425

Shah, P. and Miyake, A. (1996) 'The separability of working memory resources for spatial thinking and language processing: an individual differences approach'. *Journal of Experimental Psychology: General*, 125, pp. 4–27

Shah, P. and Miyake, A. (1999) 'Models of working memory: an introduction' in A. Miyake and P. Shah (Eds) *Models of Working Memory* (pp. 1–27). New York, NY: Cambridge University Press

Shallice, T. and Warrington, E. K. (1970) 'Independent functioning of verbal memory stores: a neuropsychological study'. *Quarterly Journal of Experimental Psychology*, 22, pp. 261–273

Shannon, C. E. (1950) 'Programming a computer for playing chess'. *Philosophical Magazine*, 41, pp. 256–275

Shapiro, K. L., Raymond, J. E. and Arnell, K. M. (1994) 'Attention to visual pattern information produces the attentional blink in rapid serial visual presentation'. *Journal of Experimental Psychology: Human Perception and Performance*, 20, pp. 357–371

Shelton, J. T., Elliott, E. M., Matthews, R. A., Hill, B. D. and Gouvier, W. D. (2010) 'The relationships of working memory, secondary memory, and general fluid intelligence: working memory is special'. *Journal of Experimental Psychology: Learning, Memory and Cognition*, 36, pp. 813–820

Shiffrin, R. and Schneider, W. (1977) 'Controlled and automatic information processing: II. Perceptual learning, automatic handling, and a general theory'. *Psychological Review*, 87, pp. 122–190

Shipstead, Z., Redick, T. S., Hicks, K. L. and Engle, R. W. (2012) 'The scope and control of attention as separate aspects of working memory'. *Memory*, 20, pp. 608–628

Siegler, R. S. (1996) *Emerging Minds: The Process of Change in Children's Thinking*. Oxford: Oxford University Press

Siegler, R. S. and Shrager, J. (1984) 'Strategic choices in addition and subtraction: how do children know what to do?' in C. Sophian (Ed.) *Origins of Cognitive Skills* (pp. 229–293). Hillsdale: Erlbaum

Simon, T. J. (1997) 'Reconceptualizing the origins of number knowledge: a "non-numerical" account'. *Cognitive Development*, 12, pp. 349–372

Smith, E. E. and Jonides, J. (1999) 'Storage and executive processes in the frontal lobes'. *Science*, 283, pp. 1657–1661

Smith, M. M. and Scholey, K. A. (1992) 'Determining spatial span: the role of movement time and articulation rate'. *The Quarterly Journal of Experimental Psychology*, 45, pp. 479–501

Sperber, D., Cara, F. and Girotto, V. (1995) 'Relevance theory explains the selection task'. *Cognition*, 57, pp. 31–95

Sperling, G. (1960) 'The information available in brief visual presentations'. *Psychological Monographs*, 74, No. 498

Sternberg, S. (1966) 'High-speed scanning in human memory'. *Science*, 153, pp. 652–654

Stevanovski, B. and Jolicoeur, P. (2007) 'Visual short-term memory: central capacity limitations in short-term consolidation'. *Visual Cognition*, 15, pp. 532–563

Sundermann, B. and Pfleiderer, B. (2012) 'Functional connectivity profile of the human inferior frontal junction: involvement in a cognitive control network'. *BMC Neuroscience*, 13, p. 119

Taatgen, N. A., Juvina, I., Schipper, M., Borst, J. and Martens, S. (2009) 'Too much control can hurt: a threaded cognition model of the Attentional Blink'. *Cognitive Psychology*, 59, pp. 1–29

Tam, H., Jarrold, C., Baddeley, A. D. and Sabatos-DeVito, M. (2010) 'The development of memory maintenance: children's use of phonological rehearsal and attentional refreshment in WM tasks'. *Journal of Experimental Child Psychology*, 107, pp. 306–324

Tehan, G., Hendry, L. and Kocinski, D. (2001) 'Word length and phonological similarity effects in simple, complex, and delayed serial recall tasks: implications for working memory'. *Memory*, 9(4), pp. 333–348

Tolman, E. C. (1948) 'Cognitive maps in rats and men'. *Psychological Review*, 55, pp. 189–208

Toulmin, S. (1953) *The Philosophy of Science*. London: Hutchison

Towse, J. N. and Hitch, G. J. (1995) 'Is there a relationship between task demand and storage space in tests of working memory capacity?' *Quarterly Journal of Experimental Psychology*, 48, pp. 108–124

Towse, J. N. and Hitch, G. J. (1997) 'Integrating information in object counting: a role for a central coordination process?' *Cognitive Development*, 12, pp. 393–422

Towse, J. N. and Hitch, G. J. (2007) 'Variations in working memory due to normal development' in A. R. A. Conway, C. J. Jarrold, M. J. Kane, A. Miyake and J. N. Towse (Eds) *Variation in Working Memory* (pp. 109–133). Oxford: Oxford University Press

Towse, J. N., Hitch, G. J. and Hutton, U. (1998) 'A reevaluation of working memory capacity in children'. *Journal of Memory and Language*, 39, pp. 195–217

Towse, J. N., Hitch, G. J. and Hutton, U. (2000) 'On the interpretation of working memory spans in adults'. *Memory and Cognition*, 28, pp. 341–348

Towse, J. N., Hitch, G. J. and Hutton, U. (2002) 'On the nature of the relationship between processing activity and item retention in children'. *Journal of Experimental Child Psychology*, 82, pp. 156–184

Towse, J. N. and Houston-Price, C. M. T. (2001) 'Reflections on the concept of central executive' in J. Andrade (Ed.) *Working Memory in Perspective* (pp. 240–260). Philadelphia, PA: Psychology Press

Tuholski, S. W., Engle, R. W. and Baylis, G. C. (2001) 'Individual differences in working memory capacity and enumeration'. *Memory and Cognition*, 29, pp. 484–492

Turing, A. M. (1948 [1992]) 'Intelligent machinery' in D. C. Ince (Ed.) *Mechanical Intelligence* (pp. 117–127). Amsterdam: North-Holland

Turing, A. M. (1950) 'Computing machinery and intelligence'. *Mind*, 59, pp. 433–460

Turner, M. L. and Engle, R. W. (1989) 'Is working memory capacity task dependent?' *Journal of Memory and Language*, 28, pp. 127–154

Turvey, M. T., Brick, P. and Osborn, J. (1970) 'Proactive interference in short-term memory as a function of prior-item retention interval'. *Quarterly Journal of Experimental Psychology*, 22, pp. 142–147

Unsworth, N., Brewer, G. A. and Spillers, G. J. (2009) 'There's more to the working memory capacity – fluid intelligence relationship than just secondary memory'. *Psychonomic Bulletin and Review*, 16, pp. 931–937

Unsworth, N. and Engle, R. W. (2007a) 'On the division of short-term and working memory: an examination of simple and complex span and their relation to higher order abilities'. *Psychological Bulletin*, 133, pp. 1038–1066

Unsworth, N. and Engle, R.W. (2007b) 'The nature of individual differences in working memory capacity: active maintenance in primary memory and controlled search from secondary memory'. *Psychological Review*, 114, pp. 104–132

Unsworth, N., Heitz, R.P. and Parks, N.A. (2008) 'The importance of temporal distinctiveness for forgetting over the short-term'. *Psychological Science*, 19, pp. 1078–1081

Unsworth, N., Schrock, J.C. and Engle, R.W. (2004) 'Working memory capacity and the antisaccade task: individual differences in voluntary saccade control'. *Journal of Experimental Psychology: Learning, Memory, and Cognition*, 30, pp. 1302–1321

Unsworth, N., Spillers, G. J. and Brewer, G. A. (2010) 'The contributions of primary and secondary memory to working memory capacity: an individual differences analysis of immediate free recall'. *Journal of Experimental Psychology: Learning, Memory, and Cognition*, 36, pp. 240–247

Vallar, G. and Baddeley, A. D. (1982) 'Short-term forgetting and the articulatory loop'. *Quarterly Journal of Experimental Psychology*, 34, pp. 53–60

Vallar, G. and Baddeley, A. D. (1984) 'Phonological short-term store, phonological processing and sentence comprehension: a neuropsychological case study'. *Cognitive Neuropsychology*, 1, pp. 121–141

Van den Berg, R., Shin, H., Chou, W. C., George, R. and Ma, W. J. (2012) 'Variability in encoding precision accounts for visual short-term memory limitations'. *Proceedings of the National Academy of Sciences*, 109, pp. 8780–8785

Vandierendonck, A., De Vooght, G. and Van der Goten, K. (1998) 'Interfering with the central executive by means of a random interval repetition task'. *Quarterly Journal of Experimental Psychology: Human Experimental Psychology*, 51(A), pp. 197–218

Vergauwe, E., Barrouillet, P. and Camos, V. (2009) 'Visual and spatial working memory are not that dissociated after all: a Time-Based Resource-Sharing account'. *Journal of Experimental Psychology: Learning, Memory and Cognition*, 35, pp. 1012–1028

Vergauwe, E., Barrouillet, P. and Camos, V. (2010) 'Verbal and visuo-spatial working memory: a case for Domain-general Time-Based Resource Sharing'. *Psychological Science*, 21, pp. 384–390

Vergauwe, E., Camos, V. and Barrouillet, P. (2014) 'The impact of storage on processing: implications for structure and functioning of working memory'. *Journal of Experimental Psychology: Learning, Memory and Cognition*, 40(4), pp.1072–1095

Vergauwe, E., Dewaele, N., Langerock, N. and Barrouillet, P. (2012) 'Evidence for a central pool of general resources in working memory'. *Journal of Cognitive Psychology*, 24, pp. 359–366

Vergauwe, E., Hartstra, E., Barrouillet, P. and Brass, M. (2014) 'Domain-general involvement of the posterior frontolateral cortex in working memory: an fMRI study of the time-based interplay between maintenance and processing'. Manuscript submitted for publication

Warrington, E. K. and Shallice, T. (1969) 'The selective impairment of auditory verbal short-term memory'. *Brain*, 92, pp. 885–896

Wason, P. C. (1966) 'Reasoning' in B. M. Foss (Ed.) *New Horizons in Psychology*, Volume 1 (pp. 135–151). Harmondsworth: Penguin

Watkins, M. J., Watkins, O. C., Craik, F. I. M. and Mazuryk, G. (1973) 'Effect of nonverbal distraction on short-term storage'. *Journal of Experimental Psychology*, 101, pp. 296–300

Waugh, N. C. and Norman, D. A. (1965) 'Primary memory'. *Journal of Experimental Psychology*, 72, pp. 89–104

Welford, A. T. (1952) 'The "psychological refractory period" and the timing of high speed performance: a review and a theory'. *British Journal of Psychology*, 43, pp. 2–19

Welford, A. T. (1967) 'Single-channel operation in the brain'. *Acta Psychologica*, 27, pp. 5–22

Wheeler, M. A. (1995) 'Improvement in recall over time without repeated testing: spontaneous recovery revisited'. *Journal of Experimental Psychology: Learning, Memory, and Cognition*, 21, pp. 173–184

White, K. G. (2012) 'Dissociation of short-term forgetting from the passage of time'. *Journal of Experimental Psychology: Learning, Memory, and Cognition*, 38, pp. 255–259

Wickelgren, W. A. (1970) 'Time, interference, and rate of presentation in short-term recognition memory for items'. *Journal of Mathematical Psychology*, 7, pp. 219–235

Wickens, C.D. (1984) 'Processing resources in attention' in R. Parasuraman, J. Beatty and R. Davies (Eds) *Varieties of Attention* (pp. 63–101). New York: Wiley

Williamson, V., Baddeley, A. D. and Hitch, G. J. (2010) 'Musicians' and non-musicians' short-term memory for verbal and musical sequences: comparing phonological similarity and pitch proximity'. *Memory and Cognition*, 38, pp. 163–175

Wilson, B. and Baddeley, A. D. (1988) 'Semantic, episodic, and autobiographical memory in a post-meningitic patient'. *Brain and Cognition*, 8, pp. 31–46

Woodman, G. F., Vogel, E. K. and Luck, S. J. (2001) 'Visual search remains efficient when visual working memory is full'. *Psychological Science*, 12, pp. 219–224

Zbrodoff, N. J. and Logan, G. D. (2005) 'What everyone finds. The problem-size effect' in J. I. D. Campbell (Ed.) *Handbook of Mathematical Cognition* (pp. 331–345). New York and Hove: Psychology Press

Zelazo, P. D. and Frye, D. (1998) 'Cognitive complexity and control: II. The development of executive function in childhood'. *Current Directions in Psychological Science*, 7, pp. 121–126

Zhang, W. and Luck, S. J. (2009) 'Sudden death and gradual decay in visual working memory'. *Psychological Science*, 20, pp. 423–428

INDEX

Entries in italic refer to figures or tables.
Added to a page number 'n' denotes notes.

accuracy: arithmetic problem solving 13, 16; cognitive load and 63, 64, *177*; postponement of processing and 110; reasoning 9, 17; retention interval and task 81; task difficulty and recall 79, 80
ACT-R model 13, 43, 44, 120, 122, 123, 124, 125, 143
action schemata 10
activated cues 185, 186, 188
adaptive behaviour 65
adaptive choice: maintenance mechanisms 104–5
adaptive gating mechanism 122
adolescents: attentional refreshing 156; processing efficiency 154, 155; time-based resource sharing 146–9
age: attentional refreshing 148–9, 156; counting speed 26; non-operation of TBRS 149–51; processing efficiency 23, 26, 154–5; rate of decay 159–60
age x pace interaction (task) 154–5, 157
Alloway, T. 169
Altmann, E.M. 89
Anderson, J.R. 13, 15, 16, 52, 120, 121, 126, 127, 166
anti-learning process (Hebbian) 172
arithmetic problem solving 11, 43, 50; tasks 11, 13, 15, 34, 37, 38, 39, 103
articulation rate 21, 23, 24, 26, 27, 153, 156, 163
articulatory loop 8, 11, 12, 23, 32, 38, 142, 188n; capacity limited 27; maintenance 105, 106, 107, 113, 119, 121; temporal constraints 19–22; temporal decay through operation of 28; word length effect 94
articulatory rehearsal 28, 38, 95, 101–111; cognitive cost 34; as counteraction to temporal decay 20; developmental change 153; and forgetting 73; inner speech programme 20; phonological similarity effect 85; prevention, and poor recall 132; prevention, and rapid decay 78, 80; recall performance 133; Type I and II 134–5; verbal maintenance 113; word length effect 27, *see also* concurrent articulation
articulatory suppression 6, 7, 20, 27–8, 35, 54, 56, 96, 103
articulatory system: competition 6, 7
Atkinson, R.C. 2, 4, 5, 9
attention: activation from 39, *see also* focus of attention
attention control 10, 149, 151, 178
attention-demanding tasks 113, 115, 123
attentional capture 53, 79, 82, 147
attentional demand 52, 63, 99, 102, 103, 104, 105, 128; and articulation rate 27; and concurrent maintenance 37; recall performance 29, 133
attentional distraction 73
attentional focusing 44, 117, 119, 124, 137, 172
attentional interference 12, 13, 27
attentional load 27
attentional maintenance 110

Index

attentional refreshing 45–6, 94, 101–111, 135; and age 148–9; delayed recall 131, 132, 133; efficiency 156–8; intermittent 78, 79; length of processing and period of 82; qualitative change in 150–51; suppressors and 78
attentional resources: age, and need for 23; binding information and recruitment of 125; cross-domain information 136; developmental increase in 152; limited capacity 43–4
AuBuchon, A.M. 81, 82
automation 169
Ayres, T.J. 55

baba span task 34–5, 36, 37, 52, 55, 57
Baddeley, A.D. 1, 2, 4–8, 9, 11, 13, 14, 15, 16, 17, 19, 20, 21, 32, 34, 38, 39, 41–2, 56, 62, 75, 76, 80, 85, 93, 94, 95, 103, 105, 113, 117, 120, 121, 122, 123, 129, 136–7, 144, 185, 186, 187, 189
Barrouillet, P. 42, 45, 47, 53, 54, 57, 58, 65, 68, 78, 82, 83, 86, 88, 128, 147, 154, 155, 156, 167, 173, 174, 175, 178, 182, 183
basal ganglia system 122
Bayliss, D.M. 97, 99, 100, 149, 168
Beaman, C.P. 143
behaviourism 4, 17
Berman, M. 140
Bertrand, R. 160
binding process 123, 124, 125, 136, 183
Binet, A. 160
Borst, J.P. 143
Bower, G.H. 2
brain: working memory architecture 45, 109–110, 120, 121, 122, 127, 129, *see also* neural networks
Brass, M. 128
Broca's area 109–110
Brodmann's area 109
Brown, G.D.A. 76, 77
Brown, J. 72, 73, 74, 76, 83, 84, 86
Brown-Peterson tasks 32, 73–4, 74–5, 79, 93, 111, 127, 131, 173
Buchanan, M. 106
Buckner, R.L. 121

Camos, V. 42, 82, 85, 102, 103, 105, 106, 132, 133, 160, 165
Carpenter, P.A. 12, 13, 14, 42, 70n, 162
Case, R. 12, 13, 19, 23, 24, 26–7, 28, 34, 36, 37, 38, 42, 55, 70n, 122, 153–4, 155
Cattell's culture fair test 163
central bottleneck 43, 44, 45, 47, 49, 65, 129
central executive 8, 10, 11, 32, 113

central processes/processing 8, 44, 45, 53, 61, 124, 125
central system 122–9; fixed capacity 181–3; and peripheral system cooperation 183
change detection task 190
Chein, J.M. 129
Chen, Z. 141, 179, 182
Chi, M.T.H. 23
children: articulation rate 21, 27; developmental increase in short-term memory span 12; processing efficiency and memory span 21, *22*; reactivation of memory traces during processing 42; recall, arithmetic problem solving 37, 42; school achievement and performance in complex span tasks 162–5; serial resource-allocation strategy 30, *see also* pre-school children; school-aged children
choice reaction time (CRT) tasks 53, 78, 98, 104–5, 125
chunk decomposition 141, 179, 182
cognition: high-level 14, 162, 165, 178, 190; information processing approach 1, 2–8; numerical 183, *see also* hub of cognition
cognitive complexity 191–2
cognitive control 129, 176, 177
cognitive cost(s) 29, 33, 34–5, 36, 37, 40, 165, 166
cognitive demands/mental effort 34, 35, 39, 47, 58
cognitive development 22–3, 33, 151
cognitive flexibility 39, 151, 153
cognitive load 46–9, 79; children's working memory 147–8; empirical evidence for 50–60; and forgetting 38; inhibition tasks 68; neural sensitivity to variations in 128–9; processing efficiency 154–5; processing-storage function 66–7, 69; recall performance 55, 57, 61–2, 65, 96, 98, 99, 133, 148, 174–5; time pressures as an alternative to 175–8, *see also* complex span tasks
cognitive maps 1, 2
cognitive psychology 5, 8, 17, 190
cognitive revolution 1, 2, 37, 151
colour discrimination task 61, 63, 67, 114
complex processes 191
complex span tasks 14; computer-paced 59, 63, 98, 107, 161–5; delayed recall 131; displacement of memory items to long-term memory 130; individual differences 161–5, 167–8; performance 97; phonological similarity effect 85; selective interference 95; stimulus similarity effect 84; verbal and visuospatial 97, *see also individual tasks*

comprehension 5–7, 13
computational simulations: ACT-R model 13; decay of memory traces 66; information processing approach 1, 2; TBRS model 144n
computer-paced span tasks 59, 63, 98, 107, 161–5
conceptual memory 123
concurrent articulation 6, 20, 50, 92, 107, 112, 133, 153, 183, 189
concurrent maintenance 34, 37, 38, 40, 41, 53, 57, 62, 110, 123, 161
concurrent memory load 6–7, 9–10, 14–15, 16; selective interference 178; spatial storage 62; task decrement 41, *see also* cognitive load
conditional reasoning 190
Conlin, J.A. 84, 165
consciousness 3, 4, 10, 46, 118
consolidation 6, 90, 92, 123–4
contextual cues 8, 85, 125
contextual information 125, 141
continuous allocation hypothesis 16
continuous operation span tasks 50–52, 54, 57, 59, 132, 154, 178
control: in modal model 4; in thinking machines 2, *see also* attention control; cognitive control; time control
Conway, A.R.A. 18, 190
Corsi block task 96
cortical structures 120, 121, 122
counting 33, 43, 55, 70n, 167
counting span tasks 6, 12, 24–6, 29–30, 30–31, 34–5, 36, 37, 43
counting speed 26, 28, 29, 36, 40, 154
covert retrieval 39, 45, 94, 113, 115, 130, 142
Cowan, N. 20, 30, 39, 44, 45, 80, 81, 82, 99, 113, 114, 115, 121, 124, 128, 136, 137, 138, 141, 149, 159, 168, 169, 178, 179, 180, 181, 182, 185, 191
Craik, F.I.M. 134
cross-domain information 123, 136, 182
Crowder, R.G. 71, 74, 75, 93
cue-based retrieval 8, 44, 75, 83, 85, 125, 127, 141, 181, 185, 186, 187–8
culture fair test (Cattell's) 163

Daneman, M. 12, 13, 14, 42, 70n, 162
decay of memory traces: developmental changes in rate of 159–60, *see also* temporal decay
declarative knowledge 121, 166
declarative memory 13, 117, 119, 121, 137, 138

declarative module 120, 121
delayed recall 130, 131, 132, 133, 134, 135
Dell'Acqua, R. 123, 124, 125
The demise of short-term memory 74
Dempster, F.N. 24, 27, 55
developmental difference: articulation rate 21; attentional refreshing efficiency 156–8; memory spans 12, 23, 26; processing efficiency 153–6; rate of decay 158–60; shift in maintenance strategies 149, 150, 151, 169; short-term memory 27
developmental psychology 151, 156
Diamond, A. 151
difficulty: cognitive load and 7, 58–60
digit span tasks 52–3, 54, 55, 67, 89, 90
Dillon, R.F. 80
discrimination: failure of 76–7
discrimination tasks 76
distraction tasks 32, 72, 73, 76, 79, 84, 86
distractor-removal hypothesis 172, 173–5
distractors: novelty-gated encoding 171; semantic 142–3, *see also* interference
distributed item representations 84
domain-generality 97, 101, 122, 123, 129, 180, 181
domain-specificity 31–2, 97–101, 99, 101, 180
dorsolateral prefrontal cortex 45, 109, 110, 122, 127
dot location task 62, 63
Drew, T. 79
dual-task *see* concurrent memory load
Duff, S.C. 11, 14, 15, 39
Dulany, D.E. 125
durable storage 124
duration of articulation 20
duration of task 29, 30, 33, 47, 57–8, 80, 150
Dux, P.E. 129

Ebbinghaus, H. 4
"elementary activities" tasks 59
elementary process: individual differences 166–7
Elliott, E.M. 113
Elsley, J.V. 125
embedded-process model 137, 179
encoding: novelty-gated 171; and recall 29; time factor 172
Engle, R.W. 16, 31, 32, 43, 50, 76, 79, 121, 122, 128, 141, 142, 162
enumeration span task 163
episodic buffer 94, 117, 118, 119, 123, 124, 126, 136, 181, 187
episodic memory 132, 188
equation solving tasks 11, 13, 15, 37, 39

equilibrium 175, 192
Etchegaray, J. 45
Etherton, J.L. 124
Evans, J. St. 190
event-based interference 89–92
executive attention 178
executive control 43, 53, 110, 122
executive functions 126–7, 128, 144n
executive loop 115, 118–19, 122–3, 127, 128
executive-attention domain-general system 122

Farmer, E.W. 95, 96
feature overlap 84, 85, 86
feature overwriting 84, 85, 86, 87, 90
flexible work space 7, 8
fluid intelligence 14, 163, 165
focus of attention 2, 39, 44, 45, 137, 138, 179, 180, 181
forgetting: and cognitive load 38; consolidation of visuospatial information and slower 124; short-term 185, *see also* working memory loss
free recall 18n
Friedman, N.P. 165
Fry, A.F. 165

Gaillard, V. 158, 163, 167, 168, 184
Galanter, E. 1
gamma oscillation sub-cycles 183
Gardner, H. 2
gating system 46, 122
Gavens, N. 57, 147, 154
general working memory 9, 41
goal buffer 120, 121–2
goal maintenance 122
goal-directed memory 43–4, 46, 65, 124, 125, 127
Goldman-Rakic, P.S. 1, 119
Greene, E.J. 45
Guttentag, R.E. 30

Haberlandt, K. 1, 190
Hale, S. 165
Hammerton, M. 7
Hanten, G. 109
Hartstra, E. 128
Hebb effect 172, 185
high-span individuals 162, 166, 167, 168
hippocampus 120, 121
Hitch, G.J. 2, 4–8, 9, 11, 12, 13, 14, 15, 16, 17, 27–8, 28–9, 29–30, 31, 33, 36, 37, 38, 39, 41–2, 46, 70n, 95, 103, 113, 121, 137, 149, 151, 189

Houston-Price, C.M.T. 33, 36
hub of cognition 1, 2, 190
Hudjetz, A. 101, 102, 132
Hulme, C. 21, 23, 24, 26, 28
Hunter, I.M.L. 5

identification processes 27
Idiart, M.A.P. 183
"if ... then" rules 44
imaginal module 124, 143
immediate memory 3, 8, 72, 141
immediate recall 11, 28, 130, 132, 133–4, 185
immediate serial recall 21, 27, 28, 34, 56, 77, 85, 87, 93, 156, 169
individual differences 160–68
inferior frontal junction (IJF) 129
information processing approach 1; Baddeley and Hitch study 4–8; need for working memory in 2–4, *see also* processing
inhibition experiments 67, 68
inner speech programme 20
intentional module 120
interference 7; domain-specific 99, 101; event-based 89–92; infra-span memory loads 8; memory of phonologically similar items 45; similarity-based 72, 73, 84–7; trade-off hypothesis 12, 13; types of 83–4, *see also* attentional interference; proactive interference; retroactive interference; selective interference; temporal interference
interference control 129
interference-only view 89
Istomina, Z.M. 160

James, W. 4, 142
Jarrold, C. 142
Johnson, M.K. 45
Johnson, M.R. 45
Jolicoeur, P. 99, 123, 124, 125
Jonides, J. 34, 110, 140
Just, M.A. 13

Kahneman, D. 47, 58
Kane, M.J. 43, 61, 79, 122
Kelley, M.R. 75
Kemps, E. 70n
Keppel, G. 73, 74, 75, 93
Kintsch, W. 96
Klauer, K.C. 62, 63, 96, 97
Kliegl, R. 82

La Pointe, L.B. 16
Lange, E.B. 86
Langerock, N. 136, 182
language 5–7
Lebière, C. 166
Lépine, R. 59, 161, 178
Lewandowsky, S. 58, 76, 77, 78–9, 79, 81, 82, 83, 88, 90, 172, 174, 175, 176, 177
Lewis, R.L. 140
Lewis, V. 9, 16, 17
lexical-decision tasks 32, 139–40
lexicality effect 169
Liefooghe, B. 45
limited capacity memory system 3, 9, 15; attentional resource 43–4; phonological loop 27; resource-sharing 33, 37, 41; storage space 6; work space 7, 8
linearity (processing-storage function) 66
Lisman, J.E. 183
Loaiza, V. 131, 132–3, 134
location judgement tasks 53, 58, 65–6, 67, 68, 82, 99, 107, 147, 152, 174
Lockhart, R.S. 134
Logan, G.D. 26, 124
Logie, R.H. 11, 14, 15, 32, 39, 41, 60, 120, 137
long-term memory: activated above the threshold 38–9, 121, 125, 129, 130, 135, 137–41, 166, 185, 187; difference between working memory and 129–30; distinction between short-term memory and 4; information storage 11; and mechanisms of maintenance in working memory 132–4; semantic 188; short-term memory as activated part of 4; traces of transient working memory representations 130–32, *see also* declarative memory; episodic memory
low-span individuals 122, 166, 167, 168
Lucidi, A. 167
Luck, S.J. 18, 81

M power 23, 151
M space 23, 24
McCabe, D.P. 130, 131, 132–3, 134
McGeoch, J.A. 73, 188
McKeown, D. 80–81
McKone, E. 138, 139, 140
macro-level switching 151
magical number four (Cowan's) 179, 182–3
magical number seven (Miller's) 3, 183, 184
magnetic resonance imaging (MRI) 128
maintenance 11, 18; active mechanisms 45; arithmetic problem solving 38, 39; disruption/prevention 20, 46, 123;

domain-specific mechanisms 97–101; effect on processing 110–115; emergence of strategies 152–3; long-term memory and mechanisms of 132–4; number and nature of mechanisms 94–5; in the phonological store 20; of representations 125–7; sequential function supposition 17; task switching and disrupted 46; time factor 68; of verbal memory 81; verbal rehearsal 85; visual search tasks 79, *see also* articulatory rehearsal; attentional refreshing
Marchetti, C. 60
Martin, R.C. 109
medial temporal cortex regions 120
Meiser, T. 96, 97
Melton, A.W. 76, 185, 186
memory load: impacts of 17, 41, 114; memory stress 6, *see also* concurrent memory load
memory span: development, controversy over 22–3; developmental differences 12, 23, 26; processing efficiency 21, 28; and reading rates 20–21
memory traces: attention and creation of 44; decay *see* decay of memory traces; effect of accumulated distracting material on 77; reactivation *see* attentional refreshing; covert retrieval
mental models 117, 125, 187
Mercer, T. 80–81
micro-level switching 151, 156
Miller, G.A. 1, 2, 3, 4, 11, 17, 179, 183
mind *see* cognition
miscueing 85
Mitchell, K.J. 45
Miyake, A. 1, 45, 95, 96, 101, 165
modal model 4, 8, 9, 16, 18
modality-specific systems 96, 97, 120
Models of Working Memory 1
monochromatic display task 61, 63, 114
Morey, C.C. 99
motor buffer 120
multi-capacities view 180, 181
multi-component model 7, 9–11, 38, 40, 94, 101, 136–7
Murdock, B.B. 4
Murray, D.J. 6, 20

N-back task 67
Nairne J.S. 75, 76, 94, 185, 186, 188
naming-colour span task 150
Naveh-Benjamin, M. 34, 55
Navon, D. 37

Neath, I. 76
neo-Piagetian approaches 184
neural lesion studies 109
neural networks: support of maintenance mechanisms 109–110
neuroimaging 95, 109, 120, 128–9
Newell, A. 2, 44, 63, 65, 115
Nicholson, R. 21, 23
non-articulatory mechanism: maintenance of verbal memory 81
non-unitary model (working memory) 94, 95, 99
Norman, D.A. 10, 89
novelty encoding 87–9
novelty-based interference 84
numerical cognition 183

Oberauer, K. 58, 67, 78–9, 79, 81, 82, 86, 101, 102, 118, 121, 132, 137, 138, 142, 172, 173, 174, 175, 176, 177, 180
object-file model 183
old-new recognition task 138–9, 140
operating space 12
operation span tasks 31, 33, 34, 37, 43, 59, 130, 132, 162, 165, *see also* continuous operation span task; digit span tasks; word span tasks
operational efficiency 23, 24, *see also* processing efficiency
output decay: word length effect 30

pace effects (task) 76, 88–9, 90, 149, 150, 156–7, 178
paced-timing trials 81–2, 86–8
parity judgement tasks 32, 54, 65–6, 67, 68, 80, 103, 111, 112, 113–14, 133, 183, 184
Parmentier, F.B.R. 125
Pascal, B. 191
Pascual-Leone, J.A. 22–3, 184
Pashler, H. 44, 45
past: remembering 121
pattern matching/recognition 126
perceptual memories 119, 123, 124, 125
peripheral buffers 119, 120, 121, 122, 123, 124
peripheral interference 61
peripheral systems 120–22, 183
Perruchet, P. 125
Peterson, L.R. 72, 73, 74, 86
Peterson, M.J. 72, 73, 74, 86
phoneme overlap 85, 86, 87
phonemic similarity 7
phonological buffer 119, 137
phonological characteristics: impact of 105–9

phonological loop *see* articulatory loop
phonological overlap 86
phonological short-term memory 109, 120
phonological similarity 45, 56, 85, 86, 87, 104, 105, 106, 107, 153
physiologically inspired models 46
Piagetian approach 151
Pillsbury, W.B. 72
pitch discrimination task 99
pitch memory 159
Plancher, G. 58, 88, 173
Plans 2, 3
planum temporale 120
Poole, B.J. 79
Portrat, S. 82, 132, 147
Posner, M.I. 5
postponement: maintenance activities 110, 111, 113, 114–15; of storage and reactivation activities 44
Potter, M.C. 123
practice effect 35
pre-load technique: reasoning experiments 5, 6
pre-school children: processing speed and processing efficiency 23; qualitative change in refreshing 150
prefrontal cortex 45, 109–110, 122, 127
Pribam, K.H. 1
primary memory: modal model 4
primary-secondary approach 141–3
priming decay 139–40
proactive interference 45, 73, 74–7, 81, 83, 93, 127
problem state resource 143
procedural memory 122, 123, 137, 138
procedural system 118, 122, 123, 124, 125, 127, 128, 136, 143
process-based interference 83, 85
processing: attention and 43–4; common resource theory 7, 11, 182; complex span tasks 14; maintenance and 110–115, 134–5; multi-component model 9–11; postponement of storage and reactivation 44; records, degraded 186; separation of functions between storage and 11; time and refreshing period 82; time-based resource sharing 63–70; trade-off between storage and *see* trade-off hypothesis
processing efficiency: developmental increase in short-term memory span 12; domain-general 180; equated with speed 180–81; factors impacting on 23, 169; individual differences 168; and memory span 21, 28; time as index of, in the

search for a trade-off 22–8; working memory development 152, 153–6
processing speed 169; assessment of processing efficiency 23; concurrent cognition 192; effect on storage 54; and memory span 24; processing efficiency equated with 180–81
production rules 44, 123, 125, 126–7
psychological refractory period 44

qualitative change: maintenance strategies 149, 150, 151, 169

rapid decay 71–7
rapid switching 38–9, 46, 128
Raven's progressive matrices 163
Raye, C.L. 45, 109, 110, 127
reactivation, of memory traces 42; processing and postponement of 44, *see also* attentional refreshing; covert retrieval
reading span 13
reading span tasks 14, 31, 33, 34, 43, 52–3, 54, 55, 59, 101–2, 147–8, 154–5, 162, 163, 165
reasoning 17, 20, 190; Baddeley and Hitch experiments 5–7, 8, 9; tasks 17, 38, 95–6
recall performance: articulation rate 21, 156; attentional demand 29; attentional refreshing and articulatory rehearsal 103, 104; cognitive load 55, 57, 61–2, 65, 80, 96, 98, 99, 133, 148, 174–5; memory decay hypothesis 29–30; and reasoning time 17; task switches 46, 102; word length effect 20, 27, 106
recency effect 74
recent-probes task 140
reconstruction-order procedure 75
refreshing *see* attentional refreshing
Reid, L.S. 80
Reitman, J.S. 73
Repovs, G. 94
representation-based interference 63, 79, 83, 93; feature overwriting 90; reading span task 102; resulting from similarity 84–7; through novelty encoding 87–9
representational overlap 84, 85
representations 2; constructing and consolidating 123–5; long-term memory traces of transient 130–32; maintaining and transforming 125–7
retention delays 49
retention intervals: arithmetic problem solving 39; baba span task 34, 35, 36; cognitive load tasks 49, 52, 58; counting span task 35, 36; decay hypothesis 72–3; distracting material 77; parity judgement task 32; proactive interference 75; two-tone comparison procedure 81; visuospatial domain tasks 62, 63; word pair task 79
retrieval buffer 120
retrieval confusion 83, 85, 86
retrieval cues *see* cue-based retrieval
retroactive interference 72, 77, 83
Ricker, T.J. 79, 80, 83, 114, 124, 177
Rohrer, D. 45
Rose, N.S. 130

Saito, S. 101
Saults, J.S. 99, 113, 159
Schneider, W. 26
Scholey, K. 70n
school-aged children: time-based resource sharing 146–9
Schunn, C.D. 89
Scott, D. 75, 76, 80
secondary memory: modal model 4; primary memory retrieving memory traces from 141–3
selection task 190
selective interference 60, 60–61, 62, 94, 95–7
self-organising consciousness theory 125
self-paced tasks 49, 59, 63, 76, 78, 88
semantic distractors 142–3
semantic judgement 123
semantic memory 109, 188
semantic similarity 86, 87, 142, 143
sensory memory 44, 124, 129, 144, 159, 160
sensory store (modal model) 4
sensory systems 4
sentence-verification task 14–15
sequential functioning 17, 110, 111, 123, 167
sequential tapping task 96
serial memory scanning 113, 115
Serial Order in a Box *see* SOB model
serial recall 27, 53, 125
serial recall tasks 34, 125
serial resource-allocation 30
Shah, P. 1, 95, 96
Shallice, T. 5, 10
Shannon, C.E. 2
shopping span task 160
short-term memory 2; as activated part of long-term memory 4; consolidation 124; demise of 73–4; developmental differences 27; developmental increase in 12; distinction between long-term memory

and 4; existence of 184–8; hypothesis of equating with working memory 5; models 4; phonological 109, 120; and processing rate 26; and rapid forgetting 71–7; in reasoning language and comprehension 5–7, 17; semantic 109; temporal decay 140, *see also* conceptual memory

short-term storage space 12; memory capacity 23; and processing efficiency 24

Shriffin, R. 2, 4, 5, 9, 26

similarity-based interference 72, 73, 84–7

Simon, H.A. 2

Simon, T. 160

SIMPLE model 76, 77, 90

simple reaction time (SRT) tasks 53, 103, 104, 105, 178

simple span tasks 14, 23, 107, 130, 131, 142, 156, *see also* word span tasks

single-item focus of attention 138, 181

slave systems *see* peripheral systems

Smith, E.E. 109

Smith, M.M. 70n

SOB model 78, 84, 87, 88, 89

SOB-CS model 84, 87, 171–2; evidence contradicting 172–3

socio-economic background 163

source activations 13, 16, 43–4

spatial fit tasks 61, 79, 111, 123

spatial location tasks 62, 82, 99, 124, 173, 181, 182

spatial maintenance 60, 62, 63, 177

spatial processing 61, 62

spatial processing tasks 61

spatial recall 61, 96

spatial storage 61, 62, 63, 97, 98, 112, 113

square location tasks 53, 58, 82, 99, 152

standard model *see* multi-component model

Sternberg, S. 113, 115

Stevanovski, B. 99, 124

stimulus similarity effect 84

stimulus-response associations 122

storage: and attention 44; common resource theory 7, 11, 182; durable 124; multi-component model 7, 9–11, 95; pace of processing and 54; processing and postponement of 44; separation of functions between processing and 11; time-based resource sharing 63–70; trade-off between processing and *see* trade-off hypothesis, *see also* spatial storage; verbal storage; visual storage

storage capacity: attempt to measure 23; limited 6; multi-component model 11, 113; short-term 7, 12, 38

Stroop tasks 67, 122

subcortical structure 122

substitution 13

"sudden death" (memory) 81

Supervisory Attentional System (SAS) 10

suppressors 77, 78

supramarginal gyrus 109

Sylvester, A. 72

symmetry task 61

Taatgen, N.A. 124

Tam, H. 153

task set reconfiguration 129

task-switching model 17, 28–33, 39, 46, 102, 128–9, 149, 152

temporal decay (hypothesis): counteracted by articulatory rehearsal 20, 21; duration of task 33; new evidence against 77–80; new evidence in favour of 80–83; occupation of articulatory loop 28; recall performance 29–30; and refreshing *see* attentional refreshing; and serial functioning 42–6; short-term memory and 71–7, 140; unpopularity of 72

temporal distinctiveness 76, 77, 81

temporal interference 12, 42

temporal lobe 109

theta neuron network oscillation 183

Thomson, N. 106

time control 79

time, and working memory 19–40; articulatory loop functioning 19–22; consolidation 124; maintenance 68; a preliminary test 33–8; rapid switching mechanism 38–9; task-switching model 28–33; time as an index of processing efficiency in the search for a trade-off 22–8; time pressure 47, 59, 175–8, *see also* temporal decay; temporal distinctiveness; temporal interference

time-based resource sharing 41–70; age and non-operation of 149–51; alternatives to 170–78; cognitive load *see* cognitive load; cue-driven reconstruction 187–8; effect of processing on concurrent maintenance 110; factors of working memory development 151–60; fixed capacity limit of central system 181–3; individual differences 160–68; limited capacity attentional resource 43–4; neurological evidence 128–9; processing-storage function 63–70; in school-aged children and adolescents 146–9; temporal decay

and serial functioning 42–6; in the visuospatial domain 60–63, 98
time-sharing strategy 6, 41–2
Tolman, E.C. 1, 2
tone discrimination tasks 123
total processing space 12, 23, 24, 26, 33
Toulmin, S. 144
Towse, J.N. 12, 17, 28–9, 29–30, 31, 32, 33, 34, 36, 37, 38, 39, 42, 46, 70n, 149
trade-off hypothesis 11, 12–14, 16, 66, 115, 155; attentional interference and 27; counting span task 24–6, 28, 30, 40; increase in memory span 23; simple span tasks 23–4; supporting evidence 33, 37, 39
traditional span tasks 165
transformation: of representations 125–7
transient mental models 117, 125, 187
Tuholski, S. 79, 166
Turing, M.A. 2, 191
Turner, M.L. 31, 32, 50, 162
Turvey, M.T. 73, 75, 76
two-tone comparison procedure 81
Type I articulatory rehearsals 134–5
Type II articulatory rehearsals 135

unbinding process 172
Underwood, B.J. 73, 74, 75, 93
unitary view of working memory 4, 11, 14, 18, 40, 73, 74, 89, 94, 95, 180, 185, 186
Unsworth, N. 76, 141, 142
updating experiment 67, 68
updating memory 126–7, 129
upgrading span tasks 163, 167

Vallar, G. 34
ventrolateral prefrontal cortex 109–110
verbal buffer 120–21
verbal information 11, 19–20
verbal maintenance 97, 100, 103, 105, 107, 109, 112, 113, 119, 137–8
verbal material: rapid forgetting 73
verbal memory 8, 26, 28, 110, 124, 142; tasks 96, 112; temporal decay 81–2
verbal processing 97
verbal reasoning task 7, 95
verbal recall 96, 99, 177
verbal rehearsal *see* articulatory rehearsal
verbal storage 97, 98, 99, *100*, 112
verbal-specific system 113
Vergauwe, E. 98, 99, 101, 111, 114, 124, 128, 129, 173, 181, 183, 188n
Vinter, A. 125
visual information 81
visual maintenance 60, 61, 62, 63, 177

visual memory 8
visual processing 62
visual recall 61, 96
visual representations 81, 124
visual search tasks 79, 175, 177
visual similarity 7, 153
visual storage 61, 62, 63, 97, 98, 99, *100*, 113
visuospatial buffer (sketchpad) 120–21, 123, 137
visuospatial domain: consolidation 124; maintenance 60, 61, 62, 63, 100–101, 115, 119, 177; processing 96, 97; reactivation 94; recall 61, 96, 99; storage 61, 62, 63, 97, 98, 99, *100*, 112, 113, 120; temporal decay 82; time-based resource sharing 60–63
visuospatial fit task 98
visuospatial processing tasks 61, 95–6, 98, 99, 111–12, 114
Vogel, E.K. 18

WAIS reasoning matrix 163
Warrington, E.K. 5
Wason, P.C. 190
Watkins, M.J. 73
Waugh, N.C. 89
Welford, A.T. 44
White, K.G. 79, 80
Whiteman, H.L. 75
Wilson, B. 11
Woodman, G.F. 79
word length effect 20, 21, 27, 30, 56, 74, 94, 106, 107, 109
word span tasks 11, 14, 15, 23–4, 130, 132
work space: limited capacity/flexible 7, 8
Working Memory 9, 10
working memory: capacity 178–84; difference between long-term memory and 129–30; as a dynamic system 15–17; existence of 184–8; information processing approach 1, 2–8; limitations in performance 183–4; limited capacity 3; as long-term memory activated above the threshold 38–9, 121, 125, 129, 130, 135, 137–41, 166, 185, 187; multi-component model 7, 9–11, 38, 40, 94, 101, 136–7; origins of term 1; physiologically inspired models 46; primary-secondary approach 141–3; slowness 119; time and *see* time and working memory; trade-off in *see* trade-off hypothesis, *see also individual models*
working memory architecture 117–45; central system 122–9; comparison with

226 Index

other models 135–43; overview of model 117–19; peripheral systems 120–22; working memory and long-term memory 129–35

working memory loss 71–93; event-based and temporal factors 89–92; and interference 83–9; short-term memory and rapid forgetting 71–7; temporal decay 77–83, *see also* forgetting

working memory reconstruction 94–116; attentional refreshing and articulatory rehearsal 101–111; domain-specific mechanisms of maintenance 97–101; effect of maintenance on processing 110–115; selective interference paradigm 95–7

Zhang, W. 81
Zhao, Z. 62, 63